METHODISM

OF

THE PENINSULA;

OR,

SKETCHES OF NOTABLE CHARACTERS AND EVENTS IN THE
HISTORY OF METHODISM IN THE MARYLAND
AND DELAWARE PENINSULA.

BY

REV. ROBERT W. TODD.

INTRODUCTION BY

REV. BISHOP JOHN F. HURST, D. D.

WIPF & STOCK · Eugene, Oregon

Wipf and Stock Publishers
199 W 8th Ave, Suite 3
Eugene, OR 97401

Methodism of the Peninsula
Or, Sketches of Notable Characters and Events in the
History of Methodism in the Maryland and Delaware Peninsula
By Todd, Robert W.
ISBN 13: 978-1-60608-498-4
Publication date 2/26/2009
Previously published by Methodist Episcopal Book Rooms, 1886

To the Memory of

A Father, whose life was the embodiment of industry, frugality, temperance, honor, and devotion to truth and God; who hated shams; who loved mercy, and whose highest wish for his son was that he might be good and useful:—

A Mother, refined, modest, beautiful; whose life was a benediction; who made home sweet and attractive; who walked the shining way, and led thither the wayward feet of her child; whose memory still blooms fresh and fragrant, from a grave, where almost two-score years ago, fell the tears of a bereaved boy in his first great sorrow:—

To the
Memory of this Sainted Twain,

ENROBED, CROWNED, AND WAITING AND WATCHING ON THE
FARTHER SHORE, THIS VOLUME IS AFFECTIONATELY
INSCRIBED BY

The Author.

TABLE OF CONTENTS.

CHAPTER I.—THE PLACE AND THE PEOPLE.

Planting and Growth of Methodism in the Peninsula, 9. Lost Chapters, 10. Our Methodist Fathers, 11. Personnel of Methodism, Past and Present, 12. Old-time Environments, Society and Customs, 14. Climate, Topography and Products, 17. Author's Scope and Purpose, 19.

CHAPTER II.—OUR QUAINT ITINERANT FATHERS.

Thomas Ware, 21. Dr. Chandler, 25. Benj. Abbott, 28. Henry Bœhm, 29. The First Camp-meetings, 35. George Wiltshire, 39. Bishop Asbury, 46.

CHAPTER III.—HEROES OF ERIN.

The Typical Irishman, 50. William Barnes, 51. John Henry, 63. Adam Wallace, 69.

CHAPTER IV.—PATRIARCHS OF THE CHESAPEAKE.

Joshua Thomas, 85. Haney Bradshaw, 102. Captain William Frazier, 110. Garretson West, 113.

CHAPTER V.—EPISODES AND COLLISIONS.

John Collins, 124. The politico-religious, 125. Solomon Sharp, 127. William Bishop, 129. Untimely Fun, 131. Vanquished Heroes, 134. James Brooks Ayres, 137. Jas. A. Massey and Geo. Cummins, 142. Thos. Childs, 150. Nathan Hunter, "Esquire," 152. Jonas Bissey, 153. "Daddy" Appleton, 155.

CONTENTS.

CHAPTER VI.—HYMENEAL AND BAPTISMAL.

Wedding in a "Bugeye," 161. "Jeems" Henry Smith's Romantic Nuptials, 163. Wedding Fees, 166. Asbury's Namesakes, 167. "Governor" Hicks' Baptism, 167. Honoring two Preachers in one Cognomen, 168. Baby Christening at Camp-meeting, 169.

CHAPTER VII.—WHITE SOULS IN COLORED ENVELOPES.

Slavery and the Peninsula, 172. Tom and the Blackeyed Peas, 173. Slave Philosophy, 174. Uncle Zeke's Text, 177. The Old-time Negro at the Primitive Camp-meeting, 178. Praying for the Preachers, 183. "Uncle Jeems" King, 185. Frost Pollet, 187. Emancipation Scenes, 193. Negro Education and Improvement, 199.

CHAPTER VIII.—UNCLE STEPHEN, THE SLAVE PREACHER.

Stephen's Genealogy, 202. Childhood and Youth, 205. Conversion, 210. Marriage, 216. Longings for Freedom and Buying His Time, 217. A Buried Master and Buried Hopes, 218. Buying His Time Again at the Vendue, 220. Rescue of his Wife and Three Children, 221. Stephen and Two Babies on the Auction Block, 225. Sad Parting, 230. Emancipation, 232. Call to the Itinerancy, 236.

CHAPTER IX.—OLD TIME SCHOOLS AND SCHOOLMASTERS.

Starting to School, 238. The Old Log School-house, 239. "Master" Marshall and His Methods, 243. Nathan Wilson, the Fighting Quaker, 249. Master Elisha M——, 253. "Chinquepin" School, 255. "Professor" Samuel Wiseman, 256. Marion Dawson, and the Historian's Graduation, 257.

CHAPTER X.—HUMORS OF A MODERN ITINERANT.

Address to Bishop Foster, 260. Our Senior Bishop's Cane, 263. The Old-time Presiding Elder, 267. The Quart'ly Conf'rence, 272. The Conservative Mule, 278. Ode to ye Olde Meetin' 'Ouse, 281. Fun in the Parsonage, 286. "When I was Seventeen," 288. Wooden Wedding, 290. Tin Wedding, 292. Professor Robinson's Silver Wedding, 297. Wash-day, 300. Church Anniversary, 303. Episcopal Methodist Centenary, 309. The Eldership and the Harmonious Quartet, 319. Rev. Lucius C. Matlack, D. D. *In Memoriam*, 321.

INTRODUCTION.

BY BISHOP JOHN F. HURST.

THE author of the following volume asks me to write some introductory words. My mind goes rapidly back to the man, first of all, before I can reach his book. We met many years ago, when students at Dickinson College, and soon learned that we had come from the same region, the Eastern Shore of Maryland, and were starting out on the race of life together. Later along, we entered the ministry, and nearly at the same time. But our field of labor has been different. The author has always preached on the same beloved Peninsula, while my field has been otherwhere. But he has kept his asthma, and I have lost mine. Now and then we have met, saluted, passed a few words of brotherly exchange, and then each has gone out upon his own path. Now there comes a note from the friend and brother of the old times, and with it most of the sheets of his "Methodism of the Peninsula." A mere glance at it brings up all my earliest memories, and gives a touch of sadness to the picture.

The country which the author describes stands completely alone in its territory and life. At an early period in its colonial history, it was almost as individual and separate in usages and tastes as if it had been a different continent. It took all its types from the James River Colony of 1607, and not one from the Plymouth Colony of 1620. The old Cavaliers of Jamestown had only to cross the mouth of the Chesapeake, and treat with the Indians, and build log-cabins, and take possession, and then trust the generous waters for food. Very early the whole Peninsula became a safe retreat. The Indians were away—carried off by the irresistible westward current. Life was easy, and so secure that, before the Revolution, we find the whole Peninsula covered with families from the more insecure territory on the western side of the Bay. These families seem to have enjoyed great favor with the government. Even during the Revolution, and long before, we meet with Eastern Shore names, such as the Tilghmans, Lloyds, Sullivans, Goldsboroughs, Henrys, Decaturs, and many others. Slavery planted itself here with a strong hand. Fred. Douglass came from the Lloyd farm, whose broad acres were ploughed by five hundred slaves. One of my earliest recollections, when living in Cambridge, was the Georgia-man, or slave trader, who sat in a split-bottomed chair in the verandah of Bradshaw's Hotel, and sunned himself, and waited for propositions from slave owners. We boys feared him as a hobgoblin. I saw him every morning, on my way to school, in the opening of the year, for it was at this time that he made his annual northward journey for business purposes. But the war of 1861-65 put an end to all that. The Eastern Shore furnished its full quota of brave soldiers for the colored regiments.

The Rev. Mr. Todd has not only been a careful observer of these various phases of Eastern Shore life, but he has been industrious in recording them. His profession having been that of the ministry, clerical experiences naturally predominate in his book. The Methodist Episcopal Church has nowhere had a more difficult task to perform than here, and nowhere has it won more signal triumphs. Bishop Asbury was regarded a Tory during the Revolutionary War, and was sheltered from danger by Judge White, of Delaware, who entertained him in his own house until the danger was over. The Methodists were considered a dangerous class of innovators, judged from any point of view. The old bricks can still be seen in Cambridge, of which had been constructed the jail in which Freeborn Garrettson was once imprisoned for some irregular ministerial exercises. The trees of some of the historical camp-grounds are still standing, while the premises bear to-day the same names as in the olden times. In the seasons of controversy the quiet villagers often lost their equilibrium. The farmers would come to town, and spend the whole day in learning the latest news of the outside world. The day when the "Maryland" or the "Osiris" landed at the Cambridge wharf was sure to attract many people down to the landing, while each stranger who stepped ashore was certain to attract all eyes.

The ecclesiastical life was well defined. All denominations were reflected here in miniature, save only the Congregationalists. I do not remember to have seen any church representing this communion, at any time during my youth, on the Eastern Shore. I question, however, very much whether an enterprise so fully reflecting the spirit of New England would have been permitted by the people at any time before the Revolutionary War, so completely was the territory in the hands of the Church of England. The Baptists, too, had but little favor. The Presbyterians gained no little strength, and it is a fact that the first Presbyterian church ever built on this continent was erected near Snow Hill, the present residence of the author of this work. The Rev. Mr. Makemie was the pastor. He organized other churches at Pocomoke, Wicomico, and in Joseph Venable's Land. Spence wrote: "There is no body of land, of the same size, in the State, the soil of which was, and is so poor." But there was freedom of conscience, as well as security from the Indian depredations. The charter to the Roman Catholic proprietor, granted by Charles I., June 20th, 1632, contained a clause of perfect religious freedom to all emigrants. A man "might live in peace, whether Jew, Mohammedan, or Pagan; whether Atheist, Deist, or Polytheist; provided he neither molested his neighbor, nor endangered the public morals." *

But after the Independents passed out of power in England, and the Revolution of 1688 had been effected, it was a good time to pay up old debts. The Presbyterians, of even the Eastern shore of Maryland, had to give account of themselves. The Established Church of Virginia took the lead in the persecution of all dissenters. Happily for the Puritans of New England, they were too far off to suffer seriously. They held the power in their own hands.

The Rev. Mr. Todd has confined his attention to his own Church. The peculiarities of the camp-meeting services, the idiosyncracies of the negro race when at worship, and all the strong features of the primitive and provincial life, are traced with a freshness and justice which we have seen nowhere else. As a study in dialect, his work must take an influential place in our local American history. He has caught up the fading colors of the old time, and given them a permanence for which we have ample reasons to thank him. The Eastern Shore has undergone a thorough transformation within the last three decades. It was coming on before the war, because of the inflowing population from the North, and especially because of the approach of railroads. But the war was a revolution. The old usages are now

---

* Foote, Sketches of Virginia, 1st series, p. 46.

rapidly disappearing, and the Eastern Shore is soon to be but little different from the Western.

As a faithful panorama of the old times in the Delaware and Maryland Peninsula, I take pleasure in commending this work. It is evidently the product of careful observation and much labor. Is it an exaggeration? No. Any man who has been "raised" on the Eastern Shore will see the justice of the delineations. Do these narratives reveal any general and exceptional popular ignorance? No. I question whether in any part of New England, at the corresponding time, the average intelligence was greater than throughout most of the Peninsula. It was as much the custom, with all who could command the means, to give a good education to their children, as to open the "road gate" for the entrance of guests, to any number and for a stay of any length. The early Virginia colleges were largely patronized by Eastern Shore young men, while Princeton and Dickinson, all the way along, have been educating them. Therefore, I would place this work, not in the ranks of history, for such it does not claim to be; but in the domain of sketches of character and life, pertaining to a region which has thus far almost entirely escaped the pencil of the artist and the pen of the American historian. As such, it must be regarded as of value to all students of the religious and local history of our whole country, and more especially to the members and friends of the Church in whose service the author has spent a successful and honored ministerial life.

BUFFALO, N Y., June 2d, 1886.

METHODISM OF THE PENINSULA.

CHAPTER I.

THE PLACE AND THE PEOPLE.

THE territory bounded by the waters of the Atlantic Ocean, and those of the Delaware and Chesapeake Bays, is classic ground in the history of American Methodism. Although not planted here until several years after the formation of the New York and Western Maryland Societies, Methodism took root promptly and grew rapidly; so that, at the time of the organization of the Methodist Episcopal Church in 1784, the Peninsula reported a much larger membership than any other territory of similar extent in the United States. This phenomenal growth cannot perhaps be attributed to any exceptional congeniality of this section, in the beginning, towards Methodism; for here the pioneer fathers met their most stubborn and malicious resistance, even to the extremity of stripes and imprisonment. Doubtless it is to be accounted for by that strange philosophy, in accord with which, God is able to subdue all things unto Himself and make the wrath of men to praise Him. Be that as it may, the Peninsular battle field has been the scene of the most heroic valor and of the noblest achievements; and from its old grave yards and cemeteries, in the day of eternity, will go up a vast army of approved candidates for special crowns of glory.

The great story of Peninsular Methodism has been told, its historic annals pictured by the able pen of the renowned historian, by the rhythmical measures of the poet, and by the facile pencil of the artist. But, much as has been written and represented, the half has not been told. Thousands of honorable names belonging to this history are written only in God's book of remembrance. Many noble and heroic deeds have never found a human chronicler. There are here enough "lost chapters," could they but be gathered, to fill a great library. But where there were once entire, large, living volumes, only torn leaves and isolated paragraphs can now be found.

One department of Peninsular Methodist history— the heroic and the pathetic; the quaint and the humorous—has remained almost untouched. Its traditions have receded and faded, until, in many cases, they have almost lost their plausibility. Some of these traditions, indeed, exist only in corrupted and distorted forms, and detached from the names of the real actors. In the course of a ministry of thirty-three years, within the bounds of what is now the Wilmington Conference, the author has gathered and treasured many well authenticated incidents of the above described class, belonging to local Methodist history. Furthermore, some of the experiences of the writer, and many of his literary efforts have been tinged with a somewhat facetious coloring; and they, of course, legitimately belong in the same archives.

These historic treasuries are, however, so fragmentary as to time, location and characters; that, in the best arrangement it will be possible to give them, they must necessarily appear as a medley, rather than a continuous melody—as scattered chapters of gleanings, instead of consecutive history.

Sin and its dire consequences excepted, God made man as he is, and takes him as he finds him. It is no part of the mission of the Christian religion to obliterate, or blur and repress man's natural characteristics; but to quicken, and by proper channels, conduct them to their appropriate objects and terminations. To the most saintly, there is as really a time to be merry and laugh as, on suitable occasion, to be sober or weep. The human creature who never, by sunny smiles or the sweet ripple of innocent, joyous laughter, gives play and expression to this sportive attribute and capacity, bestowed by his beneficent Creator, is an abnormal and wretched misanthrope.

Our Methodistic fathers were normal specimens of a God-made race. They could both weep with Jeremiah, over the slain unfortunates of the daughter of God's people; and rejoice and shout for joy with the inhabitants of Zion. They could thunder the dread maledictions of Jehovah, in sorrowful threats of a lake of literal fire and brimstone, as the portion of the reckless and finally impenitent sinner. And, with equal facility and holy earnestness, as to them it seemed proper; they could sometimes convulse an audience by their ludicrous caricatures of the solemn visaged hypocrite, or by their mimicry of the insane and grotesque antics of the silly despisers of God.

Furthermore, the mission of Methodism and of our itinerant fathers, was not specially to the great and noble; for, usually, they do not condescend to subjects adapted to "babes and sucklings." It was not to the cultured, the fashionable, the æsthetic.; for they were already enfolded in other churches. But it was to the masses, just as God made them; just as sin had deformed and defiled them; just as the churches that preceded us, had passed by on the other side and left them, covered with wounds and blood—steeped in ignorance and sin, that our Samaritan Church came on her holy mission, with sometimes but a donkey for a burden-bearer, and a wayside inn for a sanatarium. As one result, almost anything—everything possible happened that was uncouth, among the ignorant and unkempt multitudes; from the vacant, open-mouthed, stare and senseless whoop of the ignoramus, to the ludicrous antics of the outlandish clown, and the ribald jeering of the vile blasphemer. Not infrequently, has Methodism saved and enfolded, even such wretched outlaws and enemies as these; and every phase of society, human and inhuman, has been represented in her fellowship. One result of this was, that in our first century, and perhaps even beyond that point, our Methodist gatherings oft times became the theatre for comedies and farces, that no stretch of patience could now endure or charity tolerate.

To be faithful, the historian must recite "the truth, the whole truth, and nothing but the truth." Upon the stage he places before us, he must represent all phases of his subject. Otherwise, his readers will have but partial or distorted views of the society and the events he professes to dramatize. The *personnel* of Methodism to-day, upon the Peninsula, suffers nothing by comparison with that of any other denomination. As to the masses of her members, it was not so in the beginning. Perhaps some may question the propriety of placing on record the few somewhat ridiculous incidents found in this volume, belonging to the earlier and humbler stages of our history, and to isolated localities. The author thinks the reasons above given justify all he has written.

Doings and incidents, which in the light of one age or state of society, would be deemed proper, or at least admissible; at another time or amid other surroundings, would be condemned as boorish and reprehensible, if not positively wicked. In order, therefore, to take a fair and philosophical view of the history of our fathers and their times, it is indispensable that we duly consider their environments, and the influences that gave direction to their actions and sentiments.

For nearly two hundred years from the settlement of the Peninsula, by reason of its isolation, very little of foreign blood or new material had been incorporated into the composition of its people. They grew, therefore, by uninterrupted association and intermarriage, as well as by similarity of pursuits and employments, to be a homogeneous population. An inhabitant of the Peninsula has a longer list of relations—more cousins and uncles and aunts—than a denizen of any other clime in the world, except perchance it be some ocean islander. At old time quiltings and corn-huskings, much of the time was spent in recounting and retracing the genealogical tables, until it often seemed as if each was kin to every other person. And so habituated were these good folk to claim relationship and call each other cousin, even down to the fifth or sixth degree, that many from mere force of habit, addressed all their acquaintances by that endearing title. On this account also, they adopted the same idioms and provincialisms. They followed the same usages and customs. They enjoyed the same recreations. They transacted business, or plowed, planted and reaped by the same unvarying rules their fathers had observed before them; esteeming it little less than sacrilege for one of their number to attempt anything in a new way, or to advance any new theory. So completely isolated were they formerly, by reason of difficult communication with the rest of their fellows, and the scarcity of books and newspapers, that they scarcely felt at all the throbbings of the great world outside; and, in course of time, they came to be like the Gentiles, "a law unto themselves," and, like the Jews, "a peculiar people."

Another thing that ministered to their exceptional peculiarity, was the absence of general education. This phase of the old-time Peninsula life is treated in another chapter, and need be here but casually mentioned. Here and there a family, having arisen to a position of opulence, would break through the conventional crust that had formerly hampered them, and seek outside the culture impossible to obtain at home. The schools of the Peninsula were widely scattered; for the most part their curriculum did not extend beyond the merest rudiments, and less than half the population could keep their own accounts or write their names. Ignorance is always singular, and an ignorant people must needs be a peculiar people.

Of course this condition of Peninsular society in the olden times, was intensified by the introduction and spread of the institution of slavery. The poor African heathens brought with them their weird jungle superstitions; which, in due time, were translated into plantation jargon, and recited by the kitchen and cabin-fires to the wondering children of the mansion, who never wearied of listening; until, in their distorted imaginations, ghosts stalked forth in the darkness, as the stars for multitude; and witches and wizards, thick as crickets on the hearth, or bats in the air of a summer evening, played at hide-and-seek about every old building and deserted tenement, and along every fence and thicket. To this day, many ignorant whites, and perhaps one-half the colored population of the Peninsula, have as much faith in witches and ghosts as they have in the existence of a Great First Cause; and, by charms and exorcisms, take more pains to propitiate the goblins than they do to secure the favor of their Redeemer. To correct these superstitions is the work of the churches and the schools; but as men remember best and have most faith in what they learn in infancy, their complete eradication will require at least three generations of freedom.

Methodism has done more than all other influences to purge out this leaven of superstition, and these peculiarities of ignorance; but very much yet remains to be accomplished. She now, in her various branches in the Peninsula, preaches the Gospel of light and truth to more than forty thousand members, and to twice as many adherents; teaches nearly fifty thousand children and youth in her Sunday-schools; and, by her literature and her reflex influence, is largely directing the general thought and moulding public sentiment. She leads the vanguard of the temperance legion, and guards the rear of the militant column that, having already half triumphed, is surely pressing on to the complete prohibition of the legalized liquor traffic in all our beautiful territory.

Another thing that distinguished the Peninsula in

olden times, and that is not yet quite obliterated, was the far-famed hospitality of its people. Attentive kindness to multitudes of uncles and aunts, and cousins, induced a like kindness to other multitudes who were liable at any moment to become such by marriage; and, by this time, the habit of hospitality had grown into fixedness of character; and indeed, so marked was it, that the stranger was made to forget he was away from home and kindred; and was himself, forthwith metamorphosed into a cousin to all the denizens of the neighborhood where he chanced to be sojourning. The difference, aforetime, between the great progressive people to the north of us and ourselves, was that the wide-awake, thrifty Pennsylvanian, used in the home, what he could not sell to best advantage; whereas, the Eastern Shore man, and his Delaware neighbor, sold and put in his pocket, what he was unable to pack into the stomachs of his household and their jolly visitors.

With great variety of climate for so small a territory, and with almost every variety of soil, our Peninsula will produce everything, from the hardiest vegetables and the cereals, to the fascinating narcotic and the snowy cotton; from the winter apples of Newfoundland, to fruits and flowers well nigh tropical. Almost all species of game are supplied by its rivers and forests, and every aqueous luxury abounds in its diversified waters. Said Bishop Janes to a company of ministers and laymen, in Hon. Jacob Tome's parlor, during the Port Deposit Conference: "Having seen about all our own country, and much of the world beyond, were I a young man about to settle down to agricultural pursuits—if I wanted a home, and all that word implies, I should pass by all the world and invest my money in Peninsular land. And if I were a young Methodist minister, about to enter upon my chosen life-work, I would knock at the door of the Wilmington Conference."

What an outrage upon nature and the will of the Creator, plainly indicated in the metes and bounds of our territory, is that unaccountable blunder of the powers managing political divisions, by which we are partitioned off into three State governments! This great wrong ought somehow to be remedied; but, perhaps, cannot be until Peninsular Methodism shall have so developed the Maryland section, that it shall more highly esteem its grand future possibilities, than its past proud history; shall have so modified the vanity of Accomac and Northampton, that they shall cease to glory in an ideal, but defunct chivalry; and shall have so taught little Delaware the alphabet of modern progress, that she shall break loose and drift away from her precious old fossils of political bourbonism. Who shall declare that a Peninsular State—Virmadel, or Delmavir, or Mavirdel—is without the domain of future possibility?

It is with matters pertaining to this peculiarly circumstanced territory, and these peculiar people, that one of their own number, to the manor born, essays to deal. The task is by so much the more difficult, because it is hard to step outside ourselves, so to speak, and see ourselves as others see us. As an acceptable and wholesome meal cannot be constituted of mere spice and flavoring, but requires some substantial ingredients; no more will thoughtful, serious, hungry souls be content with a literary production having only its humorous flavor to recommend it. The author hopes to meet this reasonable demand of the Christian reader's appetite, and aid in the symmetrical development of his higher and better nature. He hopes also, by this humble effort, to stimulate others to undertake a similar task; so that the remaining fragments of the rich and heroic history of Peninsular Methodism may be gathered and preserved, to be sometime remoulded by the pen of a more accomplished historian, for the instruction and entertainment of future generations.

From these sketches, many a tempting bit of spicy and attractive history, must needs be omitted, because the still living actors might fail to enjoy the diversion; or indeed, to see that there is anything entertaining in the recital. Most living persons better enjoy a laugh when it is not at their own expense. Besides, it is much safer for the historian to employ the weapons of his wit upon those only who will not be likely to cherish resentment. Not being apprehensive of personal danger from ghosts of any religious persuasion, the author anticipates no risk or harm from the liberty he proposes to take with the *ante mortem* idiosyncrasies of departed worthies, lay and ministerial, now among the probationary graduates of the Methodist Episcopal Church. He will not hesitate to take all legal advantages of these crowned warriors. He will represent only chosen fragments of their earthly doings. He will watch the opportune moments in their life dramas; pull aside the curtains sometimes just at those critical junctures, when he shall happen to surprise them in some strange freak or adventure, or ludicrous episode; and will give his readers a chance for a quiet little peep here and there, and for an occasional smile; meanwhile, presenting sufficient of their life histories to make those glimpses intelligible. The author is by no means certain that he shall present these historic incidents in the order the actors would prefer; for, not being a medium, he has not had opportunity to consult them. If they have any "complaints or appeals," they must wait for an adjustment until the unintentional transgressors shall have graduated to their "Quarterly Conference."

CHAPTER II.

OUR QUAINT ITINERANT FATHERS.

REV. THOS. WARE was born and grew up to manhood in the State of New Jersey. As a Revolutionary soldier, he aided in expelling the Briton and in procuring American Independence. On the expiration of his term of service, he returned to his home. Here he heard that flaming herald, Caleb Peddicord, preach; and under his ministry was awakened and converted. He had not been more valiant as a follower of Washington than he now became as a soldier of Jesus Christ. His burning zeal pushed him out preaching without license or church authority. Mr. Asbury came to Jersey where Mr. Ware resided; heard of his remarkable gifts; sent for him; and at the conclusion of an interview, in which he made the impression on the young man's mind that he was about to receive a severe reprimand for his presumption, Asbury tenderly embraced him, and at once commissioned him for Dover circuit. "Here," says Ware, "I was caught, and how could I decline?" Accordingly, in 1783, the young soldier of the cross came, with a timid and heavy heart, to the capital of Delaware.

Mr. Ware was not the only young man who began his itinerant life in Dover. Tradition tells of a junior preacher who once came thither, evidently without "a timid and heavy heart," and thus introduced himself on the occasion of his first appearance in the pulpit: "Some p-preachers allers p-p-put their best foot fo'most only on great occasions, or when they're a g-goin' to preach in a place the first t-time. But I w-want you to understand I allers p-put my best f-foot fo'most; and I don't 'spect to p-preach no better to-day nor I shall any other t-time." He was soon given to understand that he could employ both his best and his worst foot in some more appropriate itinerant field. Memory still vividly and painfully serves another of Mr. Ware's itinerant descendants, of his introduction to a junior preacher's life, thirty-three years ago; and of an embarassment so overwhelming, as he stood before his Dover congregation for the first time, that, for some moments, he could not tell the book, chapter and verse of his text. Not infrequently, during that year, did the poor fellow get his theological skein into such a terrible tangle, as to extort from him the mental wail, "O, for a lodge in some vast wilderness!"

Like this latter young minister, Mr. Ware sometimes lost his *ware*-abouts, and broke down. On such occasions, he tells us, he would stand and sob, like a boy who had stumped his great toe, until he became calm and collected, when he would gather up the loose ends as best he could, and proceed with his discourse. Sometimes the tears of a sympathetic membership would mingle with those of the discouraged and humiliated preacher;

and he was always soothed and comforted by the fraternal and loving manifestations of the eminent ladies and gentlemen leading in the Dover Methodism of that day. Their descendants inherit their kindly instincts.

During this year, Mr. Ware was invited to occupy the pulpit of the Church of England chapel at Duck Creek Cross Roads, afterwards called Smyrna. This church was probably without a pastor at that time, its rector having no doubt fled to the mother country. There was then no Protestant Episcopal Church in existence; and the communicants of this chapel had not received the revelation that Methodist preachers are not to be ecclesiastically recognized as Christian ministers. The young itinerant accepted the invitation, and proceeded with the services. But before he had finished his introduction, three desperate looking men came marching up the aisle, one of whom announced himself a vestryman, seized Ware by the collar and proposed to expel him headlong from the church. A Mr. Skillington, a giant of a man, seized the irate vestryman in like manner, and aimed a blow with his huge fist that must have felled the ruffian to the floor but for the intervention of Judge Raymond. This honorable conservator of the peace, begged Mr. Skillington to withhold the merited blow, and finally pacified him, when he expelled the intruders by a threat of commitment.

While travelling Kent circuit in Maryland, the following year, Mr. Ware went on one occasion to hear a young English clergyman read his trial sermon.

While he was vigorously pounding Mr. Wesley, and the Methodists—many of whom were in the congregation—after the fashion of that day, and branding them as enthusiasts, he took occasion to say: "The preaching of the Methodists can only enkindle an enthusiastic flame—a mere ignis-fatuus." At this point, an interesting and pious Methodist lady, who enjoyed the confidence and esteem of the entire community, rapturously cried out: "Glory to God! If what I now enjoy in my soul be enthusiasm, let me always be an enthusiast!" It was quite manifestly evident, that the spontaneous and pious rebuke was approved by the parson's congregation; and the young gentleman was thrown into serious confusion. If he would have gracefully retreated or apologized; he labored under the difficulty, that, nothing of this sort having been contemplated, the apology *wasn't written*. After much hesitation and embarrassment, he rushed on through his reading, but stumbling and making matters worse all the way. In the interview with the vestrymen that followed, he quarrelled with them on the salary question; told them they might all perish before he would serve them for a less sum than he had named; and finally wound up the interview in a towering passion, with an avalanche of abuse on the heads of the poor Methodists, very greatly of course to their advantage.

In Wilmington, where, ninety-five years ago, there was one Methodist congregation, with Thomas Ware as its pastor, there are now twelve Methodist Episcopal

Churches and chapels, besides several of other Methodist denominations. Mr. Ware had been absent from the Peninsula several years. Of his appointment to Wilmington he says: "This was my first station; but I sighed for the back-woods, which were a Paradise to me compared with this suffocating borough." Poor Thomas Ware was not the only preacher well-nigh stifled by a city appointment.

Wilmington seems also to have been affected with a mystical miasm on the subject of religion. The Methodists were unsparingly denounced by the Hicksites and their natural allies, the Deists, as "hirelings and will-worshipers;" and, worse still, the sons of Belial were accustomed to surround the old Asbury Church by hundreds, with ribald blasphemies and wicked threats, while the long-suffering congregations were composed of scarcely fifty persons. On account of the outrageous conduct of these ruffians, women dared not venture to the church after dark; and, for their accommodation, it became necessary to hold evening services before sundown.

Mr. Ware afterwards travelled Cecil circuit. He relates the following interesting incident concerning a quarterly meeting occasion, where Dr. Chandler, Presiding Elder, was in charge. The weather was heavy and threatening, and the congregation gathered from many miles around, and with little opportunity for adequate shelter in the neighborhood, became anxious and restless. On Saturday of the meeting, Dr. Chandler arose, and calling the attention of all, said: "Mark my words; there will be no rain in this vicinity until this quarterly meeting is ended." He then exhorted the gathered saints to banish all anxiety, and worship God as if the sunlight were smiling upon them. "The morning of the Sabbath," says Mr. Ware, "was the most dark and threatening I ever saw. The clouds of heaven seemed surcharged; and there was a general expectation that the Doctor would prove a false prophet. But the rain was withheld until the services were all ended and the people had reached their homes, when the very windows of the skies seemed to be opened; and the rainfall exceeded anything known in that region within the memory of the oldest inhabitant."

A similar circumstance, but yet even more remarkable, occurred at the first camp-meeting held on the Peninsula. It was near Smyrna, Delaware, in the year 1805. Dr. Chandler, apparently sub-bishop for the entire territory of the Peninsula, presided. One day during the meeting, a terrific thunder-storm arose, and the congregation became excited and restless, but lingered on the persuasive words of the minister of God. Just at the juncture when the preliminary gust burst upon the encampment, and the alarmed audience began to scatter, Dr. Chandler sprang to his feet, and interrupting the speaker and calling the congregation to prayer, he pleaded mightily that God would stay the rain, that the preacher's message might be concluded. Instantly the dark rolling cloud began to part; a little spot of blue ether opened above;

and, although it rained furiously on either side, and indeed all around within a few rods, scarcely a drop fell within the consecrated circle.

The above was not the only instance where the divine protection was apparently vouchsafed to a camp-ground in response to the pleadings of God's people. In the year 1836, an army of locusts, probably the *Caloptenus Atlantis*, attacked the forest where the historic and renowned Spring Branch campmeeting was held. It was located in the neighborhood Bishop Asbury called "Perdens," near the site of the present town of Felton, Delaware. These destructive insects encompassed the forest, as the Assyrian army environed the Prophet. Day after day the wave of destruction rolled in, converging towards the apparently fated camp-ground. Every evening, after the day's work was ended, devoted souls visited the scene, and prayed the God of Elisha to interpose his protecting power, drive back the ravening Egyptian insect army, and save the foliage as a canopy for his worshippers. The entire grove was denuded by the tide of destruction, until it reached the outer margin of the tenting-ground, where the desolating wave ceased; and, apparently, not a single leaf was touched within the divinely enchanted spot.

Should one of our modern Peninsular camp-grounds —"Wood-lawn" and, possibly, "Wye" excepted—be thus threatened, could any really sincere, intelligent and pious soul offer a petition for its protection? What would the Head of the Church think of such a prayer?

Reader; forgive this profane step on your modern holy-ground, and let us change the subject.

Another of the remarkable characters moulded by the divine hand, through the influence of American Methodism, was Rev. Benjamin Abbott. Like Ware, he was a product of New Jersey; but did no little itinerant and evangelistic work within the bounds of the Peninsula. His early opportunities for education were meager; and Christ found him and thrust him forth into the Methodist field of evangelism, an illiterate and poorly furnished young man. But while cultured mockers at first felt inclined to ridicule the uncouth, asinine jaw-bone, with which he was equipped for the battle against indifference and vice; they very soon learned to stand in awe of the more than Samsonian strength with which his rude armor was wielded. His power over an audience was ofttimes simply wonderful. One incident will illustrate scores of a similar character, that might be produced.

Mr. Abbott was, on one occasion, delivering his Master's message at a private residence, crowded with a promiscuous company, gathered from all the surrounding regions. Though angular and verbally uncouth, the sermon was so direct and earnest as to compel attention. But when he came to make the application, somewhat in the style of Nathan to King David—"Thou art the man!"—such was the fiery, magnetic influence attending his utterances that the people fell, shrieking for mercy, all about the house. The few saints present shouted for joy. The wicked, terribly affrighted, rushed for the doors and windows; and, in their mad haste, fell out pell-mell in heaps, where they lay wailing in penitential agony. So great became the outcry that Mr. Abbott was forced to discontinue his appeal. With the purpose of drowning the heartrending cries of distress, he announced a hymn and requested that it be sung. A brother attempting to raise the hymn was struck by the overwhelming power and pitched under a table, where he lay as a dead man. A second person made the effort, and he instantly lay sprawling and bellowing upon the floor. The preacher himself then tried it; but the mysterious influence that disabled the two laymen, came upon him in such measure, that he could do naught but cry out in amazement at the wonderful manifestation of supernatural presence and power. The meeting continued throughout the day and during all the following night; attended by "signs and wonders" in the conversion of many sinners, and in the entire sanctification of most of the former believers present. Such things can only be explained upon the hypothesis, "It is not by (human) might or power, but by my Spirit, saith the Lord."

A long, strong, beautiful life, that stretched all the way through the first century of American Methodism, was that of Rev. Henry Bœhm. In his stalwart young manhood, as travelling companion to the then enfeebled Bishop Asbury, he traversed almost every part of the Peninsula. Afterwards, as Presiding Elder and in the pastoral relation at various points, he became a prominent factor among the agencies of God in building up Peninsular Methodism. Indeed, some of the first years of his ministerial life were spent within this territory. Mrs. Ann Hewit, of Elkton, died in 1883, ninety-three years old. The writer heard this devoted saint tell of her conversion at Purnell's Meeting House, near where Felton afterwards sprang up, when she was a little girl but about ten years old. But little attention was given to children in those days, and the penitent child was kneeling alone in a corner; when, near the close of the meeting, Mr. Bœhm, the young preacher, approached her, raised her head gently, and exclaimed, "Why, if this isn't my little Annie!" and then spoke so encouragingly and lovingly to her, that in a little while she was rejoicing in the salvation of Him who said, "Suffer the little children, and forbid them not to come." It must have been a most delightful episode, when seventy-five years afterwards, the same devoted man of God met this precious mother in Israel, and heard from the lips of her he once called "my little Annie," but whom he had supposed long since dead, the above story of her conversion through his instrumentality. Since that day they have met again.

Father Bœhm's "Reminiscences" cover an ample stretch of time and space, and are of a general interest that will well repay perusal. His references to the Peninsula are frequent, and are sometimes tinged with a vein of humor that shows he was by no means an ascetic.

In this he was no doubt influenced by his associations, which were with men of the most genial natures and habits. No set of men who ever blessed the world with their sunny presence, could better tell or more heartily enjoy an innocent joke, than the old itinerants of early Methodism. Of course they had due regard to King Solomon's rule of "a time and a season to all things." In fact, the more we study them in the mature light of the century whose dawn ushered them upon the stage, the more we are convinced that they were of just such materials as Methodist preachers are made of to-day.

There are sour spirits in the Church here and there, who comfort themselves annually with a summer spell of hydrophobia, or horror of watering-places patronized by ministers of the gospel in search of rest and relaxation. "Just think of such men as Asbury and Bœhm and Chandler fooling away their Lord's time after that fashion!" say they. But they did; and modern preachers who visit the seashore, are but following the example of the ancient Methodist worthies. Young Mr. Bœhm visited at least two watering-places the same season, while preaching on the Peninsula. He employed his vacation in July, in a visit to his brother's farm in Pennsylvania, whereon was a watering-place of refreshing, flowing springs. One hot day, with the mercury at 90°, he amused himself mowing in his brother's meadow until he was dripping with sweat and nearly sun-struck. Then, on his way to the house, he waded neck deep through a pond of the flowing spring water, to "cool himself off." The experiment was successful. In fact, he very nearly cooled himself off permanently. Dr. Chandler, being a Medical Doctor as well as Presiding Elder, took his case in hand; bled him well; administered stimulating restoratives, and cared for him until he became convalescent and able to travel a little; when he took him by easy stages to the seashore near Lewes, Delaware, to recuperate his prostrate energies. So depleted was he, that when bathing, he was frequently knocked topsy-turvy by the breakers. On these occasions, Dr. Chandler, he tells us, would indulge in a hearty laugh and exclaim: "Ah, my boy; that is the medicine for you!"

An incident related by Mr. Bœhm, will serve to illustrate the depth of ignorance that once prevailed in certain portions of the Peninsula. On one occasion, Rev. Freeborn Garrettson, travelling at night through the wilds of lower Sussex, became hopelessly bewildered and lost amid the labyrinths of the great Cypress Swamp. At length, seeing a light and following its guidance, he was led to a friendly cabin and received under its hospitable shelter. After some little conversation with his host, he ventured upon the subject of religion, and wound up by inquiring whether he were acquainted with the Lord Jesus Christ; when he was astonished by the manifestly innocent reply: "No, sir; don't know 'im; an' I've never hearn wher the gentleman lives at!"

Mr. Bœhm once heard the celebrated Lorenzo Dow, while on one of his hurried trips through the Peninsula, preach at old Union Church, on Duck Creek circuit. He had travelled all night and until 10 o'clock, A. M., to be in time at his appointment. He preached to three thousand people within and without the church. His text was, "Watchman; what of the night?;" and the sermon was characteristic. When he concluded his discourse, he leaped out from the pulpit window; remounted his horse, and rode away to Duck Creek, where he preached again to a great multitude. On that occasion, this wonderful man rode eighty miles and preached five sermons without sleep.

The prophet Elisha was not the only instance of a man of God providenfially fed by a bird of heaven. A widow Rouark, a Methodist lady of "ye olden times," resided on Hooper's Island in the Chesapeake Bay. Rev. Jos. Everett, one of the early itinerants, one day quite unexpectedly, and just before the hour for dinner, sought the hospitality of her home. Spring chickens had not yet ripened, and the pious widow was greatly distressed that she had nothing suitable to set before her distinguished visitor. Excusing herself, she left the house, and started forth from the yard, in tearful agitation and distressing perplexity as to what expedient she could possibly hit upon to relieve her mortifying embarrassment. But, at that moment, the burden of her heart was strangely lifted. A fish-hawk, sailing over her head, dropped at her feet a fine large bass-fish, which she received with joyful gratitude, and dressed and served to her reverend visitor.

The following interesting incident is related of Mr. Harry Ennalls, one of the prominent early Methodists of Dorchester county, Maryland. He was probably the same man from whom the historic Ennalls' Spring campground derived its name. On one occasion, Mr. Bœhm and other ministers were at Mr. Ennalls' house, in company with Governor Bassett, of Dover, and the elder James Asheton Bayard, United States Senator of Delaware. For some unexplained reason, at evening family worship, ignoring his ministerial guests, Mr. Ennalls himself led in the devotions. He made the service the occasion of a special and very fervent prayer in behalf of his distinguished senatorial guest. At the conclusion, Mr. Bayard, apparently much agitated, paced back and forth across the parlor floor for a time; and then, turning to Mr. Ennalls, inquired with some severity: "Harry, what did you mean by shaking your brimstone bag over me that way?" "To save you from hell, sir," was the prompt response. The narrator informs us that the Honorable Senator seemed visibly impressed, and was silent and apparently thoughtful throughout the evening. Was that honest, brave seed-sowing of Harry Ennalls harvestless? The gathering of the angel reapers in the day of eternity shall reveal the answer.

Mr. Bœhm was accustomed to act as amanuensis for Bishop Asbury, when engaged, with his Presiding Elders, in making the appointments. On such occasions, not infrequently the anxious preachers were disposed to importune him to ascertain, if possible, what was likely to be their fate. The humorous reply with which he was accustomed to effect his escape when thus waylaid, was: "Secret things belong unto the Bishop; but those things which are revealed, belong unto the preachers and to their children." In those days the propriety of an appointment was supposed to hinge largely upon the condition that both preacher and people were kept in profound ignorance of it until the awful hour of its *ex cathedra* promulgation. Now, sometimes, both preachers and people are wont to reveal some very curious and interesting secrets, on the question of appointments, to the Bishop!

As already stated, camp-meetings were introduced within the Peninsula in 1805. Two were held that year on Dover circuit, which embraced at that time, fully one-half of Kent county, Delaware. The first was held in a grove about three miles south of Smyrna, on the Dover road; and the second at a place called Miller's Mill, a few miles west of Dover, and not far from Union Church on the present Wyoming circuit.

Modern Methodists are very orderly and quiet—perhaps even cautiously undemonstrative in their camp-meeting worship. In fact it is not impossible we have cultivated the comely flowers of decency and order so industriously as to materially shorten the crop of wheat. But there was ofttimes a quaint fervor and heartiness—a holy and boisterous enthusiasm, in the conduct of these early camp worshippers, contrasting somewhat strangely with our present polished manners and good behavior. We whisper our prayers, if not in the

> "Holy awe, that dares not move;
> And all the silent heaven of love;"

at any rate, in the exercise of our æsthetic good taste; and the accommodating leader of the camp prayer-meeting thoughtfully sings the Doxology to announce the occasional conversion at the serene altar of sacrifice. But at the old time camp-meetings, the cries of the stricken penitents, and the shouts of the liberated prisoners were often distinctly heard at the distance of three miles! The powerful presentation, by our Methodist fathers, of the "glorious Gospel" from the then novel but truthful standpoint of Arminianism, was new, striking and mightily effective in the production of overwhelming awakening, and a corresponding anguish of repentance. The glorious relief of conscious salvation was also proportioned to the burden of terrible conviction. The numbers involved in the sweep of these great spiritual tornadoes would likewise naturally add to the excitement of the individual participants; and altogether it is not at all wonderful that the noise of the primitive camp-meeting was ofttimes like the "sound of many waters." This will appear even the less remarkable when we read the salvation statistics of these meetings. The young itinerant, Henry Bœhm, was the first secretary of the first camp-meeting association; and was charged with the spiritual book-keeping of the meetings, so far as tangible and visible results were concerned. The following is a summary of his record for the first meeting near Smyrna:

On the first day, there were 47 persons converted and 9 wholly sanctified. The results of the second day were 100 converted and 75 wholly sanctified. The next morning there were 62 converted and 53 wholly sanctified. In the Pentecostal tornado of Sunday and Sunday night, there were 420 converted and 190 wholly sanctified. And during the entire meeting there were 1100 persons converted and 600 wholly sanctified. At the second meeting, near Dover, "so mightily grew the word of God, and prevailed," that there were 1320 professions of conversion, and 916 of entire sanctification! When we consider the disparity between the population of these rural districts and that of Jerusalem at the solemn festive gathering of Pentecost; when we remember the supernatural advantages attending the Apostolic ministry, and their nearness to the startling events of the redemption they proclaimed; we are constrained to the declaration that the spiritual results above given, have never been exceeded in the history of the Christian Church.

Neither the institutions, usages, nor methods of our Church were ever invented or devised; but were rather expedients—the spontaneous outgrowths of newly recognized exigencies. For more than three decades from the beginnings by Strawbridge and Embury, no special arrangement was devised for the accommodation of penitents seeking pardon. The custom seems to have been for them to pray as best they could, wherever they might happen to be seated; or, perchance to kneel in their place; or, if mightily convicted, to fall upon the floor, writhing and wailing in the agony of their penitential sorrow. Probably the first Methodist preacher who ever invited awakened sinners to leave their places in the congregation, and to come forward and kneel at the "altar" or communion rail, was Rev. Dr. Chandler. The innovation was introduced in 1799, at Bethel, near Chesapeake City, then called "Back Creek Church," on Cecil circuit. About a score of persons accepted the novel invitation; among whom was the afterward renowned Laurence Laurenson. "That," says Mr. Bœhm, "was the first time I ever saw or heard of mourners being invited to the altar." The result of the experiment proved its utility. The interest became concentrated; penitents were much more conveniently counselled; the meetings became more orderly; and thus the unpremeditated expedient of this humble but mighty Methodist revivalist, introduced in this little Peninsula chapel, has gradually been adopted throughout Methodism; and indeed, substantially so, by all the evangelical Churches of Christendom; and the Methodist "mourner's bench," once so mercilessly ridiculed by our sister Churches, has, under some form and name, come to be universally recognized as an important factor in the successful conduct of revival meetings.

Some of the older Methodists, who will follow with interest these fragmentary etchings, will perhaps remember a quaint itinerant, known extensively in his day, throughout the Peninsula, as "Father Wiltshire." If the writer were asked to paint his ideal of an "innocent abroad," he would at once proceed to draw a sketch of Rev. George Wiltshire.

He was a little, old, shrivelled-up Englishman, about five feet in height, presenting somewhat the appearance of a dilapidated and rusty pair of cast-off scissors; albeit, in fact, he was but one side of a pair of scissors; for he was a stereotyped and helpless old bachelor. His little head was as round as an orange, and as bald as a turnip; and had apparently met with some accident in his juvenile days that drove it down close between his projecting shoulders. The front side of this quaint little protuberance, was wrought into a visage very much after the pattern of the face of a screech owl, and would have furnished a first-class study for the celebrated comic artist, Thomas Nast. Nevertheless, it was a face that would beget no painful or alarming misgivings; for it was a truthful index to the solemn honesty of the good man's matter-of-fact nature.

Father Wiltshire's ways, movements, conversation, preaching—everything about him; everything he did—was stamped with his own original peculiarity. His hands and feet were generally very much in his way; he was forever stumbling into something ridiculous; and whenever his ludicrous oddities of speech or manner would "bring down the house" in a roar of laughter, as was not infrequently the case, his astonished look would betray his utter amazement at the conduct of his auditors

—for he could never discover anything to provoke merriment. Though by no means a censorious ascetic, he was rarely, if ever, seen to smile. His profound honesty and kindness of heart, however, always insured him a welcome at all the principal Methodist homes of the Peninsula; and won to him the sincere esteem of many kindly hearts.

Once on a time, it is said, at a camp-meeting, an impulsive but indiscreet sister, whose hospitality he had sometimes enjoyed, dared to give public expression to her esteem and reverence, by imprinting a kiss on his furrowed cheek. Instantly putting himself into the attitude of an insulted tom-cat, and drawing back with clenched fist, he exclaimed: "Sister! If it wasn't for the grace of God, I'd knock you down—knock you down, sister!"

Who, that was present, can ever forget a scene in which Father Wiltshire was the chief figure, at one of the sessions of the old Philadelphia Conference in the Union Church, Philadelphia? On some unsatisfactory pretext, Rev. D. R. Thomas, M. D., had taken the responsibility of leaving his appointment early in the Conference year, and had settled in New York to the practice of his profession. He now sent a request to be granted a supernumerary relation. There was no little discussion in the case, during which, Rev. A. Manship ventured the opinion that, remaining a single man beyond the time of life at which Methodist preachers ought to be blessed with a good wife, had rendered Brother Thomas peculiar, as was invariably the case under such circumstances; and that his old bachelor notions had doubtless made him unacceptable, and led to his deserting his work.

At this moment, Rev. W. L. Gray, in those days ever on the alert to precipitate an episode in the Conference, crept to the side of Father Wiltshire, as he crouched upon the kneeling cushion, with his hand behind his ear, listening intently at Mr. Manship's impulsive and characteristic eloquence, and whispered in his ear:

"Father Wiltshire; if I were you, I would resent that insinuation. Manship is whipping you over Thomas' shoulders."

"D'ye think so, brother—think so?"

"Yes; I'm sure of it; and I wouldn't stand it!"

The intense, wild stare of the old veteran showed that he had taken the bait, and was ready for the fray. He poised himself for the onslaught; and the moment the last word dropped from the lips of the unconscious offender, Father Wiltshire sprang to a perpendicular with the promptness and agility of a Jumping Jack; and electrified the conference and the immense audience with the following deliverance:

"Mr. Bishop; I reckon the dear, good brother who's just fired off, has been a slinging his insinuations at poor, old George Wiltshire. And I rise, sir, to make my defence. It's true, Bishop, I never got married; I'm mighty sorry I couldn't; but I hope that aint no hanging matter. I've always thought, sir, I had good reasons for remaining single. Bishop and brethren;

when I was a young man, I thought a good deal about gittin' married, and I prayed over it; but I was poor, Bishop—very poor; and I was afraid I didn't have no right to marry some poor girl or woman, and half starve her to death. So I thought I'd better wait till I got more money. But oh, brethren; my appointments were poor, and kept me poor; and I never felt able to git married. After a while, I begun to grow old, with all the trials and tribulations of a poor, lonely old bachelor; with no particular home, and no wife to darn my stockings, or smooth my pillow when I'm 'under the weather.' And now, Mr. Bishop and friends" (at the same moment casting an imploring look, with outstretched hands, towards the galleries crowded with Philadelphia ladies),' "Now I'm old and ugly; and who'd have me now?—who'd have me now?" Amid the roars and screams of laughter that ensued, the Bishop's sobriety went by the board; and Father Wiltshire sank down to his place, wondering what on earth had happened in the conference.

In the spring of 1853, the conference was held at Harrisburg, Pa. Father Wiltshire had reached the seat of the conference, coming across the country by stage. When the session closed, he concluded to return by railroad, via Philadelphia. His car was crowded with his brother ministers. He and his capacious old carpet bag, always stuffed with all his most precious worldly possessions, monopolized one of the rear seats. As the train rolled along, the preachers were engaged in good-humored conversation; while Father Wiltshire was engrossed manipulating the contents of his carpet bag, apparently intent on making a complete inventory of all its varied treasures. Suddenly the train darted into a tunnel, whose midnight darkness was rendered the more hideous by the fitful glare of the fugitive sparks from the puffing locomotive. To one unused to such an experience, it seemed as if they might suddenly have come into the weird and doleful regions of Dante's Inferno.

In the comparative silence ensuing, a rustling and scrambling was heard, accompanied by suppressed groans and exclamations of alarm; and when at last the train emerged into daylight, the brethren beheld Father Wiltshire crouching in the middle of the car; while books, papers, collars, handkerchiefs, shirts, etc.,—the contents of the carpet bag—were scattered through the car in ludicrous confusion. Straightening himself slowly, and scanning the situation in every direction, as the look of terror on his countenance faded away into an expression of satisfaction and relief, he convulsed his brethren with the exclamation: "Thank God I'm not in Hell!"

Mr. Wiltshire's kindness of heart disposed him to give every one a fair show; and his ignorance of human nature sometimes exposed him to ridicule as the dupe of the foolish. Near Snow Hill, Maryland, lived a young man whose zeal had so far outrun his knowledge, that he proclaimed himself "called to be an apostle," and repeatedly, but vainly, sought license to preach at the hands of the pastors of the circuit. Soon after Father Wiltshire's arrival at Snow Hill, as preacher in charge, he was favored with a call by this consequential ignoramus, who thus accosted him:

"B–brother Willyshire; I think, s–sir, the L–lord's called me t–to p–preach the G–gospel."

"Well, brother," responded the preacher, "If you think the Lord has called you to preach, you shall have a chance—have a chance, brother. I will announce, Sunday morning, that you will preach in Snow Hill Sunday night. Now go home and make your preparation."

Accordingly, after preaching on Sunday morning, the good man made the following announcement: "I want you all to come out to-night—all to come out. A brother's going to preach you never heard before, and may never hear any more—never hear any more."

When the hour arrived, the church was crowded; the people expecting that some distinguished stranger was to address them. At length, to their amazement, the self-constituted herald elbowed his way through the crowd to the pulpit; and the officials who knew him hung their heads in mortification, but still hoped they might be mistaken as to his identity. After blundering through the preliminary exercises, the poor crank announced, with drawling stammer, the words of his text: "Ye shall grow up as calves of the stall," repeating them three or four times. Then he said: "B–breethering;

I'm not afeered o' the face o' clay," and again repeated his text. He now cleared his throat, scratched his head, and again declared: "I tell you, breethering; I'm not afeered o' the face o' clay!" And finally, after again repeating his text, he concluded his sermon with the announcement: "The subject matter in hand is calves!" As the poor fellow, at this point, discovered his inability to do anything with his "calves," he sat down overcome with confusion. Almost equally embarrassed, Father Wiltshire had gathered up the cape of his great coat about his head, and sought to hide himself behind the pulpit. At this point a leading official approached, while the congregation was vainly endeavoring to mantain its decorum; and shaking the pastor, said:

"Come, Brother Wiltshire; this brother's broken down, and here's a large congregation expecting preaching. Get up, and preach or exhort, or say something!"

"Wh–why, brother, what can I say?"

"Oh, I don't know, brother Wiltshire; say what you please."

Instantly the old man bleated out—"Ba-ah!"

Amid the uproarious laughter that ensued, the official expostulated with:

"Oh, Brother Wiltshire! what made you say that?"

"Wh–why, brother; what else could I say? The brother's made us out all calves!"

So completely demoralized were both pastor and people, that the laughing multitude scattered, like frolicsome calves, without even the formality of the benediction. To this day, the older Methodists of Snow Hill, who were witnesses of this disorderly scene, are wont to laugh over the calf sermon, and Father Wiltshire's strikingly appropriate application of its main proposition. The sequel proved the old gentleman's announcement prophetic. The people had never heard the preacher before; and they never did hear him any more! He was effectually cured of his hallucination.

This chapter may appropriately conclude with some humorous glimpses from the Peninsular drama in which the great Asbury acted a part. Francis Asbury was born in England in 1745, and died in Virginia in 1816. He was licensed to preach at sixteen years of age, and received by John Wesley into the travelling ministry six years later. At twenty-six years of age, he landed in America as a missionary. At the organization of the Methodist Episcopal Church in 1784, he was elected and ordained Bishop. In labors he was as abundant as Paul the Apostle, and like him, for his work's sake, he remained unmarried. "He was always poor and always generous." It is estimated that during his ministry in America, he "travelled more than 270,000 miles, visiting every part of the country; preached more than 16,000 sermons, ordained over 4,000 ministers, and presided at 224 conferences. It is to the labors of this indefatigable apostle, more than to any other human agency, that Methodism in America owes its excellent organization and wonderful growth."

In his "Reminiscences," Father Bœhm says of

Bishop Asbury: "He was five feet and nine inches high, very erect, and weighed one hundred and fifty pounds. In dress he was a pattern of neatness. He wore a low-crowned, broad-rimmed hat. His clothes were always black. He wore a frock coat, with straight collar, and buttoned up to the neck." Instead of pantaloons, he rejoiced in short clothes, or breeches with leggings, and sometimes the ornamental shoe-buckle. His preachers, originally, dressed in the same manner; but, in 1810, some of the more independent and progressive among the ministers began to substitute pantaloons for short clothes and leggings, to the great anxiety of the good Bishop, who imagined he discovered, in these innovations, the sure indication of the premature decay and dissolution of his beloved Methodism. The Church, he feared, was all going to wreck and ruin, because the preachers would wear pantaloons! What would the old hero do—what would he say, should he come back to-day and find the preachers clad in the height of the fashion, and their wives wearing hats, coats and vests; and, with bangs and bustles, becoming more and more the very antipodes of their godly grandmothers of his day, with every returning season!

Bishop Asbury was a genial spirit, full of good humor and pleasantry in his social intercourse; but very rarely betrayed anything but the most serious spirit in his writings. The nearest approach to a joke the writer remembers to have discovered in his journal, was his remark concerning the marriage of Rev. Joseph

Hartley, soon after his release from imprisonment in the Easton, Maryland, jail. On sixty dollars a year—the allowance of a Methodist preacher in those days—it was, of course, impossible to afford the luxury of a wife. Mr. Hartley "married a wife;" and, therefore, like the man in the Gospel, he could no longer "come" or go as an itinerant; and hence, he settled down on a Talbot County farm, and served the Church thenceforth as a local preacher.

Mr. Hartley had, it seems, a very exalted notion of his own ability and importance; and needed something to bring him to a becoming estimate of his mundane relations. Writing concerning his marriage and location, Bishop Asbury remarks: "I find the care of a wife begins to humble my young friend, and make him very teachable. I have always thought he carried great sail; but he will have ballast now!" Poor Joseph Hartley was not the only man who has been thus sobered!

Some very pious friends of the Church are no little distressed, oftentimes, at the fact that some of her ministers occasionally switch off from the main track of ministerial work, to deliver lectures in the interest of various causes; and, sometimes, to help replenish an empty pocket-book. If such will read Father Bœhm's book, they will discover that these brethren, they esteem so erratic, are right in the line of the apostolical succession. He says: "Mr. Asbury lectured at Perden's, and engaged the friends to subscribe 700 lbs. of pork towards the erection of the meeting-house at Barratt's." It by no means follows from this statement that the "friends" at Perden's were a *hoggish* set of people!

April would now be considered early for camp-meeting; but our good old fathers did not stand for the season or weather. On Thursday, April 18th, 1810, the Philadelphia Conference was held in connection with a camp-meeting in a beautiful grove, on the western suburbs of the town of Easton, Maryland. It was a season of great interest, well remembered by some of the old Methodists of that region, who still lingered on the shores of time in the year 1876. As connected with that conference, the following story was told the writer concerning Bishop Asbury and Billy Hibbard: At the conference roll-call, the secretary called, in its order, the name William Hibbard. There was no response, although Brother Hibbard sat prominently upon one of the front seats. Again the secretary called the name, and still there was no response. Said the Bishop, somewhat sternly: "Brother Hibbard; why don't you answer to your name?" "I will," said he, "Bishop, when the secretary calls it." "Isn't your name William Hibbard, sir?" inquired the Bishop. "No, sir; my name's Billy Hibbard." "Billy! Billy!" said the Bishop—"Why that is a little boy's name." "Well, sir," replied Billy, "I was quite a little boy when my father named me!" In the roar of laughter that followed, the vanquished Bishop was constrained to join.

CHAPTER III.

HEROES OF ERIN.

IRISHMEN have borne no insignificant part in the history of Methodism. Both across the sea and in this country, their enthusiasm and eloquence have left their lasting impress. The seed sown in New York and Maryland, by Embury and Strawbridge, was afterwards cultivated in part by faithful laborers born in the same green island. Like the Jew, the Irishman is cosmopolitan; and, like the Jew, his tribal traits are so distinct and prominent, that he is instantly recognized to the ends of the earth. The instincts of the typical Irishman are aggressive. No army has marched, in modern warfare, in which his sturdy tramp has not mingled. No assembly of statesmen has discussed political problems, but in which his brogue has been heard. No mission beacon lights the mountain tops of heathendom, to which his hand has not contributed its fagot. From the stormy days of 1780–83, when the brave and eloquent William Wright traversed our Peninsular fields and forests, proclaiming the Gospel of the Kingdom, till he fell amid the wilds of Annamessex,— through all our heroic century, down to the days of O'Niell, Carroll, Connor, McSorley, MacNichol and

Watt, of our present Wilmington Conference, the loquacious and pugnacious Irishman has mingled efficiently in the itinerant roll, and borne his part bravely in the Methodist division of the great battle against sin and the Devil.

To do justice to all the noble Irishmen who, through the century, have toiled to build up and strengthen Peninsular Methodism, would require at least a large volume. By the plan of the present work, this phase of our history must be compressed into the limits of a single chapter; and out of the many striking characters, standing out in bold relief amid the stirring scenes that loom up before us, a very few must needs be selected as representatives of their class.

No Irishman perhaps, ever so strikingly impressed himself upon the Methodism of the Peninsula as William Barnes. He was generally known, and generally preferred to speak of himself as "Billy" Barnes. He died a few years ago in a good old age, and his memoir can be seen in the archives of the Philadelphia Conference. Many of his earlier years in the ministry, were spent riding the large circuits of Delaware and Maryland; and even after he had reached the zenith of his fame, he received an occasional appointment within the Peninsula; the last being to Union Church in Wilmington, Del., but a few years before the last division of the Philadelphia Conference. While many familiar faces were missed, on the first assembling of the Wilmington Conference, the absence of none was more generally regretted than that of Billy Barnes. His presence would have saved any assembly of men from being considered common-place. No debate or routine of business, in which he took a conspicuous part, could possibly become dull. He was the comical point in the conference picture; and largely the inspiration and the spice of most of the conference episodes.

Billy Barnes was such an Irishman—so unique in his facial angles; so comical in his natural expression; so carelessly pitched together and tumbled into his ill-fitting clothes; so heavily bewigged; so almost hid behind the screen of an immense shirt collar, and so fidgety withal—that the very sight of him, even in repose, would have provoked a smile from the most discouraged dyspeptic in the land. His voice and brogue were as remarkable as his face, and his speech was the fitting exclamation point that intensified his grotesque expression. Nevertheless, as a thinker and orator, Barnes was both strong and brilliant—sometimes an electric light that dazzled and astonished his audience; and, in his eloquent pulpit addresses, the fantastic and ludicrous were often, for the time, obscured by the vivid flashes of his genius. When fully aroused and overflowing with his subject, his conceptions and sentences rushed along like the rapids of Niagara. Sometimes, under the excitement of some inspiring and favorite theme, such as, "The Lord is a great God; and a great King above all gods;" he heaped up words so rapidly that his ponderous thoughts and glowing sentences came down, pell-mell, on his auditors like an irresistible avalanche.

The following incident was related to me by my father, who was present at a camp-meeting prayer service where Mr. Barnes presided. From some unexplained cause the meeting was dull and uninteresting. Barnes became visibly nervous. Finally, seeming to grow desperate, he suddenly sprang to his feet and thus delivered himself, in rapid and excited utterance: "Braithren; y'er not prayin'. Down with ye on yer knees; an' pray for life, ivery one of ye." And, turning towards his wife, who was seated in the audience, he called out, "Mrs. Barnes; lade us, an' pray mightily. Good Lord; strike a spark from atarnal steel; set afire the magazane of sin, an' blow up the works of the Daivil!" The "Daivil," being unprepared for so furious an onslaught, and that, too, with his own fiery weapons, was vanquished; and the battle ground was held by the rejoicing victors.

As another specimen of this sulphurous phase of the fiery Irishman's eloquence, I give the concluding sentence of his terrific and scathing appeal on repentance, delivered on a Delaware camp-ground many years ago. It is said he once startled the sinners of the city of Columbia, Pa., with substantially the same fearful utterances. The sermon was on the text: "The times of this ignorance God winked at; but now commandeth all men, everywhere, to repent." The discourse throughout was a Vesuvius on fire; whose red-hot streams of molten and seething truth swept away every "refuge of lies," and left the impenitent without even the semblance of excuse. Reaching the application, he delivered his grand climax in the following fiery tornado: "Now, ye ungrateful, wicked rebels; it's yer douty to repant. If ye don't repant ye'll be damned. If ye won't repant, ye ought to be damned. And if I were in God Almighty's place, a ridin' on the Gospel locomotive on the salvation railroad; an' ye were on the track an' wouldn't repant, I'd run over ye an' niver blow anaither whistle!"

On account of Mr. Barnes' dress—especially his flowing wig and immense collar,—he was unfavorably criticised by the uncharitably disposed; who charged him with undue pride, and with being largely deficient in spirituality. Having been informed of this murmur of discontent and criticism, among the people at one of his Sussex County, Del., appointments, he improved the occasion of his next visit to preface his sermon with this utterance: "Braithren; I understand some of ye are disposed to judge Billy Barnes' tree by its laves anstid of its fruits—by what I've got on me anstid of what I've got in me; an' ye think I'm proud an' got no relagion. Now I want to say before ye all, I think so highly of my blessed Master, that if I was a goin' to atarnity to-day, I'd dress up in the very best clothes I could find in all Philadelphy, in which to make my bow on the occasion of my introduction to the great, atarnal King of Glory!"

An aged Methodist of Sussex, Del., once heard Mr. Barnes preach at a camp-meeting in that county, where it was his misfortune to be seated by the side of an ill-natured brother; who, during the earlier part of the discourse, annoyed those seated near him by growling out his discontent at the height and general dimensions of the preacher's collar. The speaker's nervous habit of pulling up his linen, whenever he began to grow excited in discourse, only intensified this listener's dissatisfaction, who continued his snarling, saying: "Yes; you've got more sail than you kin well carry—entirely too much canvass for a heavy blow—you'll capsize sartin—ought to take two or three reefs in it—can't preach fit for nothin' with no sich collar as that!" After a time, however, he became silent and attentive; and finally, at the conclusion of one of Barnes' grand climaxes, surprised everybody and convulsed those who were in a position to take in the full situation, by crying out lustily: "Halleluyer! God bless the preacher! I don't care now if his shirt's all collar!"

A ludicrous scene occurred, once on a time, on a very sandy road called "Featherbed Lane," near Concord, Delaware. While on his way from the above place, where he had preached in the morning, to his afternoon appointment, Mr. Barnes' horse, seized with a sudden impulse to do what he could in the way of spreading the Gospel, ran away. After breaking the reins in his frantic efforts to stop the excited beast, and exhausting his Irish vocabulary of soothing and coaxing terms in vain; he hit upon the happy expedient of the influence of sacred song, and lustily poured forth the melody of Balerma to the words:

> "Must I be carried to the skies
> On flowery beds of ease?"

and, by the time he had finished the stanza, the melodious charm, expressed in the brogue of Erin, together with the depth of the sand, had soothed the erratic animal down to a dignified and becoming ministerial equine gait; and, save for a good dusting and a terrific scare, Billy Barnes was *in statu quo ante terrorem*.

A more critical adventure, in which Mr. Barnes was the central figure, occurred in the old Zion Church, near Milton, Delaware. I give it substantially as related by an eye witness, Brother Atkins, of Georgetown, Delaware, father of Rev. E. C. Atkins of the Wilmington Conference. It was on a pleasant Sunday afternoon in autumn; and the heat from the first fire of the season brought out a myriad of wasps from the crevices where they had taken up winter quarters, who sallied forth in quest of spring-time game. It was Billy Barnes' appointment to preach. The hymn had been finished, and his reverence devoutly said "let us pray," and proceeded with a few high sounding opening sentences; when one of these belligerent insects accepted the invitation to *prey*, by unceremoniously alighting between Mr. Barnes' huge collar and the back of his neck.

The half expressed petition, upon the poor man's

lips, terminated suddenly in a somewhat suppressed Irish grunt; attracting the attention of the congregation, and fixing upon him the gaze of that part of the audience within range to see behind the pulpit breastworks. With a look of expectant terror upon his countenance; but with a coolness and steadiness of nerve that would have done credit to William Tell; he proceeded quietly to divest himself, first of his coat, then of his vest. Next, the extensive necktie was unreefed, and the projecting collar removed. Meanwhile his waspship had descended below the neck-band of his shirt, and was exploring the dimensions of the preacher's back. It was a critical moment. In the desperate extremity, but one thing could be done; and while great beads of perspiration gathered on his livid face, the preacher carefully took off the garment next in order. To this, fortunately, the persistent insect was clinging; and, with a grunt and a "now, then!" that fairly hissed from between his teeth, the outraged Irishman planted his foot upon his enemy, and he was *hors du combat*. Mr. Barnes then proceeded, with the utmost nonchalance, to resume his apparel; and, beginning where he had been interrupted, he finished his prayer, in which he thanked God that he had been "delavered from that nasty wasp—the ammissary of the Daivil." He then proceeded with the sermon.

During this perilous adventure, the congregation, of course, while somewhat alarmed, was inexpressibly tickled; and, as one after another was enabled to take

·in the situation, attack after attack of hysterical convulsions set in, until the church was filled with the hissing of illy suppressed laughter; and throughout the service, the sailing of a wasp near the preacher's dodging head, was the signal for renewed merriment. At his next appointment, four weeks later, poor Barnes picked up the hymn-book with a nervous jerk; tugged uneasily at the corners of his collar; gave a timorous look around and upward toward the ceiling; and again upset the gravity and decorum of his audience by the anxious inquiry: "Braithren; has the abominable old Daivil sent any of his nasty wasps here to-day?"

William Barnes was a great bundle of nerves. His nature was intense to the last degree. As a result, when mightily impressed with a sense of the honor and blessedness of his mission, he was a torrent of enthusiasm that must have vent or disaster was likely to be the result. At a Maryland camp-meeting, being appointed to preach, Mr. Barnes retired to the solitudes of the grove to pray and meditate upon the subject of his message. While here, he became mightily moved with the Divine afflatus; and came into the preacher's tent, scarcely able to restrain his glowing exclamations from the notice of the swarming multitudes without. On inquiring the time, he was informed it was halfpast 9 o'clock. He paced the floor, back and forth, like a caged lion, for a few minutes, and again restlessly inquired: "Braithren; aint it time to blow the hairn?" Being answered in the negative, his nervousness increased, until finally he astonished his brethren by the peremptory command to the preacher in charge: "Braither; go blow the hairn: I shall bust!" It is needless to add that the trumpet was, at once sounded for preaching; the safety valve of the intense nature was thus opened, and the threatened calamity averted.

But while thus high-strung, and sometimes apparently the victim of enthusiasm run wild, Mr. Barnes was not oblivious to the proprieties arising out of peculiar and exciting circumstances. He never forgot to exalt Christ; or that the chief end of the Gospel minister's message is to save souls, as the following incident will illustrate. At a great camp-meeting held near Principio, in Cecil County, Md., Mr. Barnes was given the Sunday morning appointment, an opportunity in which his very soul delighted. He was never in better trim or more completely filled with his message. As was his wont, after a brilliant introduction, in which he laid a broad and deep foundation; he announced three great propositions which he promised to discuss; and told the people that, by God's help, he would "blow the very heavens away from over the lying infidal's head, and by the airthquake of God Almighty's everlasting proclamations, tear away the yawning ground from beneath his iniquitous feet, and show him to himself and the whole univarse, hair-hung and braze-shaken over the stormy lake of endless hell!"

During the discussion of the first proposition, he gained the attention of all the thousands in the audience; and by the time he had finished the second, the assembly was moved as if by a mighty tempest. Tears flowed in wonderful profusion; and beneath the triumphant halleluia-chorus that thrilled the encampment, was heard an undertone of penitential agony from all parts of the vast concourse, that finally reached the ears of the exultant preacher. Though riding gloriously on the crest of so great a wave of triumph; and although his final proposition was climactic, and urgently invited him on to the grand conclusion; Mr. Barnes saw that now was the opportunity of this great occasion to harvest souls; and leaving *thirdly* to take care of itself, stepping to the good local preacher who was to follow him, he tapped him on the shoulder and said: "Braither; give ye'r invitation, an' let the poor, lost wretches come at once an' seek salvation!" The brother addressed, slowly arose; and, restating Barnes' third proposition, began deliberately to discuss it; when the indignant herald sprang to his side and arrested him with: "Braither; that won't do. I want ye to understand that Billy Barnes is fully competent to discuss the third proposition, and would do so if the Lord God Almighty wanted it discussed. But He don't: He wants to save souls. Give the invitation quick, braither; or I'll do it meself!" But no further invitation was necessary. The first intimation of a chance was accepted by multitudes; and scores were that day converted.

Billy Barnes was as generous and liberal as he was witty and impulsive—always ready to respond to every appeal of philanthropy or Church progress, according to his ability. At a session of the Philadelphia Conference, where a subscription was taken in aid of Dickinson College, he arose in his usual nervous manner; tugging at his ever offending collar; and, in his irresistible brogue, thus addressed Bishop Waugh: "Mr. Prasident; you may put Billy Barnes down for fafty dollars anyhow; and, Bishop, if you give him an appintment where the ecclasiastical nubbins grow long enough, he'll give fafty dollars more at the end of the year."

When stationed at Snow Hill, Md., Mr. Barnes suffered an attack of malarial illness, so very severe that his physician, Dr. Pitts, despairing of his recovery, deemed it his duty to inform him of his critical condition. At the conclusion of his tender and solemn announcement, the doctor said: "Brother Barnes, should you be taken from us, what word have you for our encouragement?" His reply upset the gravity of those in attendance, and convinced the good doctor that his patient was not yet quite ready to take the angelic degree. "Well, doctor;" said the irrepressible Irishman, "I once sarved the Daivil; an', these many years, I've been sarving the Lord Jasus Christ; an' now, sir, whichever has the best right to me can take me!" But, evidently, at no time after his conversion, was Billy Barnes on friendly terms with his Satanic majesty. He seldom preached a sermon or made a prayer, that he did not take occasion to pay his respects both to Beelzebub, and the Roman Pontiff whom he considered Satan's great lieutenant on earth. A young minister related to the writer, that, while Mr. Barnes was pastor of Union Church, Wilmington, he, being present one day, was invited into the pulpit to make the closing prayer. As he was about ending his brief petition, Billy tugged at his sleeve and whispered: "Braither; don't forget the Pope and the Daivil!"

It was during the same pastorate, that, having heard of some ill-natured criticism on account of his curly and flowing wig; he prefaced his sermon, one Sunday morning, with the following dramatic and irresistible performance: "Braithren; I understand ther's some of ye that don't like it because I wear a wag. Now, I've made up my mind to wear it or not, jist as the congregation says. Here I am: look at me. This is Billy Barnes *with* the wag. And this"—at the same moment snatching the offending wig from the top of his bald pate—"this is Billy Barnes *without* the wag! Which way will ye have him?" In the roars of laughter and vociferous responses—"*Brother Barnes with the wig!*"— that ensued, the wig critics of old Union were utterly discomfited.

Perhaps but one such man as William Barnes has ever lived. God had a purpose and a work for him in his day, and nobly did he fulfill his Master's designs. The stamp of his fervent soul, his brilliant intellect, his fiery zeal, his apostolic heroism made its enduring impress on the Peninsular Methodism he helped to build. He rests from his labors; but his works follow him; and, like faithful Abel, "being dead he yet speaketh." If some abler historian, to whom the annals of his singularly interesting and useful life are accessible, should be moved to weave them into a biography becoming the worthy subject, he would render the church a valuable service. May this little sketch inspire the preparation of a "Life of Billy Barnes."

Another Irishman, who figured largely in the history of Peninsular Methodism, was Rev. John Henry. Mr. Henry was reputed to be a thorough theologian, and a very able preacher. His mightiest appeals were to the reason. He lacked the intensity of William Barnes; and, while his ministry was a steady glow and a fair, strong breeze, it never, like that of Barnes, exhibited thunderbolts on the rampage or the tornado in a frenzy. Neither was his person so imposing, nor his appearance and manner so striking, as those of Billy Barnes. He was low of stature; stoop-shouldered; unsophisticated —almost verdant—in appearance; and rushed through the world and his work at a pace that insured him the distinction of being the constant butt of amusement to his brethren, without the least suspicion thereof on his part. His speech was ofttimes as awkward as his gait; constraining the conviction that he must have been near akin to his fellow-countryman, who said of himself: "An' shure, I hardly iver open my mouth, but I 'put my foot into it.'"

Having grown up in the blessed Isle of Saint Patrick,

Mr. Henry came to America with little conception, but with holy and intense horror, of "sarpents, lazards and all aither varmints." By reason of his servile fear of these things, he was for the remainder of his natural "life-time subject to bondage." His terror-stricken description of a creature that crossed his path and very greatly alarmed him one day, soon after his arrival in this country, was unique. Calling excitedly to the friend at whose home he was sojourning, he cried out in bewildered alarm: "O, braither, come here! Run quick: I'm much scair't! I've seen a great, ugly baste, that's hid himself in the grass that he may crape on me unawares! He's about as lang as my finger, an' as broad as he's lang; he's as ugly as Beelzebub; an' he's all swell't up with his wrath at me; and braither, wheniver he walks he goes steady by jerks!" A photographer could hardly have taken a better likeness of a toad.

In every Peninsular field where Mr. Henry labored, his singularly faithful pastoral work; his clear, strong pulpit ministrations; and his ludicrous blunders and innocent Irish bulls, left an impress that lingers pleasantly to this day in the memories of the old time saints. In 1826, with the renowned elder Cookman as preacher in charge, John Henry travelled Easton circuit, in Talbot County, Maryland, remaining the following year as chief pastor. Wonderful success attended the work of those years. Hundreds were converted—among them many prominent members of the Protestant Episcopal

Church, the leaven of whose influence still lingers in that communion. As already indicated, Mr. Henry was remarkable for the industry and effectiveness of his pastoral work, which seems to have embraced all classes and colors, and all Churches. It was no unusual thing for him to be out making pastoral calls before breakfast. On one occasion, he routed a family out of bed, breaking up their morning nap, that he might, in passing, have prayers with them. He would rush into a lawyer's office, while he was busy with his clients; and, after a few words of kind and faithful warning, call attorney and visitors to their knees on the office floor, while he offered his plea in their behalf before the Court of Heaven. And such was his innocent, matter-of-fact honesty of manner, that it was impossible to become offended with the liberty he took. Many a time has the writer heard the celebrated criminal lawyer, Hon. James Lloyd Martin, of Easton, entertain his friends with most humorous but respectful representations of the pointed, personal pastoral work in his behalf, of one whom he affectionately called "Brother Henry."

Hon. John Leeds Carr was also a prominent lawyer of Easton, and a good friend of Mr. Henry. Once, however, their amicable relations were seriously threatened. Mr. Carr was the fortunate proprietor of a small but beautiful clover lot, in which he took no little pride. Mr. Henry owned a pet horse, Bob, whom he sometimes turned on the "commons" at night; both as a means of supplementing the stores of his hay-loft, and of furnishing the animal with a little of the needed spice of variety. On a certain June night, the tempting perfume of Mr. Carr's sweetly blooming clover proved too much for Bob's moral character, and his equine sense of ministerial propriety; and, hunting a low place in the fence, he entered into temptation and found himself "in clover." The grass was tender and sweet; and, ere morning, Bob became too full for comfort, or to jump out again. In his anxiety, he tramped, and pawed, and rolled to such an extent, as to spoil utterly the appearance of the clover. On beholding this condition of affairs the following morning, Mr. Carr lost control of his temper, and determined to have redress or cut Mr. Henry's acquaintance. Rushing to the parsonage, he angrily saluted the parson with: "Brother Henry, your confounded old horse has been in my clover lot all night!" The anxious response: "An' shure, braither; an' do ye think it will hurt him?" so completely upset Mr. Carr's anger, that he instantly forgave Bob for the sake of his kindly and innocent master; and, to his life's end, used often to amuse his friends by the recital of the clover-lot story.

When stationed in Dorchester County, poor Bob having meantime left his master in bereavement, Mr. Henry borrowed a horse from a Brother Dixon, near Church Creek; who, being aware of his peculiarities, made it a condition of the accommodation, that the preacher engage to take very special care of the animal;

as, being young, he would be likely to be injured should he become heated overmuch. What was Mr. Dixon's surprise, a day or two after, when the thermometer was at 90°, to meet the reverend Irishman with his horse in a solid run, and all foaming with sweat and panting for breath! His excited expostulation was met by the cool and self-satisfied assurance of the philosophic divine, that he was "ridin' fast jist a purpose to git up a good braze for the poor baste!"

Outside the line of his theological studies and pulpit and pastoral duties, John Henry seems to have been as unsophisticated as a child. In fact, in the common affairs of every-day life, he was manifestly deficient in what men call "common sense." He never mastered the simplest problems in domestic economy; and provision for the household, and even the care of the pigs and the horse, devolved largely on his very capable companion. While residing at Camden, Delaware, his good wife one day requested him to go to the garden and get some potatoes for dinner. He soon returned with the report that he had examined all the vines and could find none. Bidding him to follow, Mrs. Henry took a hoe and showed him how to find the tempting tubers growing upon the roots. Some days after, she requested that he would gather a few squashes. As in the former case, he failed to bring any; and, when questioned about it, in expostulatory style, as good wives are sometimes wont to do, he replied: "An' shure, Mrs. Henry, you can go see for yourself. I can find ne'er a single squash in the gearden, although I've dug up ivery vine!" With fine squashes lying all around, so intently was he occupied with the lesson his wife had given him in gathering potatoes, that he failed to see them, and insisted on finding them upon the roots, to the utter destruction of the squash harvest for that season.

The following winter he was, as usual, busy in his study one day, while Mrs. Henry was engaged in the back yard superintending the butchering of the pigs. His attention was attracted by the conversation concerning the pork, when a brand new and brilliant idea in domestic economy suddenly dawned upon him; and rushing out bareheaded, in gown and slippers, into the presence of his spouse, he thus advised her: "Mrs. Henry; an' shure if I were in your place, I'd have the pags all cut up into homs!"

Like Billy Barnes, John Henry also once had an adventure with wasps. Unfortunately for him, however, it did not terminate so favorably. Stopping once over night with a Bro. Palmer, in Sussex, Delaware, soon after retiring, his lusty cries for help alarmed the household. "Sister Palmer! sister Palmer!" cried he, in evident pain and terror, "what is this? Is the Daivil broke loose? There's a fiend here a piercin' me with his arrows! O come quick! It will kill me!" Mrs. Palmer and her husband rushed up stairs to find the terrified Irishman writhing in agony; and, on investigation, discovered that he was floundering amid a nest of enraged wasps, that by some means had become detached from a collar beam and covered up in his bed. The scene, suddenly illumined by the entrance of a tallow candle, can be better imagined than described; so at this point we will let the curtain drop and take our leave of this notable Irishman. He was a simple minded, single eyed, devoted and successful harvester of souls; and left his impress for good upon the Peninsula fields he helped to cultivate.

Not so marked in the grotesque characteristics peculiar to the typical Irishman as were Barnes and Henry, yet no less distinguished for devotion, eloquence and bravery have been some of the noble sons of Erin, who, as their successors, have contended for God and right on the battle field of the Peninsula. Among these mediæval Irishmen, some of whom still live to bless the Church in other and distant localities, the most conspicuous, because of his long and very effective service in this territory, is Rev. Adam Wallace, D.D. His autobiography, which, by all means the Church should be permitted to place in her historical archives, would add much to the rich treasury of knowledge concerning this classic ground; and general Methodism can little afford to lose it. His series of letters in the *Peninsula Methodist*, under the caption of "Here and There on Snow Hill District," are doubtless but the outcropping veins and nuggets indicative of the rich bonanza lying beneath, and which his Irish pick and shovel and mint might soon turn into the literary marts and coffers of Methodism. The author of this sketch will attempt no analysis of the characteristics and accomplishments of this widely known divine. This belongs to his memoir. May it be many years before this shall be written. Neither will the writer attempt an extended review of Dr. Wallace's Peninsula labors and experiences, although the field and the memorial inscriptions are tempting, for reasons already intimated. It is properly the work of his own facile pen.

The Peninsula preacher whose ministerial life and labors stretch back over the last thirty-five years, has passed through many phases of experience, and witnessed astonishing changes. He entered upon his junior work, when the jagged edges of a rising cloud had just become visible above the far away horizon, and the reverberations of the distant thunders had just begun to make their ominous tremors felt along our peaceful shores. With anxious heart and bated breath, and clinging to his Master's cross; now swaying before the furious gusts of the tempests; sometimes starting in almost terror amid the terrific thunderbolts of the storm of civil convulsion and popular malice, that spent its fury upon him—through all, true as steel, he stood at his post. And now, still surviving and unscathed, with the cloud drifting out of sight, this faithful herald stands beneath Messiah's ensign; and, peacefully smiling, surveys the scene, with a clear bright heavens above him, and all around him our fields of Peninsula Methodism, ripening to the glorious harvest of his patient endurance and toil.

The Peninsula itinerants of a quarter of a century ago were compelled, by force of circumstances, to stand midway between the political cannonading of the two extremes, without the least possibility of making peace with the excited and unreasoning gunners of either battery. The abolition crusader of the north proclaimed his wild theory that, under all circumstances, slaveholding was, *per se*, a sin. His hot shot and exploding shells made no discrimination between the anti-slavery Methodist preacher, who held that, while "a great evil" that "ought to be extirpated," slavery and slaveholding Methodists were to be dealt with by Christian, peaceable and legal measures, and according to circumstances; and the rabid pro-slaveryist, who regarded the chattel feature of the institution, with all its harrowing enormities, as God ordained. In like manner, blinded by their frenzy, the Southern fire-eaters thought they did their God as great a service by striking down the anti-slaveryist as the abolitionist; and as he was much nearer—in fact within hailing distance of the vengeful batteries—he was, by so much, the greater sufferer. Another peculiarity of the anti-slaveryist's position was the Christly delicacy of his relations. He naturally sympathized with everything and everybody that promised to aid in the extirpation of the great evil; and could not well "fire back" in return for the abolitionist's volleys, without seeming to be on the wrong side. He had a commission to preach the Gospel to congregations that were largely slaveholders of the extreme view; and if he offended them at a point where they were so sensitive, his mission with them and their sympathizers was ended; nor could he any longer have access to their poor slaves, perishing for the Gospel of spiritual freedom. No set of men were ever more heartily despised, or more violently abused, than the Methodist preachers of the Peninsula, during all this fearful crisis; and perhaps no set of men ever more nearly did what their Divine Master would himself have done, had that crisis been the time of his advent, and our Peninsula the theatre of his work. As a class, they rendered "to Cæsar the things which were Cæsar's, and to God the things which were God's." They were branded as cowards, however, from both extremes. Men sometimes forget that it often requires less bravery to fight Egyptians than it does to "stand *still* and see the salvation of God." If there are crowns waiting in heaven for men who have been distinguished, as Christ and his angels see it, for moral heroism; some of the brightest will be worn by Peninsula Methodist Episcopal ministers, who, through the wild, terrific storm now overpast, stood for God, and country and human liberty. The incidents briefly sketched in the following paragraphs, were substantially duplicated in hundreds of instances, and in the experiences of almost every faithful Methodist Episcopal preacher, who, during those perilous times, occupied Peninsular appointments. Nor was it alone in Virginia that they had such battles to fight. The feeling was scarcely less hostile in Delaware and Maryland. The writer remembers the stampeding of a portion of a Delaware congregation at the reading from the pulpit of:

> "Ye slaves of sin and hell
> Your liberty receive;"

and will never forget the storm he raised in a Maryland congregation by the announcement, one Sunday, that on a certain night he would preach in the colored people's church. In another place, the ministers present were made to feel the weight of the public indignation, when they invited a colored Bishop to preach at a camp-meeting, from the rear of the stand, to the colored congregation encamped with us. The young bloods of the polished society of Kent, Del., gathered a great company, many of them "lewd fellows of the baser sort;" and waited on us, with the demand for a recall of the appointment, and the alternative threat of riot, blood and destruction, should we persist in the outrage against public sentiment. But Bishop Wayman preached; and C. I. Thompson, James Flannery and the writer, sat there by him, while his eloquent words were sometimes well-nigh drowned by the great murmur of discontent and yells of threatened revenge that alarmed the denizens of the camp. But to our story.

In 1854, Rev. Adam Wallace, a newly married young itinerant, was appointed to Northampton circuit, the "Dixie" of the then Philadelphia Conference. While the prominent members professedly accepted the teachings of the Discipline on slavery as right; they were so seriously intimidated by popular prejudice, that they admonished the young pastor to delay reading the General Rules; and not on any account invite the colored members to come down from the galleries to commune around the altar. To neither suggestion did the quiet Irishman yield. He both read publicly the Rules—that on slavery included—and invited the poor negroes to the same sacramental table where their masters had just communed. As they approached the altar, about half the congregation rudely stampeded from the house. An indignation meeting was then extemporized outside; and a committee appointed to notify the preacher to desist from the "incendiary" practice, or leave the state in so many hours. At the afternoon appointment, fearing an outbreak of resentment, the negroes declined the pastor's invitation to the altar. In the Southern Methodist Churches, the old custom met with no opposition from the rabble, because it was known they had no sympathy with anti-slavery ideas. There was much loud talk and great excitement; but the intrepid Irishman urged that even the Devil would respect them the more for doing right; and insisted on adhering to the principle of one table for all the Lord's disciples. Making a tour of the Peninsula, Bishop Scott opportunely visited the circuit at that time. The leading members of the charge gathered at the parsonage to greet him. In their presence, the pastor raised the question of yielding to this unreasonable prejudice by sending the sacramental elements to the galleries. The good Bishop's quiet and deliberate, "I would not do it," settled the question.

Not long afterwards, while driving with his young wife, Mr. Wallace reined up at a place where two white men, amid much excitement, were engaged in tieing, hand and foot, a venerable colored man, for the purpose of taking him off to a "trader," to be sold South from his home and family. In the struggle, the poor old man had fallen in the public road; and the pretended owners, one of whom had married the widow and the other the daughter of the old negro's former master, were needlessly bruising him, with knees planted on his breast, to tighten the cords about his suffering wrists. Leaping from his carriage, the preacher, with an expression of becoming contempt, pushed away the principal offender. Bristling up, and sulphurous with the profanity of the popular "chivalry" of the times, the other told him to mind his own business. The Rev. and really chivalrous Irishman, coolly informed the two vandals that it was his business to fight the Devil wherever he found him; that this aged man was not resisting; that if they had the right to sell him, which he much doubted, the man would accompany them unbound; but that he, the preacher, intended to follow them and contest their right to kidnap and sell the poor old man. He then spoke words of kindly sympathy to the maltreated negro, and brushed the gravel and dust from his grey-hair, as he slowly arose; when, climbing into a horse-cart, the "owners" and slave drove off to the market.

The occurrence was in front of a country store, and in the presence of several neighbors; and, during the melee, Mrs. Wallace sat in the carriage, pale and trembling with apprehension. Mr. Mears, the proprietor of the store, invited the preacher and his wife to stay for dinner, where they learned the name of the old man; that he was a member of Garrison's chapel, which he had helped to build; and that his old master had given him his liberty ten years before. The preacher learned further that these men were considered little better than outlaws and desperate fellows, who would not scruple to "knife" the man who should further attempt to defeat them in their purpose. No one, who had witnessed the transaction, would consent to aid him; a good Local Preacher implored him to leave the circuit on a visit, until the storm he had in all probability raised should blow over; but the preacher's Irish blood was up; and, "taking his life in his hand," he drove after the ruffians, leaving his wife at the parsonage; and soon ascertained that Sam had been sold for $300, and taken to the county jail, where a "gang" was being made up to start in a few days for Richmond.

His appeal to attorneys, in poor Sam's behalf, was met with the admonition that perhaps he had better go home, and say nothing further about the matter, lest he should be the means of stirring up an insurrection. Finally, a retired lawyer residing on a farm not far from the parsonage, agreed to sue out a writ enjoining Sam's removal, until the Magistrate's Court should look into the matter. The intervening days were anxious and painful. Many of the official brethren called at the parsonage, to express their dread of anticipated troubles. The next Sabbath sermons of the aroused Irishman were tinged with brimstone; and his public prayers reminded the Almighty of the sighing of the prisoner, and invoked his right arm for his protection.

A prominent Methodist, Mr. Garrison, called on Monday morning, to attend the preacher to court, and act as his friend and protector. The Chief Justice on the bench of six, was a man who had begun life as an ostler; but, being an expert gambler, had won so largely of spendthrift sons of the F. F. V's, that he had become the owner of many of their paternal plantations; and now, although despised for his origin and flagrant immoralities, on account of his wealth, he stood among the foremost in good society. Of this man's influence Mr. Wallace was greatly afraid; but when the case of "the negro, Sam" came up and was explained, he was overjoyed to hear the old reprobate give vent to his indignanation in the following phillipic: "Gentlemen; this negro's master gave him his liberty for long and faithful service. You and I have the same right and privilege. Suppose after we have chosen to do so, and are in our graves, some irresponsible vagabonds should assume to trample on our wishes in this manner; should there not be, in law and public opinion, some stern rebuke for such vandalism? My opinion, gentlemen, is, that warrants should be issued for the arrest of—and—forthwith, for doing an act which no honorable Virginian can look upon with anything but disapprobation."

Before the warrants could be issued, the kidnappers had hastily decamped for parts unknown; and the overjoyed and grateful Sam was discharged from unlawful custody, to return to his little home and his distracted wife and children. As, on the following Sabbath morning, the pastor arose in the pulpit of Garrison's chapel to announce the opening hymn, glancing toward the gallery, he discovered in his accustomed place and most conspicuous among his fellows, "Uncle" Sam with his glowing face all wet with rolling tears of gratitude. The sight awakened the crowding memories of the exciting contest, the rescue, the return of light and joy to the little cabin; and, overcome by his emotions, the preacher responded to Sam's salutation with copious tears of sympathetic joy.

The slaves of the South seemed to have become, instinctively or supernaturally, possessed of the conviction that somehow the Lord would interfere in their behalf; but were in doubt as to whether they ought to make a dash for freedom, or stand still and see God's salvation. The Northampton slaves often secretly consulted Mr. Wallace as to their proper course; and were always encouraged to expect deliverance from the God of Moses and Israel; but were advised to patiently pray and wait his time; which, the signs indicated, could not be very long delayed. Such was his advice, one dark night in a thicket, to forty or fifty slaves of one mistress, who were meditating flight to escape if possible from the heartbreaking exigencies of the dubious and cruel auction block, which appeared to threaten them.

Ten years after that weird and memorable night, this Irish prophet of deliverance from God was again in Virginia—this time as Presiding Elder. For two years we had been shut out by the war. But when Chaplain Vaugh Smith, at the head of a detachment of Federal soldiers, crossed the line and swept the shore of organized resistance, Mr. Wallace followed the standard of the union, and reopened our Virginia Churches. Most of the people sympathized with the rebellion, and were bitter in their hostility to the Methodist Episcopal Church; but a few remained loyal to Church and country. Mr. Lincoln's emancipation proclamation had just taken effect, and the old slave owners were very sore, while the unmanacled slaves were correspondingly elated.

Our Irish Elder was holding quarterly meeting at Onancock. It was a beautiful Sabbath morning; and, from an early hour, numerous squads of colored people wended their way towards the beloved old Church. Many whites also came, but they were generally either crest-fallen or angry. The Lovefeast was opened; but enthusiasm was at so low an ebb, among the ex-masters and mistresses, that the Elder soon invited the denizens of the galleries to "let their joys be known." A grand voice, remembered as having been heard at Garrison's ten years before, led the singing in the stirring words, "Am I a soldier of the cross?" and then the speaking began. Soon one of the leading spirits of the midnight conference in the thicket of ten years ago, and which the preacher had almost forgotten, arose and said:

"Christian Fren's; I's happy soul an' body dis mornin'. It's de brightest day I's eber seen. I hearn tell dat our good preacher Wallace, dat used to 'spense de Gospel to us years ago, had got to be a 'Sidin' Elder, and was a gwine to be heah; an' I started befo' sun up to come heah an' see his face onct mo' (sensation and "Yes, praise de Lord!") A comin' along dis mornin', I felt like de lame dat kin leap as de hart in a wilderness; an' my tongue was unloosened to sing hallelujah! ("Amen!") Dis 'sidin' Elder dat sets dere in de pulpit, told us, long time ago, dat salvation would come. ("Glory!") He told us one night, in de thicket, when our troubles was as deep as de ragin' waters ob de sea, dat de mornin' would break some time. When some ob us was about to run away to try to 'tain our freedom, he says to us,—'Hold on; hold fast to yer anchor in de mighty God; you folks dat runs away is afeared. Stan' still, till Moses smite de waters, an' ole Pharaoh is broked wid a rod ob iron!' Some of our people couldn't see de light; but dey sees it now, glory to de blessid Lamb! (Mighty shoutings of "Yes; yes," and "Praise de Lord!")

"De preacher settin dere says to me, says he; 'Jesse, mind you don't act de fool. Don't let de colored people

disbehave. Your time will come, shore as you live.'"
And then he continued, reaching out his hand toward
the occupant of the pulpit, "Preacher; bless de Lord!
De time you told us 'bout is heah shore 'nuff, dis free,
blessed Sunday; an', thank de Lord! we is free in body,
free in soul, an' on our gladsome march to Heaven!"
Thus did the happy Irishman, after many days, find
and gather the bread he had cast on the troubled waters
of this modern Egypt.

At Garrison's chapel, in the olden times, great crowds
of slaves were wont to assemble; and, while the white
members, on protracted meeting occasions, rallied around
the altar within, the sable soldiers of the cross would
repair to the open air, build a camp-fire; and, under the
starry canopy of the heavens, form a circle for a holy
shout. Going out one night while their meeting was in
progress, Mr. Wallace found some wicked young men
enjoying the sport of throwing blazing pine-knots within
this circle and among the weeping penitents. His
warning to desist being disregarded, he unceremoniously
knocked down two of the ringleaders, who were so completely demoralized at the preacher's temerity, that they
forgot to hit him back. His rencontre in the case of
Sam had gained him a reputation for courage. Even
a Virginia rabble could admire such a display of physical Christianity; and when these disconcerted young
fellows, so far recovered as to begin to swear they were
going to thrash the Irishman, they were hooted down
by their companions, who frankly admitted the preacher
had served them right.

Not only did Adam Wallace display physical courage in dealing with the "chivalrous" roughs of that day and section; but, amid all the exciting questions, in Church and State, growing out of the popular frenzy on the questions of slavery and secession, his moral spinal column was a tower of strength to the cause of truth and patriotism. The Methodist preacher who was brave enough to vote an honest "no," on the Philadelphia Conference "Union" resolutions of 1861, has never ceased to enjoy the respect and fraternal regard of his brethren, who voted an honest and enthusiastic "aye" on the same memorable paper; but there remains only contempt for the few cowardly time servers, whose careful sentiments, through all those perilous times, were adroitly fitted so as to appear responsive to any and every opinion that might be uttered in their presence. The unmanly, pusillanimous poltroon of a preacher, who, for a slice of popular bread and butter, became literally, "all things to all men," was only a curse to the Methodist Episcopal Church of the Peninsula, during her fiery ordeal; and was very largely responsible for the secessions by which, at various points, she was finally convulsed and dismembered. But the dough men are all dead or left behind. In her new and aggressive career, the Church had no work for sneaking imbeciles; nor had men outside, of either party, any respect for them; and they have become silent partners of Othello. Like Mr. Wallace, most of the Methodist preachers who stood at Peninsular posts of responsibility during these memorable years, were living men, of sturdy arms, perpendicular backbones, intelligent brains and loving hearts; and through their manly labors, by God's blessing, the Methodist Episcopal Church emerges from the smoke of her greatest battle-field, bearing proudly before her leader, Christ, the trophies of her greatest victories.

While by no means so quaint and peculiar as Barnes and Henry, the present generation of Irish preachers in the Wilmington Conference, are not without the striking characteristics of the typical Irishman. It is yet too soon to write memorial sketches of them; but the author may be pardoned for suggesting that, unless your rapier is sharp and your coat of mail of the best construction, you had better not invite a *rencontre* with one of them on the arena of repartee. One of our Irish coterie, whose name begins with the significant "O," on a certain quarterly conference Saturday, was seated in a Caroline County layman's parlor, with Rev. John Hough, Mr. A. P. Sorden, Rev. Dr. T. J. Quigley, Presiding Elder, and the writer. Said the Irishman: "I've got a tooth—" leaving the sentence unfinished, to dig at the offending member with his tooth-pick. "So have I," said the writer; and so said all, ending with the staid and sober Doctor of Divinity. Again the Irishman spoke, saying: "I've got a tooth with a hole in it;" which was followed with the same response, by the quartet in order. He then returned to the charge with: "An' shure; I've got a tooth that's not got any hole in it." And again, for the third time we gave forth the responsive chorus: "And so have I." But his final charge disarmed his competitors, and "brought down the house." With the provoking air of triumph of a consciously victorious gladiator, he quietly but confidently announced: "Well, braithren; I've got an Irishman's tooth!"

While some portions of our country are so marred by the ignorance, vice and lawlessness of the lower order of immigrant Irish; it is a cause for hearty congratulation that our beautiful Peninsula has attracted few, except of the better class of these swarming multitudes. In our fields and orchards; in our work-shops; in society; in our churches and in our conference, the sons of Erin have wrought with honest hands and earnest hearts. The impress of their personality remains on our territory and upon our church; and their well and deeply graven record is in heaven.

CHAPTER IV.

PATRIARCHS OF THE CHESAPEAKE.

THE isles of the beautiful Chesapeake are already renowned in story if not in song. The weird and fascinating annals of "The Parson of The Islands," written by Rev. Dr. Wallace, have both amused and astonished the church; and perhaps many who have read that book, have arisen from its perusal with the skeptical conviction that the reverend author was gifted with a glowing imagination, on which he drew very freely for his facts. From personal contact with many of the scenes and persons therein mentioned, the author of these sketches is fully prepared to vindicate the faithfulness of the historian. For some of the incidents herein detailed, the writer acknowledges his indebtedness to the above mentioned book. If this chapter shall induce many to buy and read "The Parson of The Islands," it will have demonstrated its right to existence.

The ranks of the Methodist local ministry have never produced a more pious, laborious and successful man than Rev. Joshua Thomas. He was born in Somerset County, Maryland, amid the stirring and heroic events of the American Revolution, soon after the Declaration of Independence; and lived to see three-score-and-ten of its returning anniversaries.

It will, of course, be impossible, within the prescribed limits, to give any sketch of Mr. Thomas' remarkable and valuable career that will do justice to the subject. The author can only give a little glimpse, here and there, of some of those incidents in his life, where the quaint and facetious side of the good man's nature so pleasantly protrudes.

Joshua Thomas, lived to be more than thirty years of age, with a growing family about him, before he had any experimental knowledge of the truth and power of the Christian religion; nevertheless he had been, from childhood, a believer in the truths of Revelation. On his way to the camp-meeting where he was converted, he stopped at the house of his uncle, Levi Thomas—a solid churchman—who, learning his intention, tried to dissuade him from going. Among other things, his uncle said: "Joshua if you do go there, they will have you down to worship them. They are nothin' but a lot of villainous Irishmen, who have run away from their own country to keep from being hanged. They have a great deal of larnin', but know no honest way of gettin' a livin'; so they go around the country a raisin' the Devil by their preachin' and carryin' on; and then they make people worship them and give them money to support them in their deviltry."

"No, uncle;" responded Joshua, "they will not get me down to worship them," and proceeded to the meeting.

While they did not ask or receive his homage, they did lead him to His shrine whom the wise men of the East worshipped in Bethlehem.

While Mr. Thomas' early opportunities for learning much of God and religion were very small; yet, long before he knew anything of practical godliness, he was in the habit of praying God to direct his fishing excursions to those locations where the Rock, the Tailor or the Sheepshead most plentifully abounded, in order that he might be successful in his business of catching them. Like the apostolic fishermen, he was destined to become a great fisher of men.

His early ignorance of God and religion is strikingly illustrated by an incident he relates of himself, connected with the ministry of Lorenzo Dow. "When I was about thirty years old" says he, "I attended a meetin' in Virginia; L. Dow was preachin' very powerful. A woman in the audience begun to shout. Dow stopped and cried out: 'The Lord is here! The Lord is here!' Immediately I jumped to my feet, and stretched my neck every way to try to see the Lord, but I could not see him;" whereupon the simple-minded child of thirty years tells us he reached the conclusion that the preacher was a base deceiver and fraud.

When Joshua was a young *gent* twenty-three years old, he says he "began to think he had rather have a good wife than anything in the world." There really does not seem to be anything very wonderful in Mr. Thomas' fancied precocity. The author thinks he has known some instances where young gentlemen have graduated to the same conclusion at sixteen or seventeen years of age. It isn't, however, every youth who acts in that emergency as did Mr. Thomas. Says he: "I immediately begun prayin' to the Lord that I might obtain a wife and the means to support her; promisin', in that case to do a good deal better than I ever had done." It was not long till he heard of a certain nice girl, who had given a mutual friend to understand that she "liked Joshua real well." At this good news he says his "very soul was transported;" he "never was so glad to hear anything" in his life; in a word, it made him "feel just like a man." On second sober thought, however, his poverty greatly perplexed him: how in the world could he provide for a wife? But, although not an experimental Christian, he took the matter to the Lord in prayer; and finally reached the conclusion to make sure of the nice, good girl who "liked" him, at a venture; and leave to the future the solution of the problem of support. Would that all young men were equally wise. Joshua's determination was evidently in the line of God's usual order, and the pretty little romance was appropriately finished up, of course. Nothing in the world was more natural. A neat little cabin on the Tangier Island; a straw bed; a broken table; a few wooden stools; a barrel of meal, and two little pigs; with a fisherman and his bride in the midst of their honeymoon, and you have a picture of complete earthly happiness!

But years passed away, and then came a sad, dark day that bereft Joshua of this loving girl, leaving him and several little children to mourn their loss. The widowed father had learned, meantime, the sweet lesson of holy trust at the camp-meeting heretofore alluded to; and he was therefore the better prepared to "commit his ways unto the Lord." In the exercise of a spiritually illumined faith he began, very soon, to pray the Lord to supply the vacant place in the cabin. As he kneeled in a thicket and made known to his Divine Friend his desires, and asked for his direction, a certain Miss Lottie Bradshaw's image was presented to his mental vision. Instantly he expostulated: "Lord; she is too young!" Retiring to another place, he again bowed before the Lord, and presented his request. Instantly, and for the second time, the image of Miss Bradshaw flitted before him. "Oh, Lord! She is too ugly!" exclaimed the unfortunate petitioner; at the same time arising to seek another part of the thicket, that might prove a more lucky and propitious Bethel. Long and earnest was this third prayer. Like Jacob, he wrestled with the angel for the answer of full assurance; and finally the answer came, but it was the old answer repeated—Miss Lottie Bradshaw's homely, but kindly smiling face again beamed upon the lonely widower. He calmly arose from his knees, submissively saying: "Well, Lord, I reckon you know better'n I do;" and the matter was finally settled to his unquestioning faith. Untieing his canoe, he pushed out, hoisted sail and steered for the Bradshaw homestead on Holland's Island. On arrival the following dialogue ensued:

"Good morning, Brother Bradshaw."

"How d'ye do Brother Thomas?"

"Brother Bradshaw, I think it is the will of the Lord that you should let me have Lottie to be my wife."

"Well, Brother Thomas; Lottie is rather young; but we will leave the matter to her. You can go see what she says about it: you'll find her out at the cow-pen, milking."

Mr. Thomas started and soon encountered the rosy maiden in the back yard, straining the milk. After the usual friendly salutation had passed, said Joshua:

"Sister Lottie; I've come on special business this mornin'. I've been prayin' over the matter; and I think, Lottie, understand, that it's the will of the Lord that you and I should git married!"

"The will of the Lord be done, Brother Thomas!" responded Lottie, in the spirit of humble submission to her divinely ordered fate; and, in a few days after this matter-of-fact *popping*, there was an equally matter-of-fact wedding; and what seemed to be God's order was cheerfully consummated.

Many years afterwards, at a camp-meeting on Deal's Island, the dear old saint said to a company of preachers, after relating to them the above story: "Brothers; when I married her, understand, I thought she was one of the ugliest women in the world; but now, I tell you, I think she is the *purtiest*. She has made me a lovin' wife, and a good, faithful mother to my orphaned children; and I know, brothers, understand, that the good Lord picked her out for me."

Mr. Thomas was in the habit of giving the Scriptures a literal interpretation; and accepted the directions he found therein, apparently applicable to his circumstances at the time, as the sole rule of his action. At one time he was the subject of a protracted and painful illness. Various remedies had been tried without material relief. Reading his New Testament, as he lay helpless on his bed one day, he came to the passage in James, where the Apostle says: "Is any sick among you? Let him call the Elders of the Church; and let them pray over him, anointing him with oil in the name of the Lord; and the prayer of faith shall save the sick, and the Lord shall raise him up."

The suffering saint fixed his mind on two elderly and leading members of the church—Messrs. John and Zachariah Crocket—as likely to meet the divine prescription as to "Elders," and he sent post-haste for John, who forthwith appeared at his bedside. After citing to Mr. Crocket the passage above quoted, Mr. Thomas said: "Now, Brother John; you must do exactly as the good Book directs. I have no Scriptural oil; but yander, on the shelf, understand, is a plenty of excellent goose-grease, that I suppose, understand, will do just as well. Use some of that to anoint me, Brother John; and then pray in faith."

"Brother John" was no little startled by this novel proposal, and confessed his want of confidence in the arrangement. However, to gratify his respected neighbor and Christian friend, he proceeded with the grotesque formalities of the sacred goose-grease anointing, and offered prayer for the patient's recovery. But there was no apparent relief or improvement, and Mr. Thomas said the fault was in the weakness of their faith. "Go, John;" said he, "and tell Brother Zachariah to come and try it." On "Zach's" arrival, learning all the particulars, he clapped his hands in joyous enthusiasm and exclaimed: "Why, Brother Thomas; that is the very thing! I believe it will do you good!"

"Go on, then!" shouted Joshua, "and let us believe!"

Brother Zach then went at his work with good-Samaritan zest and interest; and after a repetition of the unctuous application, he kneeled down at the patient's bedside and prayed vociferously till he got shouting-happy. Strange to tell, at this point, Joshua Thomas leaped from the bed—whole in body and in soul, and joined his friend in "walking and leaping, and praising the Lord."

An esteemed local preacher, Dr. R. W. Williams, late of Dorchester County, Md., and well known to many ministers of the Wilmington Conference, related to the writer the two following incidents, which have never before appeared in print. While Dr. Williams resided at Onancock, Va., Mr. Thomas sailed across from Tangier in his canoe, the "Methodist," to make him a visit. Upon his arrival, he learned of the dangerous illness of one of his lady friends, a Mrs. Mister, residing near the town; and at once remarked to Dr. Williams: "It comes to me, understand, Doctor, that we ought to go over and pray for Sister Mister." Although at first hesitating, on account of the apparent professional discourtesy, Dr. Williams finally yielded to Mr. Thomas' earnest importunity and accompanied him. The lady's physician was in attendance, and her friends were gathered about what, to all seeming, was her dying bed. Mr. Thomas inquired of her physician as to her condition, and received this reply: "Mr. Thomas, Mrs. Mister is *in extremis*." "What's that?—got the tremors?" inquired the simple-minded man. The doctor then explained that he had exhausted the last remedy without avail, and that the lady was at that moment actually dying. At his suggestion, Dr. Williams examined the sinking patient, and coincided with his brother physician's opinion.

"Have you any objection to my prayin' for her?" inquired Mr. Thomas.

"Pray if you feel like it;" responded the doctor. "Nothing can now do her either good or harm."

"Let us pray, then," said Mr. Thomas, at the sametime dropping upon his knees; while her physician, a high Churchman, sat upon the side of the bed looking his utter astonishment, if not his contempt, for the strange proceeding. The prayer was as follows:

"Lord; this here doctor, understand, has given this

dear Christian woman up, and says he can't do nothin' more to help her. You must take her case in hand, if you please, Lord, or else she must die. When you was here on the earth, Lord, you gave blind people new eyes; you made lame people run and jump; you healed the sick, and put life into the cold, stiff bodies of the dead. It comes to me, understand, that this good woman oughtn't to die yet; and, O Lord, I want you to make her well again, if you please, for Jesus Christ's sake. *Amen.*"

Having made this matter-of-fact, business-like presentation of her case and of his own desire unto the Lord, he and Dr. Williams left her bedside and started for Onancock, with every indication pointing to the conclusion that a few minutes, or an hour or two at most, would terminate Mrs. Mister's earthly history. Reaching a woods that lay in their pathway to the village, Mr. Thomas suddenly stopped, and quietly remarked: "It comes to me, understand, Doctor, we ought to pray again for Sister Mister;" and down he went on his knees, calling on Dr. Williams to lead in the petition.

The doctor obeyed the request, but confessedly with "little faith;" and then Mr. Thomas followed, winding up with a shout of victory. The same thing was repeated at family prayers; and the good old man literally shouted himself off to bed, and shouted out again next morning. His explanation of this extraordinary expenditure of wind and muscle, was that the Lord had told him the sick woman was getting well.

After breakfast, Mr. Thomas said, "Come, Doctor, let's go over and see Sister Mister." As they neared the house, they espied the bed and bed clothing spread out doors for airing. The appearances were very suspicious, and Dr. Williams remarked, "Bro. Thomas; Sister Mister is dead." "No she's not," said the man of mighty faith; "the Lord never tells me a not so." At that moment the husband came out to meet them; and, in reply to Mr. Thomas' confident inquiry, informed them that his wife was able to leave her bed and to be about superintending her household affairs. It was a transition from death to life and health, in a few hours, in harmony with, if not in answer to, the simple unquestioning faith of an illiterate oysterman.

On another occasion, Mr. Thomas came in the "Methodist" to convey Rev. Jas. A. Massey, the pastor at the time, to Tangier to fill his appointment. It being inconvenient for Mr. Massey to leave home, Dr. Williams consented to take his place; and the two local preachers were soon gliding over the waters of the beautiful Pocomoke Sound. But while on their way, a dark cloud arose, and a furious storm swept down the Chesapeake upon them, driving them before it into a little inlet haven on the Accomac shore. It looked as if the appointment was doomed to prove a *disappointment;* but, in the emergency and amid the howling storm, Mr. Thomas said, "Let us pray;" and, kneeling in the tossing canoe, said:

"Lord; I'm on my way to the Island with a preacher

to fill an appointment. I can't go, understand, in this here storm; and if it lasts any longer, we shall be too late; and thy poor children there will have to go hungry for the bread of life for two weeks more. Lord; you once rode on a storm across the sea of Galilee; and you know all about 'em and can manage this one better 'n I can, though I'm a good sailor; and I want you to speak to these winds right away, if you please, and tell them to be quiet, so I can go on and get Bro. Williams to the Island in time to preach, for thy own sake and for the sake of thy cause. *Amen.*"

Arising from his knees, and without waiting a moment to ascertain the result of his petition, he began at once to hoist sail. And, strange to tell, by the time his canvass was spread, the furious tempest had moderated to a propitious breeze, and the voyagers reached their destination in ample time. Numerous similar incidents may be found in the memoirs of his wonderful life. These stories there is no room to doubt. They are quaint and strange, but it may be they are so, only because the Christian Church is so profoundly unconscious of her privileges.

Mr. Thomas was an intimate friend and a great admirer of Rev. Laurence Laurenson. His admiration of this flaming herald's preaching led him to attempt once to imitate him. It being another case of David in Saul's armor, without the timely wisdom of the shepherd boy to discover its unfitness; poor Joshua, with his lofty soaring, his unsteady flopping, and his *toploftical* tumbling, cut a most painfully ludicrous figure, and was deeply but healthfully humiliated. He never tried to be anything but fisherman Joshua Thomas afterwards. It was some relief to his wounded feelings, when Laurenson made him a present of two of his elegant shirts. While Mr. Thomas never again attempted the folly above described; it is said that whenever he had an appointment to preach on any special occasion, in after years, he always put on one of the Laurenson shirts, imagining this arrangement to be the nearest possible approach to Elijah's mantle!

At a certain quarterly meeting in Somerset, a number of ministers—Laurenson and Thomas included—were guests at the same farm-house. After retiring for the night, the brethren engaged in the discussion of various Scripture passages; Mr. Thomas expressing his conviction that a particular passage he had mentioned would "make a first-rate tex' for a sermont." Laurenson, who, in his periods of cheerfulness, was keenly alive to the ludicrous, proposed that Thomas should preach them a sermon from the text, right then and there as they lay in bed. The "Parson" accepted the challenge, and began at once to work out a sermon. By the time he got through the introduction he was sitting upright on his bed. On *firstly*, he warmed up until he slid out and stood upon the floor. On *secondly*, he got excited and walked the room back and forth, with most earnest voice and gesticulation. But when he reached *thirdly*, he became so jubilant that he could stand it no longer;

but "went off" into a regular "spell" of boisterous rejoicing. John Parks, one of the company, equally inflammable, caught the electric current; and, leaping from his bed, joined in the shout with Mr. Thomas; while Laurenson and the other preachers sat up in bed, responding "Amen" to their resounding "Glory!" Meantime, the family and friends, sleeping in the lower rooms, were awakened by the "big meetin'" going on above; and arose, dressed hastily, and came up to participate; when, alas! some one struck a light! The ludicrous spectacle upset all gravity; and the descent from the sublime to the ridiculous was immediate, precipitous, astonishing, overwhelming; and threw the whole company into hysterical convulsions! Laurenson, it is said, could never think of this scene, when the light was thrown upon it, without the most immoderate laughter.

Mr. Thomas' remarks in public as often provoked mirth as seriousness and tears. Speaking at an experience meeting at Ross' woods camp-meeting in Sussex, Del., on one occasion, the quaint old man said: "Brothers; the Devil sometimes bothers God's people right smart by suggestin' that things is not a goin' on right at home. This very mornin', understand, he's been a tellin' me that the hogs are in my pertater patch, down on the Island. But I told him, understand, if they were, and ate up all the pertaters, I'd eat up the hogs next winter, understand, and that'll make accounts all square."

It was Mr. Thomas' custom, wherever he took a meal in his journeyings, at the close to call the family to prayer. On such occasions it was his habit to remember and mention each person of the company by name, and adapt his prayers to the peculiarities of their respective conditions. Having learned on one occasion of dining out, that three of the ladies constituting the company were widows, he prayed most devoutly for them, telling the Lord all about their bereft and lonely condition; and asking that they might all in due time be made happy in the possession of loving husbands and pleasant homes. Coming finally in his petition to the young gentleman visitor present, whose intentions he had divined, he prayed: "Lord, bless this nice young man; give him favor in the eyes of this lovely lady he's so much interested in; and so dispose her heart that his suit may be successful." However much this petition may have embarrassed the parties, it surely afforded the young gentleman an excellent opportunity to "pop the question."

Mr. Thomas was an earnest advocate for "decency and order" in worship, and could illy brook any interruption calculated to interfere with a devotional frame of mind. His special antipathy was to the annoyance of crying children in meeting. It was no unusual thing for him to interrupt the speaker, to volunteer needed suggestions to thoughtless mothers. One day at a camp-meeting, the parson stopped a minister in the midst of a fine oratorical flight, to appeal to a mother in the congregation, whose baby, for fifteen minutes, had kept up an annoying squall. "Sister," said he, in tones tender and pleading, "Sister, do please give that 'ere child a tater!"

With regrets we must now take our leave of the good veteran, and pass to other scenes and characters. Peace to the ashes of Joshua Thomas.

Not far away from the Tangier and Deal's Islands, in the same queenly waters, is Smith's Island, or more properly islands; for the low, marshy emerald that barely rises above the storm-tides, is divided by various little straits serving as highways, into a multitude of islands, thickly dotted over by cabins and cottages, where dwell the thrifty oystermen who inhabit those regions, and gather their sure and remunerative harvests from the bottom of the deep.

Until the era of emancipation in Maryland, with its natural accompaniment of free schools for all sections, these primitive folk were generally innocent of the offence of reading pernicious literature,—or any other literature, for that matter,—for the schoolmaster, although abroad, had never wandered that far from home.

Some years ago it was the writer's good fortune to enjoy a trip to Smith's Islands, partly in quest of healthful relaxation, but also to aid the pastor, Rev. John Shilling, in what the islanders called a camp-meeting, which, however, was held in the spacious chapel. These chapel camp-meetings are held usually about the last of August or first of September, that being a season of leisure; and all the inhabitants—men, women and children—seem to esteem it almost a disgrace not to be in attendance. The men come in their shirt-sleeves and the matrons in their slat, or sun bonnets; only the bronzed youths and rosy maidens apparently making any effort at "dressing up" or adornment. More than half the families bring to this great gathering from one to three or four live babies, varying in dimensions from the month old "squaller" to the rollicking youngster of three or four summers. A juvenile at home, during these meetings, is a rare exception. Peter's declaration; " The promise is unto you and to your children," is literally accepted on these islands, as it ought to be everywhere.

To stand near the chapel on a bright morning, when the assembly is gathering, and scan the horizon around, presents a spectacle never to be forgotten. The mingled picture of little green isles; the glistening and rippled streets of water; the scores of snowy sails, like angel wings, dotting the horizon in every direction for miles, and converging towards the humble sanctuary; the mingled snatches of cheerful, sacred melodies from many of the approaching crews, floating over the waters from every direction in sweet and witching confusion, stamp an impression on the sensitive canvass of the soul, so weird and picturesque as to remain forever indelible.

It was night when the " Bugeye " that bore us across from Crisfield arrived; and, in a little while, the tired voyager was snugly tucked away in the preacher's room at "Uncle" Haney Bradshaw's. The little one-story cottage having proven too strait, the proprietor had sawn it asunder, moved one-half twenty feet away; and, between the two parts, had erected a two-story addition for the special purpose of having a suitable and comfortable chamber for his ministerial visitors.

Haney Bradshaw was, at that time, the patriarch of the Islands; everybody's uncle; and, by common consent, proprietor of the *Hotel d' Itinerante*. Uncle Haney was *sui generis*, and perhaps even a little more so. Among his many striking peculiarities, was his propensity to coin words and phrases for his own convenience in utterance or expression. He neither knew nor cared anything for dictionaries or usage, and set all the laws of lexicographers and grammarians at defiance. The phrase, "In that form," or sometimes, "In that manner and form, sir," was interjected into almost all his utterances. Taking down his old, blackened clay pipe from the mantel, for the indispensable smoke after the meal, said he: "Formality times, in that form, sir, I allers used to stick my pipe in my waistcoat pocket, when I warn't smokin'; but Polly she kept up a reg'lar blundeguster about it. In that manner and form, sir, she allowanced it perfumegated my clothin' with a solid confunction of a dark smell, and to pleasify Polly, in that way and manner, brother, I quit the practize." This would constitute a sufficient reason for every one to cease carrying the pipe in either the pocket or the mouth.

Uncle Haney greatly enjoyed the preaching of the Gospel, and was not slow to express his high appreciation of our efforts. After our return from church one night, he took it into his head to compliment the writer in the following style: "I tell you, brother, you had a mighty bunctious tex' to-night. In that way and form, sir, you got things into a solid smother. Why, sir, if you'd 'a combusticated at that dyin' rate a little longer, I'd 'a splodified right out in the consanctum! In that form, sir, why haint they made you a Bishop long ago?" Uncle Haney was equally complimentary to a sermon preached on the Island, by Rev. Bro. H.——, of the Wilmington Conference; when, in giving an account of it to one of that gentleman's parishioners at Crisfield, he said: "I tell you, Bro. Hance Lawson, in that manner and form, your preacher's a regular Bonytholimar. He norated powerful well in the mornin', and then went home with me to dinner and tuck in a cooner load of pervisions; and I tell you, sir, I didn't think he could preach much of a sermon in the arternoon, and I jest rared my head back agin the wall for a good nap; but I tell you, sir, in that way and manner, when he let on the steam and got under full headway, he jest funked out the preachin' to excess!"

Brother H——'s description of the introductory to the above-mentioned sermon is unique. While he was looking up his hymns and Scripture lessons, a tall, lank brother, in his shirt-sleeves, and somewhat resembling a pair of oyster tongs, arose in the amen corner; and, with a very emphatic and significant gesture with his index-finger, drawled out: "Mister Preacher; it's time for to begin!" The preacher was about to arise in obedience to the admonition, when Uncle Haney came crawling into the pulpit, and said to the preacher, in what was meant to be a whisper, but in a growl loud enough to be heard all over the house: "Brother H——, Aunt Levina Bradshaw, an old 'oman ninety and odd year old, in that form, and weighin' two hundred and odd pound, fell overboard, in that way and manner, in ten foot of water, and lost everything she had in the world, even to her shoes. And I tell you, sir, it's a mighty feelin' sense-thing, in that manner and form, and I feel for the circumstances, and I want to take a collection." He then straightened up, told the same story of misfortune to the congregation; and was about to proceed to make his levy on them; when the tall oyster-tongs in the amen corner again arose, entered his protest, "Agin Uncle Haney a 'sturbin' the meetin' in that way;" and then repeated, with additional emphasis: "Mr. Preacher, I say it's time for to begin." Uncle Haney, however, went right on with his appeal, and after "'sturbin' the meetin'" for about fifteen minutes, secured for Aunt Levina a "right bunctious" collection, "in that form;" and then gave his permission for the preacher to "drive ahead." The patient dominie then arose to begin the service; when another pair of human oyster-tongs came running to the door; and, beckoning to the minister, with panting breath, implored: "Mister preacher! Hol–hold–on a while! Don't—don't say-say yer tex' now. Ther's some a comin'—comin' to meetin' what's not got yer yit!" A precisely similar circumstance occurred, on the Sunday morning of the writer's visit; and while the "congregation, a comin' from Holland's Island, what's got becalmed and not got yer yit," were laboriously "toiling in rowing" for a full half-hour to reach the point, Uncle Haney growled out: "I don't see the use 'n people's bein' so disconstitutional lazy. Why don't they git up Sunday mornin's same es they was gwine a oysterin'; and then they could git to meetin', in that form, with some kind o' temporaneous decency!" Brother Shilling improved the opportunity by extemporising a baptismal service; and, although it was "not a good day for a christenin'" Uncle Haney said, the names of twenty-nine boys and girls were taken by the pastor for entry on his record of baptisms!

Uncle Haney Bradshaw's appearance was as uncouth as his mode of expression; but, beneath all this rough exterior, there was the most child-like simplicity and earnest sincerity. One summer it was very dry and hot, and the little corn-field, a short time before so luxuriant and promising, wilted and faded, until it made the old man heart-sick to look at it. Finally, at morning devotions, Uncle Haney prayed most earnestly that the Lord would send a refreshing rain, and save his little crop from destruction. That very same afternoon, a storm-cloud swept down the Chesapeake; the lightnings sent their bolts crashing along the galleries of the heavens; and the winds shrieked their weird and awful accompaniments. But all this was music in Uncle Haney's ears, who thought only of the copious and refreshing rain, that, in answer to his prayer, was blessing his thirsty corn-field. At last it was over and the sun shone out, transforming every rain-drop on the corn-blades into a glistening diamond; and, contentedly humming "Praise God from whom all blessings flow," Uncle Haney started out barefoot to walk around his little field and mingle his rejoicings with the gladness of the corn. But, alas! what havoc met his vision! Tangled in utter confusion; with torn roots exposed to view; with many noble stalks broken and ruined; the luxuriant corn of which he had been so proud as the biggest on the Island, seemed damaged by the storm beyond recovery. Coming back with fallen countenance and doleful groans, he entered the door and saluted his wife in the following discouraged language: "Well, Polly, in that way and manner, I've about come to the conclusion that the Lord sometimes answers prayer a little too much, and does about as much damage as he does good! I don't see, in that form, but what he mought jest as well burn up the corn with heat as tear it all to flinderations with a thunderguster!" To those who knew Haney Bradshaw well, this will not seem to be the utterance of angry complaint or irreverence. He simply gave honest expression, to about what many of us feel under parallel circumstances, and without a single thought of rebellion.

In Uncle Haney Bradshaw's apparently rugged bosom, there beat an honest heart, full of generous impulses; and, at times, glowing with a fervor of feeling and a vividness of imagination that was simply astonishing. Never will the writer forget the effect of the old veteran's thrilling experience of his awakening and conversion, related on Sunday afternoon, as we sat under the pleasant shade of the great pear-tree that grew in his yard. No pen-portraiture can do the scene justice. It was largely the heaven-lighted face of the simple-minded old saint, that made the vivid impression. He began the story while sitting smoking his pipe; but, ere long, the fascinating narcotic was forgotten, and Uncle Haney was on his feet; his unstudied action most strikingly and gracefully dramatic; his lion-like voice softened and attuned to sympathetic tenderness; and tears of grateful remembrance of God's goodness stealing down his furrowed cheeks. His story, as nearly as I can remember, was as follows:

"I tell you, brothers, in that form, when the Lord got arter me, I was a permegatin' my own devices like a young devil; and I didn't want nothin' to do with the glimmerations of the Sperit, 'cause it took all the flavorin' out'n my confectionary, like. So I run this place, that place and the tother; and dove into all sorts o' mud-puddles, a tryin' to disgustify the Lord, so's he'd lemme be. Well, sir; in that way and manner, I was jest like one o' these ornery, cunnin' old crabs; that, soon's you git arter 'em, 'll cut stick for the place where your paddle's stirred up the mud, so's to scapen away and hide. Well, 'bout that time, ther was a camp-meetin' over on the Somerset Main; so, in that manner and form, sir, I 'cluded to 'tend it, and performerate all the jimmycracks I could think of, so's to bust the Lord's holts loose, and do 's I pleased a spell; and then arter a while I thought, when I was fulfilled with my own circumlutions, I'd turn to the Lord. Well, sir, in that form, when I got over there and hearn the singing, and begun to think what I was a tryin' to do, it seemed like to me every wind that whistled through the pine-tree tops, was like the growl of a chained devil that could almost reach me with his red-hot pitchfork; and I tell you, sir, I begun to feel powerful ramshacked-like, and wished myself back on the Island. Then I hearn a voice that seemed to say: 'Haney; now's the day of salvation—turn to-day.' ''Bout then my knees come right weak and trimblin'; and my heart jumped out and in—up and down, like it was a cork on a fishin' line, and all the eels and catfish in pandehonium a nibblin' at the bait. Well, sir, in that way and manner, about that time the preacher said: 'Young man; turn now, or you're lost;' and the singers struck up 'Turn to the Lord and seek salvation!' and, sir, 'bout then the earth cracked open; and the flames shot up from the stiflin' furnace; and I felt myself a sinkin' down, down, down, in that form, sir, where God Almighty's arm couldn't reach me, and the angels, they'd all forgit me. And then, thinks I—'yes; you've broke God's holts on you, sure enough; and you're lost forever!' and that's the last I remember, till three hours after—they said it was—I found myself about a mile down, a lookin' out at the top of Hell—as I was afeerd; and it was so near closed I could only see, away off, one little star, like the eye of Jesus, a lookin' down kind o' pitysome-like on me. And then, brothers, in that form, that star begun to dimensionize bigger and bigger, and come nearer and nearer; and I looked and looked, till the eyes of my 'mortal soul blazed like the top peaks of the waves in the first kisses of the mornin' sunshine; and jest then I begun to rise out'n that drearysome hole. They say the lumigatin' moon, drawin' the water, raises the high-tides from the see, and makes the rivers run up stream. And jest so, that mornin' star drawed my perishin' soul out'n damnation; and flung its arms of light, in that form, about me; and lifted me up higher and higher, and come nearer and nearer, until Heaven busted open; and then I saw that the star was nothin' but the face of Jesus, shinin' down from the mercy-seat; and, when I fully come to myself, I was in the snow-white 'cooner' of salvation, a skimmin' over silver waves of peace, tipped with pearls and gold of joysome love; and a fair breeze, in that way and manner, for the uncrumpled cove of glory, where no flurry of sin can ever blow!"

A few years after the date of the above glowing recital, Uncle Haney's "cooner," dropped anchor in the peaceful, "uncrumpled" haven, for which he was so long a hopeful voyager. Aunt Polly—dear old soul—who stood on the little wharf in front of the door, wiping her eyes with the corner of her checked apron, as the "bugeye" bore the historian away, still lingers on the shore, looking out over the waters for the approach of the kindly ferryman to bear her over.

Equally remarkable in characteristic personal traits, but with large advantage as to general knowledge and culture, is Captain William Frazier, familiarly known as "Capt. Billy," a product of the "Neck," stretching below Cambridge, between the little and the great Choptank, and projecting into the Chesapeake. Captain Frazier was somewhat of a politician, and very influential in Dorchester as a leading Whig, and afterwards as a Republican; several times, and with much credit, representing his county in the halls of legislation. For many years, until recently, he occupied an important position in the Baltimore Custom House; but has lately been invited to retire; and now again takes up his residence at the old homestead on the beautiful Choptank waters.

Says Rev. Adam Wallace, D.D., in his interesting sketches in the *Peninsula Methodist:* "The Captain's stories of sea and land; his practical sense in business and church affairs, and his unquestioned influence as the adviser of his neighbors, made him an entertaining host." Of his introduction to Capt. Billy, he speaks on this wise: " It was a chilly afternoon, when my first appointment down the 'Neck' led me to Spedden's meeting-house. They had hastily made a fire in the one large ten-plate stove, standing in the centre of the plain old church. The stove-pipe was shaky, as it had a long reach up to the flue. The house became filled with smoke. Preacher and people felt a smarting about the eyes; and we could not commence the exercises until all the windows had been opened and the house cleared of smoke. Before preaching, I suggested that the interruption would not occur again if the trustees, or some thoughtful friend, would see to the proper fixing of the pipe; and that it ought to be attended to the first thing on Monday morning.

"'Here, young man,' said a plain, sturdy and very outspoken brother in the congregation, 'you just mind your own business, and we will attend to ours: go on with your preaching.'

"I had never met Capt. Frazier, but from what I had heard of him I suspected this must be the man, and I was not mistaken. The way he knocked the wind out of my sails—to use one of his own sailor phrases—was a caution; and, with fear and trembling, I proceeded with the service. I had my turn, however, four weeks from that day. It was a backward spring, and they made a fire in the old stove; but early enough to have the house cleared of smoke before I ascended the pulpit. As I arose to give out the opening hymn,—always the signal for out-door loiterers to enter the church in a body,—the vibration of so many feet upon the floor disturbed the equilibrium of the stove-pipe; and I saw it topple. We had just raised the tune; but down came that forty-foot cylinder, parting into three sections, and every joint nearly full of the accumulated smut of time immemorial. Part fell over on the women's side, part towards the 'amen corner,' and the remainder came down with a crash among the sinners in the rear. The first man to leap to the rescue was 'Captain Billy;" and, seizing the falling pipe, he let it go again suddenly and began to blow on his hands. The pipe was very hot!

"Our singing was suspended until the dense cloud of soot settled down on the people's Sunday clothes, and the roaring fire had been put out. I kept my eye on the Captain, and, catching his, inquired: 'Well, whose business is it now to repair damages?' He possessed a streak of the ludicrous, and, moreover, had a very big, generous heart; so he made an apology that set every body in a good humor; and from that day he and I became the best of friends. We had some trouble, however, in resuming our hymn, and still more in composing our minds and faces into the proper frame for prayer. He insisted that I should go home with him; and a pleasanter home picture does not hang in all the gallery of my recollections, than I found at the old family dwelling of Capt. William Frazier."

Rev. Thos. L. Poulson, D.D., was Capt. Billy's pastor in 1860. While engaged in an extra meeting that fall, the preacher was one night detained by a pastoral duty, so that he failed to be on time for the beginning of the service. Becoming impatient, Captain Billy had sung a hymn; and, at the time of Bro. Poulson's arrival, was vociferously leading the congregation in prayer. Stealing in softly, the pastor took his position a little in the rear of the unsuspecting leader, who, in the course of his petition, took occasion to notify the Head of the Church as follows; " O Lord, we are here like sheep without a shepherd; we've got a preacher who ought to be with us, but he's out somewhere, a galivantin' around, and we don't know what he's about. O Lord, we pray thee to look after our preacher, and have mercy upon him and bless him!" "Amen!" responded the parson; when Capt. Billy, looking round at him in surprise, growled out: "Humph! you got here at last!" after which he speedily reached the "amen."

With all the old sailor's blunt ways and pugnacious antics, none of the many victims of his keen but humorous sarcasm, have ever questioned his profound honesty and Christian generosity. The writer most heartily joins in the prayer of Dr. Wallace, that "his sunset of life may be serene and cloudless; and that the Saviour he has loved so long and ardently, may be the support and joy of his failing heart, and his portion forever."

Another remarkable character, belonging in this category, was Garretson West, who lived and died at St. Michaels, Maryland. He was born in the early part of the present century, and died on the 23d of February, 1853. Mr. West was poor in this world's goods, but rich in faith and good works. His sphere was circumscribed by his lowly condition; but most admirably did he fill its measure and meet all its requirements. Owing to his environments in childhood, he was debarred from all privileges and blessings of literary culture, not receiving even the most primary elements of education. Indeed he was such a simple-minded child of nature, that the merely casual acquaintance might perhaps have adjudged him mentally weak, if not indeed bordering closely on imbecility. Such a conclusion, however, would never have been reached by any but a superficial observer; and, in such case, largely owing to his singular deadness to the things that ordinarily engage human attention, and his absorbing devotion to religious enjoyment and conversation. It might appropriately be said of him, his "conversation was in heaven." One of the most devoted and discriminating laymen of Easton, Maryland, Mr. Leonidas Dodson, Sr., says of him: "It must not be supposed that he was, in any sense, weak-minded or deficient in natural intelligence. If he appeared to be indifferent to business pursuits, and literally without care for the morrow, it was for the reason that the religious element of his nature had absorbed the man."

Garretson West was converted to God in early manhood; and, to the end, retained such a vivid recollection of that blessed hour and event, that he seemed ever to be rejoicing in the exhilarating ecstacies of his new, first love. Religious life with him was a great protracted meeting and a revival without intermissions, ending only with the victorious shout of the dying warrior. Immediately upon his conversion, he came to the front in the spiritual activities of the Church; and such was the touching simplicity and effectiveness of his humble efforts in that line, that, despite his apparent disqualification, he was instantly recognized as "called of God to be an apostle," and commissioned by the Church to be a sort of independent ranger, or evangelist without limitations or restrictions in St. Michaels and surrounding regions. Says Mr. Dodson: "Methodism in St. Michaels, Md., and its vicinity, owes more to the heroic services of Garretson West than to any other single individual, living or dead."

Early in his Christian career, recognizing his preeminent spiritual qualifications to feed Christ's lambs, Mr. West's pastor appointed him leader of a class; and so wise were his counsels, so attractive his sweet spirit, and so inspiring his fervor and enthusiasm, that even the refined and cultured esteemed it a privilege to be enrolled as members of his little flock. For like reasons, he was soon licensed to exhort; and many a time his rude and simple but really eloquent and stirring appeals, and his glowing utterances of Christian sentiment and experience, saved a dull meeting from failure, and turned apparent defeat into victory. "He was always in the lead at extra meetings and at camp-meetings. His exhortations were pungent and awakening, vehement in the denunciation of sin, and true to Methodistic orthodoxy. They were ofttimes truly eloquent, and always the outcome of a heart deeply imbued with a simple, unquestioning faith in the great verities of the Christian religion."

Early in life Mr. West followed the occupation of an oysterman. While thus engaged, it was no unusual thing for him to lay down his tongs to engage in a prayer meeting, all by himself, to which his busy brother oystermen's attention would finally be called by his lusty singing and triumphant shouting. Sometimes whenever the rakes were lifted on board with their load of bivalves, his hearty ejaculations of "hallelujah!" or "glory to God!" would mingle with the sound of the oysters as they rattled down upon the pile or on the bottom of his canoe. After laboring and rejoicing thus all day, he would spend half the night in leading the singing at some protracted meeting that happened to be going on within reach of his humble home. He afterwards secured a team, and became a carter. In this business much of his time was employed in conveying goods and freight for the merchants of St. Michaels, between their places of business and the packet wharf and steamboat landing. But if, while thus engaged, he chanced to meet any one who was willing to tarry for extended religious conversation, no matter what the exigencies of trade, he would forget his errand, and allow the needed goods to remain on the wharf for hours after he was expected to deliver them to the anxiously waiting merchants. Sometimes Mr. West became the innocent victim of little conspiracies on this line—the young men arranging to meet and stop him, at intervals, for conversation upon his favorite theme; until the merchants, weary with waiting and sometimes quite out of patience with the carter's zealous negligence, would go or send a clerk to hunt him and "jog his memory," or even gently reprimand him, and thus recall him to the duty of the hour. Says Mr. Dodson again: "Religion beamed from his countenance, and the bright smile that played upon his features was the index of the sweet power filling the soul." He was a shouting Christian, but however demonstrative— whether jumping, clapping his hands, or voicing his hallelujahs and amens in the public services or the classroom, he was *privileged*, for all knew he had something over which to shout."

At length, in middle-life, Mr. West was stricken with an illness—the result of overwork and exposure in a protracted meeting—that proved fatal. When the serious nature of his malady became known in the community, an interest little less than a panic took possession of the public mind. Persons who kept a record of passing events of importance, entered upon their journals the fact of his illness and the progress of the disease, with their hopes and fears of the result, from day to day. In all public religious services, the Church put on sackcloth and ashes; and tearful and importunate prayers were offered that his valuable life might be spared. The following transcript from Mr. Dodson's journal, written at the time, will reveal better than anything I can write, the estimate in which Mr. West was held, and the deep sense of bereavement under which a whole community bowed:

"*February* 21*st*, 1853.—Brother West still lives in a precarious situation, barely allowing hopes of his recovery. A great deal of sympathy is felt for him. He is truly a man of God, and in his death the church would experience a heavy loss.

"22d.—It seems to be the will of the Almighty to remove Brother West from the militant to the triumphant Church. No hopes are entertained of his recovery. He lives, but evidently in a sinking condition. As might well be expected of one who has labored so long and faithfully in the service of God, his humble home and lowly couch are the scenes of the highest triumph of which the mind has conception—the triumph over death. I visited him late yesterday afternoon, and experienced that, 'the chamber where the good man meets his fate, is privileged beyond the common walks of virtuous life—quite on the verge of heaven.' His chief desire was to depart and be with Christ; and frequently clapping his hands and crying 'Victory! Victory!' he gave to the numerous friends, who wept and rejoiced around his bed, the best assurance that he was standing upon the everlasting Rock, and contemplating, unmoved the waves of death that rolled beneath his feet. I shall not soon forget this most interesting visit to Brother West nor his dying prayer, as he grasped my hand and said; 'Brother Dodson, may the Lord bless you.'

"23d.—Yesterday evening, a little after sundown, the mortal sun of brother West set to rise no more. Thus has closed the life of this deeply pious, useful and beloved man. He leaves a monument in the heart of every man in the community. The whole church membership are mourners. As a mark of the public esteem for the memory of this dear brother, a notice has been posted requesting that all business shall cease, on the morrow, during the funeral solemnities.

"25th.—Brother West was interred yesterday by the Sons of Temperance, of which order he was a member. The funeral was preached by Rev. James A. Massey from a text he selected before his death—'I have fought a good fight.' The church, notwithstanding it was one of the coldest days of this winter, was crowded to overflowing; and stifled sobs and weeping eyes attested the high esteem in which the deceased was held. Never have I witnessed such universal and unfeigned sorrow. In the afternoon a meeting was called to consider the propriety of placing at his grave a monument to his memory, and the initiatory steps were taken to have a suitable one erected."

In a recent letter, speaking of the closing scenes of Mr. West's life, the same writer says: "And so living, the end came; and such an end! His physician—the late Dr. James Dawson—finding it out of the question to stop him from rejoicing aloud in the prospect of victory over death, or to prevent the constant stream of visitors who were eager to see and hear the dying hero, *gave in;* and the last days of his life were given to a glad and triumphant testimony to the power of that grace he had recommended to all in his life."

From a most interesting letter, received since writing the above account of this remarkable saint of God, written by Mr. James Valliant of Talbot County, Md., I glean the following:

"Garretson West was to St. Michael's and vicinity, what Joshua Thomas was to Deal's Island. Except that the latter was possessed of some property, and could read and write, they were counterparts of each other. * * * * Money was never of any value to him save as the means of support to the church, and of a bare subsistence for himself and his little family. Religion was his constant theme through the whole of every day of his life, and was closely intermixed with his every dream at night. That he was an enthusiast is undeniably true; but his enthusiasm was never of a nature to be repulsive to any one. He commanded not only the confidence, respect and esteem, but also the heartfelt affection of all who knew him, whether within or outside the pale of the church, and of whatever sect or creed. His mind and heart—his whole life, character, conduct and intent, were as pure as it is possible to conceive mortal man can attain. His whole life was a most beautiful commentary on the Christian religion. * * * *

"His success as a peacemaker and arbiter of differences, among his neighbors was unparalleled. As soon as it

PATRIARCHS OF THE CHESAPEAKE. 121

became known to him that misunderstanding or ill-will existed between any two of our people, of whatever sex or condition, he would avail himself of the first opportunity to visit them; and rarely indeed did he fail in effecting a happy reconciliation. The poor and illiterate looked to him for advice and comfort in all their difficulties. To these he was another Moses; and, at all times, to them his word was law. He visited and prayed with all the sick and dying; and his coming was always welcomed with gladness. His tact in imparting comfort, consolation and good cheer to the afflicted was such as few men have possessed. He could not go too often, and never failed to inspire the patient with confidence and hope.

"Though he never learned even so much as the alphabet, he was as familiar with Bible history and all the cardinal doctrines of his church as any clergyman I ever knew. Few ministers were as familiar with Scriptural texts as he. For every occasion he had ready at hand a quotation from the sayings of Christ, his Apostles or some of the prophets. He never ceased or tired of his Master's work. On the oyster rocks, with some forty or fifty others engaged in tonging oysters, his conversation was an all-day sermon. If the subject of converse should drift into the secular, his part therein soon ceased to be prominent. In our village stores on rainy days, on the street, around the domestic hearth-stone, and when visiting his neighbors, his theme was the same; or, at least, had for its main object the cultivation of a religious sentiment in the minds of his auditors; and, strange as it may appear, his converse never became irksome. Never in the town of St. Michael's, and within a radius of ten or twelve miles around, was the loss of a citizen so deeply and universally mourned." By reason of his liberal contributions for charity and to the support of the Church, "he was almost without a dollar at the time of his death. But he was decently buried by the affectionate contributions of his numerous friends, by whom a very substantial, though plain, monument was erected over his grave, in the old Methodist burying-ground."

A few years ago, when the Methodists of St. Michael's purchased and laid out a beautiful, new cemetery near the town, the dust of Garretson West was removed, and deposited in the central and most conspicuous location; and his tomb is the Mecca to which all the winding walks of that silent city of the dead lead the willing feet of visiting pilgrims. On the west face of his monument is the inscription:

"BORN IN TALBOT COUNTY IN 1800;
BORN AGAIN IN 1818;
DIED IN 1853."

On the east face is chiseled:

"THOUGH POOR AND UNLEARNED,
HE WAS A BURNING AND A SHINING LIGHT;
'ALWAYS ABOUNDING IN THE WORK OF THE LORD.'
*   *   *   *   *
'I HAVE FOUGHT A GOOD FIGHT.'"

Such a life-history as that of Garretson West is inestimably valuable to the Church; and deserves to be commemorated, on account of the encouragement to devotion and zeal it affords to those of humble surroundings and small ability. The Lord's parable of the talents exhibits the success of those of respectable and large abilities, and shows the terrible failure of him whose endowments were more humble. The life and labors of this lowly saint shows what may be experienced and accomplished by the servant of but one talent; who, instead of digging and hiding his Lord's investment, lays it out in the stock of entire consecration to God's service and full salvation from sin. Like the loaves and fishes, blessed by the handling, the breaking and the words of Jesus, the devoted life and efforts of Garretson West were divinely distributed to the satisfaction and enjoyment of a great multitude of many thousands.

CHAPTER V.

EPISODES AND COLLISIONS.

AMONG the eccentric and noted characters of Peninsular Methodism of olden times, was Rev. John Collins. He was naturally angular and irascible; and seems never to have had his nature so sweetened by grace as to cease entirely the production of porcupine quills, which it was his wont to project among his auditors upon every provocation. He was particularly distinguished for the severity of his rebukes to those guilty of any breach of order or decorum in church.

Once on a time, when Mr. Collins was preaching at Concord, Delaware, a stalwart young man named C——y, dressed in a fine new suit, with his pants tucked in the tops of his No. 12 cow-hide boots, arose in the midst of the sermon and stamped his way down the aisle and out at the door. The preacher paused and shot a fiery glance after him, but said nothing. In a few moments afterwards, John S——t arose and started for the door; when the indignant parson saluted him with: "Young man, you had better stop and sit down. Your new clothes are not near so good a fit as that other young man's."

On another occasion, however, the scolding preacher

met his match in the person of an unfortunate slave of the bottle, who had tarried outside to take an extra sip from his flask, after the congregation had gone into the house and the services had begun. On coming in, he found but one vacant seat, and that was uncomfortably near a red-hot stove. He accepted the situation, however; seated himself, and began attentively to listen to the sermon. It was not long until the heat of the fire and the poison of the bad whiskey produced their natural effect; and the poor fellow was made deathly sick. Noticing his distress, Mr. Collins vociferously ordered: "Take that drunken hog out of the church!" Turning upon him a reproachful look of injured innocence, the suffering toper retorted: "I'm not—hic—not drunk—hic—at all. It's the—hic—'s the nasty preachin's made me sick!"

Two incidents will serve to illustrate a phase of Methodist history within the Peninsula, that may be styled the politico-religious. The first happened during what Mr. Nasby calls "the late onpleasantness." The scene was a camp-meeting, at that time in progress in Kent County, Delaware. A lively meeting was going on at the front of the preaching stand. A young man, whom my Democratic readers will agree was not very well furnished in the upper story, had just "got through"—to use the expressive language of such characters—for about the sixth time within a few years; and, in the exuberance of his excitement, mounted a bench and began to exhort his companions and tell his experience.

Among other things, he alluded to his recent godless course, and said: "O friends! what a poor mis'able sinner I has ben! I've don a'most everything that's mean. I've broke Sunday! I've lied! I've cussed! I've cheated in measurin' osters! I've sold 'ale wives' for herrin's! And O! my dear friends, last fall I—boo-hoo! last fall, I voted the Dimmycrat ticket!" Poor, unfaithful Al! when last heard from, he was in the insane department of an alms house; but whether it was remorse for his ecclesiastical defections or for his political sinning was not known.

Let not the other side of the political house serenely chuckle over what they may be disposed to consider a well-deserved thrust from this poor, conscience-stricken crank; for the glass compartment of the body politic in which they reside bears marks, here and there, of equally effective *religious* stone-throwing. In a Delaware village but a few miles distant from the scene of the above episode, and a few years later, the Democratic part of the Methodist congregation had so grown in grace, that they could no longer consent to remain in church-fellowship with their Ephraimitish neighbors; and calling to their aid a minister of a sister denomination having professedly "nothing whatever to do with politics," they drew with them to his ministry most of the denizens of the village; and finally built and occupied a fine new church. At the dedication the tide of enthusiasm ran high. Religiously and politically it was a family gathering of kindred spirits. Finally, a zealous and doubtless sincere and honest sister, unable longer to restrain her pent-up joy, broke forth into jubilant exclamations in the following incisive language: "O, glory! Glory, hallelujah! We've got a new church, with forty good members; and, bless the Lord! there's not one ugly, dirty Black Republican among 'em!"

Rev. Solomon Sharp was one of the mighty heralds, whose clarion notes of war against the King's enemies were heard echoing through all the forests and valleys of the Peninsula. There seems to be but little left on record as to his life and labors; but from the most authentic traditions remaining, it is apparent, that although comparatively uncultured and given to an enthusiastic quaintness bordering on superstition, he was, nevertheless, a man of mighty faith and valiant in the wielding of his simple, spiritual armor.

There is said to have been great musical power, and singular magnetic effectiveness in his utterances. In 1856, the writer made the acquaintance of an aged gentleman whose name was Weeden, living on Kent Island. When a boy, Mr. Weeden heard Solomon Sharp preach his first sermon on the Island, under the spreading branches of a monster apple tree. A great crowd was gathered; and, the better to see and listen, the boy climbed into the tree above the speaker. He described Mr. Sharp's voice as "clear and full of music as a silver cornet." His appeal was indescribably terrible to the consciously wicked; and many fell under his words, like soldiers slain in the thick of the battle. Two gay young men who came up to the outer margin of the throng, and, with an air of laughing indifference, began to listen, soon changed their aspect to one of seriousness; and, finally, seized with the horrors of sudden conviction, turned and started to flee from the alarming scene. Pausing in his impassioned verbal torrent, Mr. Sharp's powerful voice rang out the admonition: "Young men; if you run away, I warn you it is at your eternal peril!" And then, lifting his eyes to Heaven, and raising his clarion voice still higher, he uttered the short, sharp petition: "O, Lord; harpoon them!" The well-aimed volley took instant effect. One partly fell under the incisive dart, but recovered himself and ran out of sight. The other wheeled as if lassoed by an angel horseman; and running straight back to the presence of the preacher, fell crying for mercy on the ground, and there struggled until the chains of Satan's bondage were broken.

At another place on the Island, pointed out to the writer, Mr. Sharp was once preaching to a gathered company in a private house. During the discourse, a respectable and usually respectful lady—a Mrs. Carter—began to rave and froth at the mouth in a most unaccountable manner, presenting the horrifying symptoms of an evil influence, similar to the demoniacal possessions of olden times. Although, when in her normal condition, she was given only to the use of mild and modest language, she wildly and profanely raved against the preacher and his message. She charged him with blasphemous hypocrisy; and averred that, although Christianity was divine, he and his co-workers present were the friends of the Devil; and finally dared the astonished soldier of the cross to a contest for the spiritual mastery. Taking advantage of a pause in her tirade of accusation, occasioned by a convulsion that brought her down prostrate, and rendered her speechless, Mr. Sharp stretched forth his hands towards her; and with an emphatic stamp of his foot, and kingly tone of utterance, he said to the influence that inspired her: "I command thee, in the name of the Lord Jesus Christ, to come out of the woman!" Instantly the writhing lady became calm and apparently unconscious. The sermon was concluded; and, in the solemn prayer-meeting that followed, this "accuser of the brethren" revived, and the announcement was made, "Behold, she prayeth!" In a little while, she was clothed and in her right mind, and sitting with joy at the feet of Jesus. Her descendants to this day are among the most reputable citizens of Kent Island. It is said that Mr. Sharp always insisted that he was divinely inspired to his authoritative, apostolic words and work on the above occasion; and that he plainly saw the Devil, somewhat in the form of a crestfallen and mean-looking dog, sneaking out at the door, with his caudal appendage drawn close down into a discouraged curl between his legs.

Rev. William Bishop was one of the men whose stirring biography the Methodist Churches should not have been permitted to lose. We sometimes feel almost indignant at the last preceding generation of Methodist itinerants, who might have gathered the materials, accessible until within the last quarter of a century, out of which the most thrilling histories might have been constructed. As it is, alas! the lives and doings of these heroes of Peninsular Methodism are now so dim and distant as to present only their shadowy outlines.

"Billy" Bishop, as he was familiarly called, was somewhat celebrated for his expertness in "cracking a joke." The author is indebted to the venerable John Tucker, of Dover, Delaware, for the following incidents, which he heard from the lips of the veritable Billy himself:

On a certain quarterly meeting occasion, Mr. Bishop, with other ministers and a number of the laity, enjoyed the hospitality of a Mrs. Coombe, in Camden, Delaware. This lady also had a reputation for genial humor and pleasant repartee. Mr. Bishop, being a stranger and not suspecting an ambuscade, on passing his cup, asked Mrs. Coombe for "half a cup of coffee." "Excuse me, Bro. Bishop," replied the lady, "but this is my best china, and I prefer not to break my cups in half." The twinkle of the preacher's eye acknowledged the bon-mot, while an audible smile rippled all around the table. At the next meal, the gentle hostess said: "Bro. Bishop, take another cup of coffee." "Thank you, sister," replied he, "but you needn't trouble about getting another cup: the same cup will do—filled up again!"

At one time, after he became widowed, Mr. Bishop was in attendance at a General Conference in the city of

Baltimore. He was understood to be the fortunate possessor of about $8,000—a neat little competency for a minister at that day; and there was some little interest among his brethren—and it was thought, indeed, among some of the sisters also—as to the matrimonial possibilities in Billy's case. He had been several times recommended to make the acquaintance of a certain "good looking" and well-to-do widow, residing in the city; and she had been bantered about Mr. Bishop. Finally, an interview was arranged. In company with several delegates, he was escorted by her guests to the widow's house and duly introduced. In the course of the evening, after a little promiscuous bantering on the part of the company in the way of pleasantry, the comely widow found occasion to speak of her business cares and responsibilities, in her relation as guardian to her children; remarking that the farm in Harford County was the property of her son Thomas; that another, in Baltimore County, belonged to John; and that the city property was the heritage of her daughter Lida. Billy Bishop's exclamation, in response, was decidedly more expressive than elegant or gallant:—"Umph! Take an old goose, and she picked!" It wasn't a match!

Many amusing scenes have transpired in the midst of circumstances of solemn import; and usually the ludicrousness of an event is intensified by its untimeliness. When people most feel they oughtn't laugh, it is often most difficult to refrain. Two or three incidents from the unwritten history of Peninsula Methodism will illustrate the above philosophy. In a revival meeting at a country church on Princess Anne Circuit, Rev. William J. O'Niell called on a sincere, quiet brother to lead in prayer. At the end of a very brief petition, he added: "Lord, with these few remarks we close, and remain yours truly. *Amen.*" The result can be imagined.

Rev. J—— D——, a sedate member of the Philadelphia Conference, was once stationed at Cambridge, Maryland. When the winter season came on, and the people could take time to let the Lord revive his work, an extra meeting was duly announced; and the reverend pastor took no little pains to prepare an initial sermon to inaugurate the campaign, that would tend to stir the Church into new life, and arouse the drowsy worldlings to a proper realization of their unhappy condition.

The auspicious Sunday night arrived. An immense congregation greeted the preacher, crowding the church to its utmost capacity. The sermon on "Awake thou that sleepest" was a decided success, and held the audience enchained, except a little negro boy who had accompanied his mistress; and who, notwithstanding the stirring message of the preacher, had tucked himself into a corner of the gallery and gone fast asleep.

At the conclusion, the earnest minister poised himself for a rousing appeal to the spiritual sleepers of the assembly. With a voice clear and shrill as a blast from a silver trumpet, he called out the initial word of his text—"Awake!" The little "darkey" aforesaid, mistaking the sharp call for the voice of his mistress, rubbing his eyes, lazily responded—"Ma'am." The unexpected shock brought on a general attack of merriment. Excited "risibles" refused utterly to yield to the philosophy of the "fitness of things." The discomfited preacher heroically struggled for a few moments with his facial contortions; and finally so far managed his curled-up and refractory mouth, as to be able to say, between spasms of snickering amusement: "We'll close—the serv—close the services—of the—the evening by singing the Benediction!"

The scene of the following protracted meeting incident was St. John's Church, on Annamessex circuit. Rev. Adam Wallace was presiding Elder, and was conducting the service for that evening, it being the occasion of his quarterly visitation. The church was minus an altar-rail, a movable bench being used instead for the accommodation of penitents. On this occasion the said bench was near the stove, and was occupied by a notorious rowdy of the neighborhood, who was lounging thereon, apparently asleep; while near by, in the amen-corner, sat a good old sister absorbed in her pious meditations.

"Come!" said the eloquent Elder, as he pleaded with the unconverted, "Come any way, just as you are. Fall down before the Lord and seek salvation!" At this juncture, while two brethren were quietly removing the "mourner's bench" to its appropriate place before the pulpit, without disturbing the youth thereon lying, he lost his balance and rolled off sprawling on the floor.

The noise and confusion of the fall arrested the attention of the meditative old sister before mentioned; who, supposing a stricken penitent had come and fallen at the altar, lustily cried out: "Thank the Lord! There's one sinner on his back, anyhow!" Rising slowly and sullenly, with an expression of outraged indignation scowling from his features, he scornfully replied: "I ain't no sinner on his back!" As Uncle Haney Bradshaw was wont to say: "It was a feelin' sense time, in that manner and form;" and the solemnity of the service for that evening was effectually destroyed.

At a Quarterly Meeting once held at Bolingbroke, on Easton Circuit, Rev. John T. Hazzard, the Presiding Elder, was greatly annoyed on Sunday morning by late arrivals, squalling children and other interruptions, and consequently was quite dissatisfied with his effort. He consented, however, to preach again that night, and open the extra meeting Rev. Charles I. Thompson, the junior pastor, was appointed to conduct.

At night again, many of the people were late; and the church, being small and crowded, no little confusion was the result. The last person coming in was a young colored man, who had great difficulty in working his way through the crowd standing in the rear aisle, leading to the gallery stairway. Mr. Hazzard paused with a discouraged air, while the boy clambered noisily to the head of the stairs; where, on account of the crowded condition of the gallery, he took his seat. Resuming his discourse, the preacher strove hard to turn the tide of battle—and with a fair prospect of success—when, alas! the aforesaid negro, who meantime had gone fast to sleep, lost his balance and came tumbling down the steps, crying, "O Lord! O my Lord!" with every thump; and finally, bursting open the stair door in his disorderly descent, and screeching with fright, he rolled out among the demoralized crowd of whites below.

The now utterly vanquished Presiding Elder closed the Bible with an impatient "slam," saying: "It's been nothing but a constant scene of interruption all day, and I'll not try to preach another word!" Springing into the breach with the agility of a young lion, the valiant junior preacher delivered a stirring exhortation, beginning with the bold declaration: "We are not going to let the Devil whip us off in this fashion!" and finally ended with a mighty appeal to the King's enemies to surrender to Emmanuel.

With startling promptness and precipitation, the hardest case in all that region—a stalwart six-foot sailor, weighing nearly two hundred and fifty pounds—sprang to his feet, threw off his coat and vest, and rushed for the altar; where he fell, yelling, kicking, striking out right and left, and writhing under the terrible contortions of a mixture of wild fire and bad whiskey; until screaming women and astonished men scattered hither and thither; and the "tall son of Anak," having seriously hurt a number of the men vainly trying to hold him, was master of the situation. Notwithstanding Brother Charlie's confident words and brave onslaught, the powers of darkness had prevailed, and the meeting broke up for that night without the formality of even "singing the Benediction!"

Sometimes incidents transpire "in meetin'" that are so childlike, so sincerely devotional, but at the same time so amusing, that the only appropriate and religious thing to do is to laugh at them. Occasionally, incidents of this character reveal a beautiful blending of tears and smiles upon the same Christian face. Of such an incident Dr. Wallace speaks in one of his letters in the *Peninsula Methodist.*

While he was holding a woods meeting at Cokesbury, on Georgetown circuit in 1856, a man of the world, well advanced in life and influential in that region, was gloriously converted; and, although wholly unlettered, at once came to the front as an effective worker. Being very anxious for the conversion of his wife, he took Brother Wallace home with him to talk with her on the subject of her soul's salvation. At length she yielded to her convictions, and presented herself at the "mourner's bench." Her rejoicing husband, for a time, was wellnigh wild with excitement over her surrender to Christ; but finally became sufficiently composed to offer audibly the following petition: "O, Lord! I have got all I kin hold. It's a runnin' over! Do please give some of this sweet religion to Nancy. Poor sould! she wants it so bad! O, my God! If I could, I'd give her all the religion I've got; for I know jest where to git a plenty more!" The kind Lord heard his and Nancy's prayer, gave her a full supply of the "sweet religion;" and that, too, without lessening the fullness of her rejoicing husband's cup.

Rev. James Brooks Ayres is well remembered by many of the senior Methodists of the Peninsula. In the division of the Philadelphia Conference, he, with most of the "Fathers," gravitated to the northern side of the line; and, on the first assembling of the Wilmington Conference, the absence of his striking and well-remembered form and features was quite noticeable. He was of medium height, compact build, ruddy face; and his well-marked features revealed no little of nervous and intellectual force, and a striking individuality. He seemed hung on wires, and went bouncing around like a ball of India rubber. One could no more calculate what Mr. Ayres would do next than he could prognosticate the gyrations of a whirlwind. His mind was logical but uncertain in its course, and liable at any moment to switch off into the most absurd vagaries. First and last, he traversed the Peninsula well-nigh all over, and everywhere left the impress of his angular personality.

The preaching of James B. Ayres was a strange mixture of strong, logical, manly reasoning, that grappled fearlessly the mysteries of the Divine administration in nature and redemption, and the most grotesque and ridiculous anecdote. Not infrequently, after preaching a sermon that would capture the minds and hearts of the thoughtful and reverent of his audience, he would suddenly shock their sensibilities and convulse the more frivolous by the most absurd and ludicrous recitals. Such was the case when the writer heard him preach a masterly sermon on a camp-ground near Sudlersville, Maryland, in the summer of 1853. Had he stopped when he was done, the effect of the discourse would have been most salutary. But reverting to some point in the sermon, he introduced a far-fetched story as an illustration, and went into a twenty-minute recital of how "John," the son of a wealthy and worldly family, somewhere on the Peninsula, had gotten under conviction for sin. His parents had tried in vain, by a series of gay pleasures, to divert his mind from the subject. A camp-meeting was to be held a few miles away. John wanted permission to attend it, but was denied. As the Sunday of the meeting approached, his wretchedness so increased, that his parents finally consented to go and spend the day, with the entire household, on the camp-ground. But it was on conditions indicated in the following colloquy:

"John," said his father, "if we take you to the camp-meeting, we don't want you to turn fool and jump up and down, like some of the Methodists do."

"All right, father; I won't jump."

"And we shall all be ashamed of you, John, if you yell amen, or glory, or hallelujah, like the Methodists do. If you must pray and be religious, do so; but you'll mortify your mother and sisters to death, if you get to imitating these outlandish Methodists."

"Well, father, I'll not say amen, or glory, or hallelujah."

"You won't do anything like the Methodists do?"

"All right, father; I promise you I won't."

To make Ayres' long story short, as soon as the family arrived on the ground, and were comfortably seated beneath the shade of a spreading oak at the far end of the block of seats from the preacher's stand, John excused himself; and going straight to the altar, where the eight o'clock prayer-meeting was in progress, he kneeled at the "mourners' bench," wrestling, like Jacob of old, with the Angel of the Covenant. Just as the trumpet sounded for preaching, John, like Jacob, prevailed, and was gloriously saved. Although all the language of Canaan bubbled up from his glad heart to his lips, John remembered and faithfully kept his promise. Rushing from the altar place, he started to make the circuit of the encampment, exclaiming at the top of his voice, "Out of the dark; into the light! Out of the dark; into the light!" At this point of his story, Ayres, in imitation of the youth, and stepping as high as a blind horse, tramped around on the floor of the stand, throwing his arms in wild gesticulation, and yelling in imitation of the young man's exclamation. Said he:

"As John came round by where the family were seated, the old man suggested—'Say glory, John.' But he tramped on, still crying, 'Out of the dark; into the light!' On his next circuit, both father and mother nervously called out: 'John, don't say that; say hallelujah!' But on he tramped, with 'Out of the dark; into the light!'"

"By the time John came around on his third circumambulation, most of the Christians on the camp-ground were shouting, and many of the unconverted were weeping. As he approached, the humiliated family arose and started off the ground. As father and son met, the old gentleman, with menacing fist almost in John's face, growled out in the fury of his vexation: 'Why don't you jump, and holler amen, you confounded idiot!' As the family coach rolled away down the road, above its rattle and the great volume of song from the assembled multitude, the disgusted parents and sisters heard John's jubilant 'Out of the dark; into the light!'" It was not so much the grim humor of the incident, as the dramatic exaggerations of Mr. Ayres in its recital, that so completely upset the gravity and decorum of his audience, and obliterated the good effects of his excellent sermon. As in the case of the kicking cow and her pail of milk, this harum-scarum old preacher had ruthlessly destroyed his own good. Fortunately, it was not always thus; and sometimes Mr. Ayres' preaching was in the demonstration of the Spirit and with power.

Mr. Ayres was a mighty hater of all iniquities; but the iniquity on which his powers of hatred were most intensely concentrated, was the moustache. In his opinion, if a man was otherwise without blemish or spot, a moustache would surely close against him the gate of heaven's kingdom. At the same camp-meeting where he preached the above-mentioned sermon, coming to a young man at the penitential altar, whose upper lip thus aroused his special antipathy, he roughly said to him: "Young man, you may as well get up and leave. God Almighty is not going to have mercy and save you with a thing like that upon your upper lip. Get up, and go shave it off, and come to God with a clean face." The poor fellow dejectedly arose and slunk away into the darkness of the woods, beyond the circle of tents, and I saw him no more.

To Mr. Ayres no meal was complete without his cup of coffee. At the Pratt's Branch Camp one summer, he had been unfortunate in the invitations he had accepted to dinner, and failed for two days to receive the refreshing beverage. On the morning of the third day he was put up to exhort after the sermon by the preacher for the occasion. He began by telling about a great camp-meeting he had just attended over in Maryland, and what a good time they had both socially and religiously; and wound up his description by saying: "Yes, my friends; and the sisters over there gave us a cup of good, strong coffee with white sugar in it, every day for dinner." Of course this clever device brought the answer, and thereafter brother Ayres always secured his cup of coffee.

In the same exhortation he soundly berated his frail brethren, among whom was the writer, for having bronchitis and other throat ailments. He insisted it was because they were too lazy, or too nice and fastidious to *holler;* and wound up his tirade with the most emphatic expression of his conviction that, preaching his way with full swing and a plenty of healthy noise, the bronchitis could not get hold of him, if it should make the effort, in forty years. A few months afterwards, the author called at the Greensborough parsonage to express his sympathy with poor brother Ayres, who, at the time and for many weeks, was bound hand and foot upon his bed of suffering by Inflammatory Rheumatism. It is due to him, however, to say that his *vocal* powers were still unimpaired; but then about the only thing in the world the poor old man could now do was to *holler;* and, with every new twist and twitch of the tormentor, he did so manfully. Years ago, the old hero passed through his last pang; and, out of great tribulation, went up among the blood-washed throng, where, no doubt, he has been induced to revise and modify some of the theories he so pertinaciously held to on earth.

The very antipodes of James B. Ayres was his contemporary, James A. Massey. Tall, angular and somewhat ungainly, with sometimes a strangely vacant look, and with facial contortions suggestive of a grotesque phase of idiocy, his presence would at once arrest the stranger's attention and start the inquiry: "What manner of man is this?" When, at last, his curiosity was gratified, he settled down to the conviction that the man before him was no ordinary personage. He was a solid, Gospel preacher, dealing in no theories, and rarely ever illustrating by incident. He was, perhaps, abnormally serious, never provoking by his thought or imagery even a mental smile. But one of his most distinguishing personal traits was his abstraction and absent-mindedness. Many are the stories, floating around in the various Peninsular fields he traversed, illustrative of this peculiarity. As an example, one will be sufficient. Walking, one day, in company with his boy, Will, a street of Princess Anne, as they passed a cow quietly grazing by the side of the pavement, Mr. Massey politely lifted his hat, saying, "Good afternoon, Madam." Will roared out, "Ha, ha, ha!" in boisterous laughter; and said, between his convulsions, "Why, fa—father, that—ha, ha, ha!—that was a cow!" "Was it?" said he; and instantly turning toward her ladyship, and again politely lifting his hat, he humbly importuned: "I beg your pardon, Ma'am!"

In 1860, Mr. Massey, with Rev. Geo. Cummins as his colleague, was assigned to Onancock Circuit, on the Eastern Shore of Virginia. The excitement on the slavery agitation was at high tide; and in the early summer, a mass meeting was held at Pungoteague, at which it was resolved to appoint a committee of nineteen, who were charged with the duty of driving the Methodist preachers from Virginia "by any means they might find necessary."

During preaching at Garrison's Chapel the following Sunday morning, this great committee appeared on the scene and entered the church; but so manifest was the Divine presence in the service, that they could not muster courage to interrupt it. They notified the people, however, that there should be no preaching allowed at Trinity in the afternoon; and that, if the minister attempted it, he would be mobbed. Mr. Cummins was strongly urged not to risk holding service. A good local preacher—Mr. Humphrey—earnestly importuned him to desist. The young hero assured him, however, that he should pay no attention to threats, and should meet his engagement; whereupon, Mr. Humphrey kindly volunteered to go, and support him by his presence. Dining at father Richardson's, Mr. Cummins met a young Doctor and an Editor, who also admonished him not to go to Trinity. Firm in his purpose, the young man assured them that he should certainly go, esteeming it his duty to God to meet all engagements in the line of his calling, regardless of consequences. The two young gentlemen then replied: "Well, if you are determined to go, we'll go too, and see you through." They meant the preacher should understand this as an assurance of sympathy and protection; but, judging by their demeanor, he rightfully interpreted their words as a menace. Nevertheless he expressed his gratification at their assurance, and added: "I shall be very happy to see you there, gentlemen."

On arriving at the church, he found the committee present in full force, and amply supported by an excited and noisy mob. Scarcely waiting for him to dismount from his horse, they surrounded him, pressing upon him so closely that he could scarcely hitch the animal. In most emphatic and sulphurous language they warned him at his peril not to attempt to enter the church. Mr. Cummins quietly assured them that where duty led it was his purpose, by God's help, to follow; adding: "Gentlemen; I see it is time to begin the service, and I shall have to ask you to excuse me from further parleying;" at the same time starting toward the door of the little sanctuary. Strangely enough, the mob parted as he proceeded, and allowed him to pass; and he entered the church and ascended the pulpit, followed by the hooting crowd. True to his promise, the good local preacher was in his accustomed place in the "amen corner"—the only friend the preacher had, all others having been effectually intimidated and kept at home.

The crowd pressed close up to the pulpit, with hats on and with segars in their mouths. The breath they expended in curses was redolent with the odorous admixture of tobacco and whiskey. Loudly and peremptorily they demanded that the preacher instantly vacate the pulpit and leave the church. In addition, they insisted that he should notify his colleague not to attempt to hold service at Garrison's Chapel the next Sabbath; and, furthermore, that he—Cummins—should agree to leave Virginia, "on pain of a coat of tar and feathers, and even worse."

Said Mr. Cummins, coolly: "Gentlemen; I shall decline to do any part of your dirty work for you. As to leaving the church and departing from the state, it is not my habit to allow anything to interfere with the attempt to perform my duty; nor do I usually dismiss a service, under any circumstances, without at least offering prayer." A somewhat waggish fellow by the name of Barnum, replied: "Mr. Cummins, I'm afraid we are not exactly in a spirit to profit by your prayers;" at which there was such boisterous hilarity that Mr. Cummins felt that any service he might attempt would be in violation of his Master's admonition not to cast pearls before swine, and wisely desisted.

Again did the mob announce, as their ultimatum, that he must instantly leave the church and promise not to preach again in Virginia, unless he agreed to take authority to do so from the Southern Methodist Church, or he would at once be summarily dealt with. Straightening himself, with defiant look and attitude, he informed them that he would make no such concession or promise; and that he would leave the pulpit and church voluntarily, only when it suited him to do so. Thereupon, a voice from the crowd exclaimed: "Phew! I do believe that Methodist preacher would fight!" By this time the brave and chivalrous knights of Dixie betrayed their want of pluck; their countenances fell; their bravado was exhausted, and the heroic and triumphant Cummins, having, like the intrepid Irishman, "surrounded forty men," including the Doctor and Editor before mentioned, leisurely walked through the midst of the mob, assuring them that when they desired again to see him, he would be in his accustomed place; and, mounting his horse, departed to his stopping place at Mr. Richardson's.

Soon after his arrival the Doctor and Editor made their appearance, and began lugubriously to condole with him. They grew eloquent in their expressions of indignation that the old commonwealth of Virginia should be so disgraced, and a minister of the Gospel so wantonly insulted. At the close of their five minutes' harangue the young preacher, looking them squarely in the face, said: "Gentlemen, it is all true. It is a burning disgrace. But I don't blame the poor, ignorant and drunken fellows, who formed the bulk of the mob, half so much as I do those who ought to know better, and who sat quietly by giving the mob their sympathy and support." At this remark, they silently exchanged significant glances for a moment; then picked up their hats and slunk away from the house.

On the following Sunday morning, Mr. Massey, despite the threats of the committee of nineteen, drove to Garrison's chapel and met his congregation. Soon after he began the service, the mob appeared upon the scene, headed by the famous committee. Dick Ayres, the leader, a stalwart man weighing two hundred and fifty pounds, ascended the pulpit to the side of the preacher, and began haranguing the crowd. At this juncture, an old sister of seventy years climbed over the altar-rail; ascended the steps; and, collaring the rowdy, by a dexterous jerk snatched him off his feet and upon his back on the floor. Then, grabbing him by his flowing hair, she pounded his head upon the floor until he begged for mercy. While the men of the congregation sat still in amazement, the ladies of the church put themselves in attitude to defend their pastor; and it was the impression of the spectators that, had not Mr. Massey counseled non-resistance and suspended the service, they would have soon cleared the church of the cowardly rabble.

The last contact of these ministers with the redoubtable committee of nineteen occurred, some two weeks after, at Drummondtown, where they stopped on their return from a funeral. The county Court was in session, and an exciting murder trial had drawn together a great concourse of the denizens of every part of the county. While Mr. Massey was hitching his horse, Mr. Cummins, taking his stand on the steps of a store-house, was scanning the concourse in search of friends he desired to see. At this moment the mob, headed by the committee, pressed around Mr. Massey in threatening manner. The old gentleman, in evident alarm, appealed to their manhood and sympathy, on the ground of his age, his calling, his southern birth and his interest, in common with them and all Virginians, in the well-being and good name of their native state. In reply, they disclaimed any purpose of physical violence; and, at the command of the leader, the crowd fell back, allowing Mr. Massey to go in peace. They then gathered about Mr. Cummins, saying: "We are authorized, Mr. Cummins, to say to you what we have just said to Mr. Massey,—that you must not again attempt to hold service at Garrison's chapel."

Said the young minister: "What will be the penalty, gentlemen, if I do?"

The significant reply was, "You'll find out what the penalty is!"

Assuming an attitude as if their master, and as if making sport of them, the hero responded: "Anything more, gentlemen?"

As if dazed and cowed by the preacher's coolness, they responded, "No;" when, master of the situation, Mr. Cummins quietly went about his business.

Both preachers continued to fill their appointments; but at the end of a few weeks, Mr. Cummins was transferred by the Presiding Elder to fill a vacancy at Salisbury, Maryland.

James A. Massey finished his conference year in peace; when, the war breaking out, a military despotism in the interest of the Southern Confederacy, took possession of all that part of Virginia; and the ministers of the Methodist Episcopal Church were, for some three years, forcibly excluded.

Mr. Massey was as honest a soul as ever trod the soil of the Peninsula. Despite his frailty, heretofore mentioned, he was a man of sound, discriminating judgment, good executive ability, and faithful in all things. He was more than once called to fill the important office of Presiding Elder; and, in all the sacred trusts to him committed, he purchased for himself a good degree. The intellectual cloud that shadowed the last few years of his life, gave way amid the glory of his setting sun; and, in the blessed regions whither he has gone, there is no night, and the endless day is without cloud or shadow. His colleague and partner in Virginia tribulation is now an influential and manly member of the Philadelphia Conference.

"Soldiers of Christ, well done!"

One of the author's conference class-mates of the spring of 1853 was an unsophisticated Englishman, Rev. Thomas Childs, of precious memory. He was a young man of frail physique, and a great sufferer from that terrible scourge, asthma; which oftentimes seriously interfered with both his comfort and his efficiency, and, at length, brought his career to an untimely termination. Although of such haughty blood, he was of gentle spirit and quiet demeanor,—possibly owing to the chastening influence of sanctified affliction. His natural abilities were above mediocrity; and his preaching was often both attractive and in the demonstration of spiritual power. Brother Childs had little of the spirit of self-assertion and egotism characteristic of the typical Englishman; but was possessed of an unobtrusive and pleasant humor, that now and then rippled over the surface, as if set in motion by some passing, playful zephyr. In our first examination on the course of conference study, Dr. George R. Crooks, chairman of the committee, was questioning the class on some abstruse point in speculative divinity. At an early period of the examination, it became apparent that, for some reason, Brother Childs was embarrassed with difficulty; and he hesitated and stumbled so much as to excite the sympathy of his class-mates. At length, on the proposal of one of the Doctor's knotty questions, he greatly amused his brother neophytes, and no doubt propitiated the favor of the examining committee, by concluding his discouraging attempt at an answer with the following triumphant apology: "Excuse me, Brother Crooks; you know I'm but a *Child*, and I cannot speak!"

At a great camp-meeting held by Dr. Adam Wallace, in Morris' woods near Georgetown, Delaware, in the summer of 1856, Mr. Childs was present and aided efficiently in the services. It became his turn to preach his second sermon at the camp on Monday afternoon. On coming into the stand, however, Dr. Wallace discovered that he was very hoarse and breathing hard from Asthma, besides suffering some inconvenience from errors of diet. Explaining where he would find a bottle of Jamaica Ginger in the preachers' marque, the kind Doctor sent him thither to take a dose, while the remainder of the straggling members of the congregation were gathering. Delaying his return until the patience of the preacher in charge was exhausted, brother Wallace went to hunt him in the tent, where he found him doubled up and writhing in the most fearful agony. Poor Childs, supposing the vial, which was nearly full, to contain about a fair dose for an adult Englishman, had swallowed its entire contents of the fiery liquid. The effect was "as if a whole torch-light procession had gone down his throat!" He was wheezing, coughing, suffocating, and gasping pitifully for water; and the sympathizing Irishman ran to his relief as soon as possible with the grateful draught. Surprising to relate, he soon cooled off, and recovered his normal condition in time to preach; and being, for the time, relieved of his severe asthmatic paroxysm, both his voice and his intellect were untrammeled, and he acquitted himself grandly. Not being assured, however, by this precedent, that swallowing two ounces of Jamaica Ginger before preaching would produce a similar result, the author, although an asthmatic, does not feel inclined to risk the experiment.

"Nathan Hunter, Esquire," as he was wont to call himself, was neither minister nor layman of Peninsula Methodism, but evidently a well-meaning friend. When the poor toper, who had staggered up against the "meetin' house," was questioned as to his relations with that Church, he said he *leaned* that way. Nathan Hunter, Esquire, may have sometimes had occasion for a similar leaning, for he dearly loved a brandy toddy; but, for other and better reasons, he claimed to be a friend and adherent of early Methodism. He resided in Caroline county, Md., not far from Greensborough. Occasionally, on Sundays, Mr. Hunter would dress up in his best linsey-woolsey, saddle old "Bill"—a white mule—and attend service at the Greensborough Methodist Church.

It so happened, on one of those Sundays, that the brother who led the singing was absent. When the good pastor announced the opening hymn, beginning:

> "Lord, in the morning thou shalt hear
> My voice ascending high."

Mr. A. nodded to B., and B. to C.; but no one dared to start a tune. There was an awkward pause, and it seemed as if that important part of the service must needs be omitted; when Mr. Hunter spoke out: "Mr. Preacher; s'pose you give them words out agin. If you will, I think I kin strike a tune." Again the minister repeated the first two lines; when, to the amazement of everybody, the self-constituted chorister fitted the first line to the then popular song—"Pretty Betty Martin, Tiptoe Fine," after the following style:

"Lord, in the mornin', thou shalt—thou shalt
Lord, in the mornin' thou shalt hear;"—

Then, discovering the impossibility of making the words further fit the jolly hoe-down, he wound up his performance by reciting, in a discouraged nasal squeak,

"My voice ascending high!"

The greatly mortified pastor said, "Let us pray;" but between the humiliation of the saints and the merriment of the sinners, begotten by the effort of the rustic soloist, the praying was nearly as sad a failure as the singing.

Rev. Jonas Bissey was a Methodist itinerant, somewhat noted in his day for both his excellencies and his peculiarities. Not, however, until near the close of his life was his ministry attended with any marked success. An experience of official criticism and complaint at conference one spring, seemed to have spurred him on to a fuller consecration and a more devoted effort; and, thenceforth, his labors were prolific of great good, and his life was a benediction to the churches where he ministered. One of the peculiarities of his earlier preaching was that he sometimes became absurdly theatrical in manner, indulging in the wildest ravings and the most grotesque antics.

While travelling Snow Hill circuit in 1843, he preached at all the appointments a favorite discourse, called by the older people to this day, "Bissey's Hellfire sermon." The text was, "These shall go away into everlasting punishment." On reaching his peroration, it was his custom to work himself up into a kind of frenzy, in which he seemed to imagine himself a lost soul, tortured in the flames of perdition. At a bush-meeting, held at Spring Hill, where he preached this sulphurous sermon, leaping from the stand, he flung himself upon the ground, rolling and writhing amid the straw, shrieking "Fire! fire! fire!" and plaintively pleading with an imaginary father Abraham to send some Lazarus of pity to the relief of his agony. Such was his apparent distress, and so vivid the woeful tragedy to susceptible natures, that more than one of his female hearers fainted away from sheer terror.

Sometime afterwards, Mr. Bissey preached the same sermon at Newark appointment. Most of the discourse was heavy and uninteresting—especially as many in the audience had already heard it once or more; and old brother M—— had yielded to the influence of "tired nature's sweet restorer," and gone fast to sleep. Struggling hard but vainly to awaken an interest, the preacher came at last to the climax, where success or failure depended upon the effectiveness of his final impassioned effort. After picturing a lost soul amid the flames of the awful pit, throwing himself into the tragic attitude of distracted suffering, Mr. Bissey began, at the top of his voice, to scream, "Fire! fire!! fire!!!" when the old brother aforesaid, awaking suddenly and supposing the church had caught fire from the stove-pipe, began to tear around among the brethren like a demoniac, drowning the preacher's impassioned utterances with his lusty yells for "Water! water!! water!!!"

Completely taken by surprise, Mr. Bissey ceased his tragic performance; looked a few moments in utter astonishment at the old farmer's unaccountable antics; and thoroughly discomfited, with his favorite sermon in ruins, he dejectedly resumed his seat. Upon explanation all around, it was hard to tell whether Mr. Bissey or old brother M—— was the more discouraged and humiliated.

In 1851, while preaching in New London Church, in Pennsylvania, in the midst of a thunder-storm, Mr. Bissey was killed by lightning in the presence of his terrified audience. His labors had been greatly blessed in all that region; and now that they were ended, his Master called him suddenly home.

This chapter may appropriately conclude by introducing to the reader a pious and simple-minded but very quaint and peculiar local preacher, known extensively in his day throughout central Delaware as "Daddy Appleton." Mr. Appleton was very zealous, but from all that appears, his zeal was not always "according to knowledge." It is altogether probable that when his brethren of Duck Creek Quarterly Conference voted him a local preacher's license, they spoiled a fairly good exhorter. Only a few scraps of his history have floated down to us of this day; and these were preserved and narrated by the late Hon. Charles Marim, whose fondness for a good story may have sometimes betrayed him into a shade of exaggeration. However, Daddy Appleton's oddity must have been extreme, and ofttimes most ludicrous.

His boy, "Giddie," as his name might import, was by no means a saint. Giddie would have fun even at family prayers; and, to make it a little more attractive to the other children, he would sometimes indulge quietly in such responsive exclamations as "halleluia!" and "amen!" On one occasion, having become a little too hilarious, he was overheard, and was duly admonished by his father that, should there be any repetition of this unseemly conduct, he would be sure to receive a good "trouncing." It wasn't many days until he was caught. One morning, in the midst of the old gentleman's prayer, Giddie's "amen!" was ejaculated just a hair's breadth too late to be entirely smothered by his father's louder tones. Leaving the petition unfinished, Mr. Appleton deliberately arose from his knees, took down the waiting rod, divested Giddie of his jacket, applied the remedy until he was *giddy* no longer; and then, as deliberately, returned to his knees and began where he left off; and when he reached the "amen," Giddie's discouraged sniffle was the only response!

Mr. Marim used to relate what he declared was a fair representation of a sermon he once heard Daddy Appleton deliver at a country chapel. During the interval of twenty-five years since he heard it, much of this unique discourse has faded from the historian's memory. A part only of the "points" made by the preacher can be recalled. Exaggeration is impossible. The text was: "And he receiv-ed him joyfully." Said the preacher:

"My dyin', mortal friends; I don't feel very well to-day. I tuck some doctor's stuff last night. Feel powerful weak-like this mornin'. When I waked up and riz this mornin', the Devil said to me, sez he: 'How are you a goin' to your appintment to-day? Your old hoss is lame; you're poorly yourself; and it's no use,— you can't go.' Sez I to Satin, sez I,—You're a liar. Guess I've got legs and kin walk; and so I will, sez I. 'And he receiv-ed him joyfully!'

"My dear sinner friends; I've got a powerful bad taste in my mouth to-day. It's from that nasty medicine, I'm shore. Sometimes I've a great mind to never take no more doctor's truck while I'm above ground. I don't see what use doctors are no how: kill about as many as they cure, I reckon, on an average. I never can preach fit for nothin' when I've got a bad taste in my mouth. But, breetherin' and sisterin', you pray for me; and may be I'll git along right well after all. 'And he receiv-ed him joyfully!'

"Now, none o' you sinners needn't think I've come here to preach this mornin' without knowin' what I'm about. There's some wonderful smart critics now-a-days, Zaccheus-like, a climbin' up sycamore trees to git above common people; and they think they kin see a mighty sight further nor other folks; and then go off a chucklin' and a makin' remarks about the sermont. Fact is, some of these folks know no more about preachin' nor a hog knows about makin' mince pies. And some folks that 'll set and nod all the time o' meetin', will go home and find fault with the preachin'. Now, how kin such sleepy-heads tell what the preacher's been a sayin'? 'And he receiv-ed him joyfully.'

"For my part, I don't see how anybody can expect me to preach much of a 'scourse, when ther's sich car-ryin's on a goin' on in the house. Some o' you young folks hev been a whisperin' an' snickerin' jest as ef you was at a show; and back yander on the gallery steps is that big, strappin' darkey with three or four combs stuck in his wool; and he's a grinnin' and a grinnin' like a baboon monkey, same's he was at a hoe-down. People as don't know how to behave are a plaguey sight wuss 'n Zaccheus; for he went to meetin' outen curiosity; but some good come outen it to him; for he come down when Jesus called him. 'And he receiv-ed him joyfully.'

"My dear breetherin'; Sinners is often as mischieve-e-ous as a lot of bothersome goats; but true Christians is jest like a flock of sheep—the worser the weather the closer they'll huddle together. I've watched 'em many a time on a rainy day. After a good mess of grass, they'll come together and lay down under the shelter of a tree or somethin'. And ef ther's one's happened to git out'n the parsture, the rest 'll all bleat for him; and, bime by, he'll hear 'em; and he'll run up and down the road a cryin' ba-a-a, ba-a-a, ontil at last he'll jump back agin; and then the whole flock 'll git up and run to meet him. 'And he receiv-ed him joyfully."

"O, my dear Sisterin'; there was my poor, dear wife Chloe: she's gone to Heaven and left me. She could beat any woman in Duck Creek Cross Roads a makin' short cake and coffee. Whenever I used to git sick while she was a livin', her good tendin' and cookin' would soon bring me around agin all right. Ah, friends, ef I'd only a had a little of Chloe's short cake and coffee this mornin', I'd a preached as good agin a sermont. I hope I shall git to Heaven, bye-and-bye, and be with her agin; and, ef the Lord will let her, I want her to make me one more mess of her good short cake and coffee. 'And he receiv-ed him joyfully!'"

It is altogether probable, that when Daddy Appleton hadn't a bad taste in his mouth, he could preach a much better "sermont" than the above specimen. Long years ago he went to join his beloved Chloe in the better land.

It may seem strange to us who enjoy the light and the opportunities of this age, that a man so ludicrously odd, and of so little culture, could ever have been authorized as a teacher of religion; but we are to remember that God can thresh the mountain with the frailest worm;

and that multitudes of the denizens of the forests of Kent, seventy-five years ago, were much more ignorant and unkempt than this simple-minded but sincere and pious child of nature. The harvest was great and the laborers were few; and though, measured by the standards of our times, Daddy Appleton would have been very far below the mark of acceptability, he may have been peculiarly fitted for some phases of a Local Preacher's work in the region and generation in which he lived.

CHAPTER VI.

HYMENEAL AND BAPTISMAL.

WHEN catering for guests, so many of whom are candidates for matrimony, it would, by no means, answer to omit some crumbs from the banqueting hall of Cupid. This masculine fairy is a quaint little scamp, and is given to the mischievous pastime of getting people into all sorts of odd "scrapes," from which, with all his fair promises, he sometimes utterly neglects to relieve them. If the youthful reader does not wish sometime to be caught in a ridiculous attitude, the prudent course is to keep out of the way of Cupid's pretty little arrows.

Some three decades ago, Rev. A. M. Wiggins, of the Philadelphia Conference, a newly fledged Deacon never having tied the silken knot, was sent to Annamessex circuit, at that time including the Tangier Island. While on his first visit to that point, he was approached one night by a young oysterman, who thus accosted him: "Mr. Preacher, me and my gal wants to git fixed up: kin you do anything for us?"

"I'm the very man that can help you," replied the parson, as the image of a five dollar note flitted athwart his eager vision; at the same time extending his hand to receive the license the youth handed him. Upon scanning the document, however, he found it was issued in Maryland, and said to the young man:

"My dear sir, I can do nothing for you on this license. It is issued from Princess Anne; and we are in Virginia. You'll have to try again."

"Well, now, Mr. Preacher," rejoined the eager candidate, "I guess that don't make no difference. You jest jump into my bugeye, with me an' my gal; and I'll have you in Maryland waters in less'n no time."

Accordingly, the parson, and a friend as witness, got into the boat with the intended bride and groom; and, in a short time, the happy candidate announced that they were within the bounds of "My Maryland," and said: "Guess you kin crack yer whip and drive ahead now, Mr. Preacher!"

The blushing maiden was in the little cabin, whither all the party repaired, leaving the graceful craft meantime to drift with the current. The cabin was about 4x6 feet, and 5 feet high in the clear, necessitating one, in the attempt to stand up straight, to stand *down crooked* somewhat in the shape of the crescent. The expectant couple sat upon the "locker," while the parson, thinking it more decorous, and more becoming to the important occasion, attempted to stand; and, book in hand, proceeded to read the marriage ritual, by the light of a tallow candle held by the friend at his side. He had read but the words: "Dearly beloved; we are gathered here in the presence of God," when the little vessel gave an unfortunate lurch, causing the parson, in the effort to maintain his equilibrium, to knock the candle to the floor and extinguish it,—the next lurch pitching him headlong into the bride's lap. He gathered himself up as best he could in the darkness. There was not a match to be found in the ship; and yet a *match* must needs be made. The preacher knew not a word of the marriage ceremony; and was necessitated to extemporize one for the emergency. It was like nothing, he said, in Earth or Heaven—like nothing from the catacombs of the early saints, or the mythological fables of the pagan annals; and the confused divine finally wound up his nondescript performance by pronouncing the bewildered couple "man and woman together;" and, landing again finally on Tangiers, launched them forth on a voyage of discovery to ascertain, as best they could, their mutual relations.

In 1863, while residing temporarily on a farm in Caroline county, Maryland, the writer was permitted to look, with pleasurable anticipations, upon some fine broods of spring chickens he had nurtured to that interesting point in their development when they were about ready for broiling. One night in June, some godless scamp, "against the peace and dignity of the Commonwealth," and the rights of a "supernumerary," borrowed about a dozen of these attractive birds; thus violating the "General Rules" by "taking up goods without any probability of paying for them." The next night the parson either heard, or dreamed he heard, a commotion in the poultry yard. Suspecting more *fowl* play, he leaped from his bed; and, without delaying to make his toilet, sallied forth on a skirmish of investigation.

"All was quiet along the lines" of chicken coops; and the preacher had about reached the conclusion that the alarm was but "the ugly phantom of a tragic dream;" but he proceeded in his stealthy and ghostly wanderings, until he reached the lawn gate; when, what was his surprise and indignation, at three o'clock A. M., to discover a horse and carriage standing before his cottage door.

"A pretty state of affairs, indeed!" said he to himself. "You are not content with what chickens you can carry off in a bag; but propose to take them away by the carriage-load! Well, we'll see about this business!" And, forgetful of the figure he cut, he strode boldly up to the side of the vehicle, and excitedly called out: "Hallo, here!"

"Hal-lo!" was the sleepy response.

"Who's here?" he angrily inquired.

"Smith."

"What Smith?"

"Jeems Henry Smith."

"Well; where does Mr. Jeems Henry Smith belong?"

"In Mashy-Hope."

"What does Jeems Henry Smith, of Marshy-Hope, want here at this time of the night?"

"Want to git married!"

"Get married, indeed! Whom do you want to get

married to!" for the parson saw but the one person in the darkness.

"Oh, I've got her here in my lap! She's asleep!"

"O, ah! yes, sir!" said the parson changing his tone and manner. "How long have you been waiting here, Mr. Smith?"

"Got yer about ten or eleven o'clock last night, sir."

"Why didn't you wake me up, Mr. Smith?"

"Feered of the dogs, sir."

"Well, Mr. Smith, you wake up your intended, and I will get ready as soon as possible and see what I can do for the relief of your case."

Accordingly the supernumerary returned to the house, in pleasant humor on account of the financial expectations incident to such a romantic occasion; awoke his dreaming spouse; dressed hastily; admitted the eager but patient couple; and soon pronounced them—not "man and woman," like parson Wiggins, but husband and wife; tendered congratulations, and invited Mr. and Mrs. Jeems Henry Smith to be seated.

In a few moments, said Mr. Smith:

"I suppose you don't mind givin' a fellow a certifick-it?"

"Certainly not, sir," responded the parson; and proceeded to fill out the coveted "certifick-it," at a cost of twenty-five cents for the neat blank.

"What's yer charge?" inquired Mr. Smith somewhat sheepishly; meanwhile fumbling his clothing and ramming his huge fists down into his trousers' pockets.

"O, Mr. Smith," replied the parson, "I never make any formal charge. I always suppose a gentleman will pay the preacher according to his ability, and in proportion to his estimate of his bride;" fully expecting that this adroit little speech would be rewarded with a liberal fee. The thermometer of expectation, however, fell rapidly to away down below zero as Mr. Smith drawled out: "Well, I haint 'zacly got the change to-night; but I'll see you in Denton next Chuseday." The author has never seen Mr. Jeems Henry Smith of "Mashey-Hope," since that memorable and romantic night; and the bridegroom's promise to pay is one of the parson's many investments and stocks still remaining on interest.

Writing of this long-overdue obligation recalls, among others, a somewhat similar incident dating back to 1860. When stationed at Cambridge, Md., the author was summoned, one blustery, bitter-cold night, to ride six miles to the Blackwater Swamp, to unite a young couple in wedlock. His young friend, "Tom" Rea, agreed to take the parson "for the fun of the thing;" but the latter volunteered to divide with him the wedding fee. This proved to be the *promise* of a pig, on the part of the very *promising* young husband. The parson has not yet made the acquaintance of his pigship; but if he had, at that date, arrived on his mundane "rootin' ground," he must, by this time, have reached *Jumbonic* proportions, and be a very valuable swine. Nevertheless, should Mr. Barnum desire this colossal animal to fill the vacancy occasioned by the "tragic taking off" of his pet elephant, he can purchase the ministerial interest therein on accommodating terms.

The "fire" probably enkindled by the matrimonial alliances involved in the above incidents will, no doubt, be ample for any ordinary "dish of hash." It now remains to provide the "water." This duty may be appropriately performed by supplying a few sketches of Peninsular baptisms.

Bishop Asbury left a provision in his will, requiring his Executor to furnish a Bible to every boy, at the time of the testator's death bearing the name of Francis Asbury. Mr. Bœhm informs us that, under this provision of the good man's last will and testament, he was under the necessity of supplying between five and six hundred Bibles; and he supposes there were at least as many more boys bearing the honored name, who, failing to learn in time of their good fortune, never claimed the legacy.

The late Governor, Thomas Holliday Hicks, of Maryland, was very popular with the masses, especially in Dorchester, his native county. Not a few boys were adorned by their parents with his honored name. Rev. Thos. L. Poulson, D.D., now of the New York East Conference, was called to officiate at the baptism of one of these fortunate Dorchester youngsters.

"Name this child," said the preacher.

"Governor Hicks," was the father's response.

"Well," said the minister, "but the Governor's name

is Thomas Holliday. You mean, I suppose, to call him Thomas Hicks, or Holliday Hicks, or Thomas Holliday Hicks?"

"No, sir-ee!" said the patriotic parent. "You christen him jest like I tell you; his name is Governor Hicks!" and so he was baptized.

The same minister was once the junior colleague of Rev. Abraham Freed, on Annamessex circuit, and was immensely popular with the colored population. During the year a day was appointed, at a central point, as a general baptizing occasion. Scores of both white and colored were present, to dedicate their little ones to God and the church, in the holy ordinance, Mr. Freed officiating. One of the colored matrons, desiring to honor her junior preacher in the name of her promising picaninny; and being apprehensive of the appearance of an invidious indifference towards the preacher in charge, deemed it best, in order to avoid such a construction, to add also her senior pastor's name. To the preacher's interrogatory therefore she gave response: "Yes, Sah; dis chile's name's Abraham Freed Thomas L. Poulsing Johnsing, Sah." "O, tut, tut!" said the modest parson, "Sam, I baptize thee," etc. After dismissal of the service, the poor, injured woman sought her junior preacher, and thus comforted him: "Neber you mind, Massa Poulsing! Dis chile's a gwine ter have your name, sartin! An' now Massa Freed's done gone christened him 'Sam,' he sha'n't have no part in de oner at all—so he sha'n't!"

HYMENEAL AND BAPTISMAL. 169

At a camp-meeting once held at Lloyd's Spring, for Easton Circuit, the pastor, Rev. Dr. T. J. Quigley, appointed the hour of one P. M., of Tuesday, for a great baptismal service. A promiscuous and motley crowd, gathered mostly from the out-of-the-way swamps and thickets, was in attendance. It was a baby-show that would have deprived the great American showman Mr. Barnum, of his prestige. There were

> Babies great and babies small;
> Babies short and babies tall;
> Babies fat and babies lean;
> Babies soiled and babies clean;
> Babies romping, tumbling, falling;
> Babies crowing—babies squalling:
> Candidates for Church probation
> Full enough to stock a nation.

Two young ministers, Revs. C. I. Thompson and J. Frank Chaplain, were in attendance on the dignified Doctor of Divinity; the one to bear the baptismal water, and the other to preserve a list for the Church Registry. The service proceeded, with becoming decorum, to a point where the officiating minister said to the little, comical-looking grand-dame who presented her screaming young hopeful: "Sister, name this child."

Her reply—"Mary 'Lizabeth, after its mammy"—upset the gravity of the young ministerial attendants; but they still stood their ground, and the good old Doctor applied the water, solemnly saying, "Mary Elizabeth, I baptize thee."

The next case, however, was a stunner. Taking the young *rooster* in his arms, Dr. Quigley, for the fortieth time, said, "Sister, name this child."

"Peter Tomato Pickler," was the reply.

"What!" propounded the astonished parson.

"Peter Tomato Pickler," reiterated the mother.

"What did you say?"

Again the matron, indignant at the preacher's apparent dullness of comprehension, deliberately and emphatically answered: "*Peter—To-ma-to—Pick-ler!*"

"*Peter;* I baptize thee," said the protesting dignitary, and reached for the water; when he discovered the bowl upside-down in the straw, and his convulsed attendants making their hasty exit over the altar fence.

On a certain occasion, Rev. John Henry, the celebrated Irishman, whose unique peculiarities are elsewhere delineated in these sketches, was engaged to baptize the child of a lady of some prominence on the Maryland side of the Peninsula. The service was in a church, at the close of the Sunday morning preaching. The old colored nurse—the indispensable appurtenance of a baby moving in good society, in "ye goode, olde times" of slavery—was on hand in the gallery, of course, to grace the occasion with her presence and to see the work well done. The lady-like mother had an unfortunate lisp; and when she presented little Lucy at the baptismal font, and Mr. Henry propounded the question as to name in the usual form, the response was:

"Luthy, thir."

"What did you say, sister?" exclaimed the astonished Irishman.

"Luthy, thir," reiterated the innocent, but confused lady.

"Why, sister," said Mr. Henry, "Lucifer is the name of the Daivel! You must not so disgrace the boy." And, hastily selecting a name himself, he proceeded with: "John Wesley, I baptize thee;" and was about to apply the water, when the old nurse aforesaid convulsed the already amused audience by screeching out from the gallery: "O, Mistah Preachah! Stop—don't! He's a gal!"

The necessary explanations were then made by the lady's husband, and little Lucy was appropriately "christened."

CHAPTER VII.

WHITE SOULS IN COLORED ENVELOPES.

IN many places, in the Peninsula, in the *ante bellum* days, the soil had become greatly impoverished by the system of farming begotten of the "peculiar institution." Sometimes large slaveholders were profligate, or fond of gaiety and sporting, giving no personal attention whatever to their plantations, but leaving everything to overseers, or to a "foreman" selected from the "gang" of field hands.

If a few hundred dollars were needed to meet some exigency, at no very distant point could be found some Jim Vaughn, Marcy Fountain or Patty Cannon, ever ready to supply the coveted money in exchange for "likely" negroes. Thus the improvement of the soil, so constantly depleted, was neglected; the crop of slaves became the matter of prime importance; and, if the exhausted fields produced sufficient to keep this human harvest in luxuriant condition, it mattered little to the gay lords of the soil whether there was aught else for the market.

This condition of affairs was quaintly, but aptly described by Col. A. J. Willis, himself a Caroline County slaveholder, in a speech delivered in the Maryland Senate a year or two before emancipation was effected. Advocating some measure proposed by what afterwards became the emancipation party, he said: "Gentlemen on the other side of the Senate seem disposed to test every measure introduced by its probable effect upon slavery. If they can have their way, they will soon damn their pet institution. What is slavery worth to us now, Mr. President? Fields; corn; hogs; 'niggers.' It takes a big field to raise a little corn; the hogs eat up all the corn; the 'niggers' eat up all the hogs; and what have you got on hand at the end of the year? Just what you had to begin with—fields and 'niggers.' Mr. President and gentlemen of the Senate: I'd rather have a string of a dozen herrings than a dozen negroes!"

When the persecuted fields became so impoverished that they would no longer produce "nubbins," they were planted in black-eyed peas; and when the soil was "so poor it wouldn't sprout peas," it was "turned out" to grow up in scrub pines. It not infrequently happened that peas were more plentiful than corn; in which case, as pigs could not be persuaded to eat the former, it fell to the lot of the slaves to consume vast quantities of them. Poor Tom, one of Gen. P——'s field hands, having dined on black-eyed peas daily for four months, at last reached the point of indignant protest. Coming into the "Quarters" one day, he was confronted, for the one hundred and twentieth time, with the inevitable bowl of smoking peas seasoned with rusty bacon; and being ignorant of the fact that his master was just at that moment passing by, he broke forth in the following emphatic strain:

"Now, Mary Liz, mind what I tells ye. De Oberseer's done gone got to change de livin'. We's eat peas till we's as po' as the ole field whar dey growed—we's jest turned to pea mush! Dis nigger's a gwine ter try to 'vour dis one mo' stinkin' mess; an' den Is'e a gwine ter quit, ef I dies. Mars Gen'l may save a few dollahs on co'n; but I specs he's a gwine ter lose a thousan' dollah niggah some o' dese days! Fo' I tells ye, I aint a eatin' no mo' peas, ef I has to"——

"Who's that, aint a goin' to eat peas?" stormed the General, at the same moment confronting Tom with the glare of a tiger.

"Not dis nigger, Mars!" answered Tom, as he scooped in a small ladlefull between sentences. "Dis nigger 'vours de peas to all tarnations!"

Despite his condition of physical and mental bondage, the negro was not incapable of moral distinctions and logical conclusions, albeit he sometimes followed the latter until he lost sight of the former. Jerry and Hercules, who belonged to Mr. C., a leading farmer of Caroline county, Md., will serve as an example. Said Jerry to his fellow-servant:

"Herc; you know de Book it say ye mustn't steal. Now, you an' me 'longs to meetin'; an' so we mustn't steal. What am stealin', Herc? Gim' me your 'pinion as a resorter in de Church."

"Well, sah;" replied the sage Hercules, "it am takin' on de sly, fo' you own use, what am anodder man's goods."

"Now, Herc; fo' de 'lustration, s'pose dis case: Dere am Mars Jimmy's turkeys up de ole apple tree. You an' me is Mars Jimmy's niggers. Dat is, turkeys an' niggers bofe 'long to Mars, don't dey?"

"Dat am sho'ly so," responded Hercules.

"Well, now den," resumed Jerry, "s'pose Mars Jimmy's niggers, Herc and Jerry, eat one o' Mars Jimmy's turkeys to-night, what harm dat be to Mars Jimmy? What he lose from de apple tree, he gains in de health an' strength ob de boys, don't he? Turkey still his'n, aint he?"

"Dat's so, Jerry," was the reply; "it am all in de family."

But next morning when the old turkeys counted their children, they were not "all in de family." One had fallen a victim to Jerry's moral philosophy; and the consciences of the logical twain were about as comfortable as their capacious and well-stuffed stomachs. Even to this day, despite the better teachings of the public school and the Christian pulpit, it is to be feared there are some among our colored population, who reason themselves into the belief, that because, in the days of slavery, they or their fathers wrought in uncompensated toil, for the benefit of others, and for the general prosperity; therefore the families thus benefited, or the community in general, have no moral or equitable right to complain if they "collect de wages owin' on de ole score." With some, the law of limitations is ineffective to bar this twenty-two-year-old debt; unless the limitations be prison walls. Such cases, however, are growing more and more rare, as the years of our higher civilization roll on; and, in the Maryland counties of the Peninsula, it is no unusual thing for the jails to be without a tenant charged with theft for many months together. For some reason—perhaps because the governing power in Delaware denies education to the negro unless he pays for it out of his own hard earnings; and denies to him the right of suffrage, even when he and his party are willing to pay for it—we cannot say so much for the Delaware counties. There accusations are numerous; convictions follow almost as a matter of course; and the whipping-post has many victims. Juries are composed almost wholly of the governing class; and it would not be wonderful if they should have the acuteness to see that every colored man convicted of crime is an opposition voter permanently disfranchised.

In the days of slavery but few of the colored preachers and religious teachers were able to read. By the laws of most of the slave-holding states, teaching negroes was constituted a penal offence. To them learning was contraband, and to be obtained only as some of them were wont to obtain their Thanksgiving and Christmas turkeys—by stealth. The old time local preachers and exhorters among the colored people had, therefore, to depend largely upon their powers of memory to recall appropriate texts of Scripture, as bases for their discourses, or as illustrations of religious doctrine and experience.

One of these ebony-skinned sons of nature in the lower part of the Peninsula, renowned in his day for a punctilious observance of dignified ministerial forms, always used the Hymn-book and Bible in his announcement of hymns and texts; as he explained to his white pastor, "fo' de 'pearance ob de thing to de 'sembly;" carefully turning the pages, and scrutinizing the books, with an immense pair of brass-bowed spectacles astride his nose. It was his custom, before going into the congregation, to avail himself "ob de larnin' ob brudder Aaron," a fellow-servant and member of the same congregation, in order to insure accuracy. One day, after considerable manipulation of the pulpit Bible, he settled down somewhere about the middle of the volume; and with a great show of confident ceremony, thus announced his text: "Preach de Gospel. Bees instantly work in de season, an' outen de season;—dat is, ef dey kin—'prove, 'buke, 'zort; all along a sufferin'. Dese words, breethering you'll 'scover in de second varse ob de fourth chapter ob de second 'pistle of Saul o' Tarshis to Clover." This was more than "Brudder Aaron" could stand; who at once interposed with: "Uncle Zeke, dat are a mistake. Dere am no such a 'pistle in de Book. It am Paul de 'Postle's 'pistle to Timothy." Instantly Uncle Zeke, nothing daunted, responded: "Dat's a fac', Uncle Aaron; it's kinder dark in heah. I seed it war some sorter grass: I 'scovers now, it am Timoty an' not de Clover."

Another old colored brother, residing in the neighborhood of Chestertown, Maryland, and who was environed by similar disadvantages, one day announced for "de tex fo' de 'scourse ob de casion," the following unique scripture: "Whar ders two or three gits togedder in my name, an' I'm dar too, ders six or seven ob us."

In those days of yore, the simple faith of the unlettered African oftentimes attached to the Deity a very decided, and really a kind of corporeal personality. What, with others of better culture, would have been irreverent or bordering on the idolatrous, was, with him, but the legitimate outcome of a most reverent and anxious feeling after God. He accepted the terms and words in which, in accommodation to human conceptions and consciousness of need, God has been pleased to speak of himself and of his relations to his children, as being strictly literal in their import; and, not unfrequently, in his innocent ignorance, did he exaggerate and distort them. At a camp-meeting held on Kent Island in 1856, the writer one day heard a manifestly sincere and earnest colored man, in his address at the throne of grace, make the following petition: "O, Lord! O, Lord! We is mighty po' an' helpless critters! O, Lord! we needs ye pow'ful bad! O, Lord! Don't take no time to git ready; but come 'long anyhow, jest as ye is, in de ole workin', ebery-day close—we's in sich a bad way an' big hurry! O, Lord! O, Lord! Harness a pow'ful strong an' mighty white hoss to de ark; an' git out yer sharp, flashin' sword; an' ride an' cut an slash all ober de camp-groun'!"

In the old-time Peninsula camp-meetings, the colored people were always provided for; a portion of the circle to the rear of the preacher's stand being invariably set apart for their occupancy and use. Here they drew up their covered carts, and erected their nondescript tents. The latter often consisted of poles stuck into the earth, and bent and tied together; over which they spread such articles of bed-clothing as they might happen to possess, to afford the needed shelter. Not infrequently their tents were of patchwork, after the pattern of Joseph's coat, or a modern crazy-quilt; and added a ludicrous feature to the weird scenery of the primitive encampment.

In front of their tents, and generally in the most open and sunny spot obtainable, was their shouting-ground, or meeting-place; where, after the sermon, they were wont to gather for the great revival effort. This service was usually opened by the formal announcement of some solemn hymn, such as, "And am I born to die?" or, "Hark, from the tomb the doleful sound;" which was sung to a melancholy minor, in the slowest time possible, and slurred and tremoloed into all sorts of fantastic shapes, until the author of old "Mear" or "China," had he listened from the other world, would surely have been unable to recognize his own production. When this opening piece had at last dragged to its conclusion, "Brudder Jacob Isr'el Potter," or "Isaier Ishm'el

Carter," or some other recognized dignitary, was called on to "lead in de revotions at de throne ob grace."

Beginning in slow and measured sentences, in indistinct monotone, the petitioner was wont to rise by degrees from apparent formalism to warmth; from warmth to earnestness; from earnestness to intense enthusiasm and excitement; when the prayer and the responses struggled with each other for the mastery in the midst of a confused babel of glowing metaphor and red-hot exclamamation; and the conflict was finally terminated by the surrender of the tired lungs and wrecked voice of the leader, to the overpowering noise of superior numbers. The "amen" said, one of the younger and more active "brethering" would spring to the lead in the song-service; and the transition from E flat to C marked the beginning of the jubilant era of "de meetin'." As the leader struck the first notes of the song, peculiar motions, confined to no particular portion or member of the body, indicated the time in which the piece was to be rendered; and significant glances in the direction of the chief "men-singers and women-singers" brought them, one by one, into position for effective action, in hollow circle facing inward. The space thus inclosed was devoted to penitents; and there, kneeling on the bare ground—ofttimes prostrate in the dust—many a wounded spirit, from the double bondage, human and satanic, found the liberty of Christ and the "balm in Gilead." Many of the most jubilant songs of the negroes pointed with glowing metaphor to this blessed, spiritual freedom, and to the coming good time when the Immortal Liberator should break their last fetter. The following stanza and chorus, heard a thousand times in my boyhood, will serve as an illustration:

> "O! sinner; run to Jesus;
> Wid a mighty hand he frees us;
> An' ole Satin neber tease us,
> Ef de Lord do appear.
>
> *Chorus:* Den you will git free
> In de year ob jubilee;
> Yes, childring, we'll be free
> When de Lord do appear!"

Under the inspiration of sentiments like these, what wonder if ebony faces shone with somewhat of the supernatural fire that illumined Moses' countenance! What wonder if the suddenly unfettered spirit signalled the glad occasion by "walking, and leaping, and praising the Lord!"

Usually the tide of enthusiasm, on the colored side of the encampment, arose and intensified as the days and nights rolled by; and reached the climactic point on the last night of the meeting. By general consent, it was understood that, as to the colored people, the rules requiring quiet after a certain hour, were, on this last night, to be suspended; and great billows of sound from the tornado of praise and singing rolled over the encampment, and was echoed back from hill and wood for miles away, until the morrow's dawning. To those in the tents, this hour was usually signalled by the sound of hammer and axe, knocking down the plank partition walls separating the white and colored precincts; and, in a few moments, the grand "march 'round de' campment" was inaugurated, accompanied with leaping, shuffling, and dancing, after the order of David before the ark when his wife thought he was crazy; accompanied by a song appropriate to the exciting occasion. Some of my readers will recognize the following couplets:

> "We's a marchin' away to Cana-ann's land;
> I hears de music ob de angel band.
>
> *Chorus*—"O come an' jine de army;
> An' we'll keep de ark a movin';
> As we goes shoutin' home!
>
> "Come, childering, storm ole Jericho's walls;
> Yes, blow an' shout, an' down dey falls!
> *Chorus*—"O come, etc.
>
> "We's all united heart an' hand;
> An' fully able to 'sess de land.
> *Chorus*—O come, etc.
>
> "When we gits dere we'll all be free;
> An' oh, how joysome we shall be!
> *Chorus*—"O come," etc.

The sound of the hammer aforesaid became the signal for a general arising all around the camp; and, in a few moments, curtains were parted; tents thrown open; and multitudes of faces peered out into the early dawning to witness the weird spectacle. Sometimes the voices of the masters and veterans among the white people would echo-back, in happy response, the jubilant shout of the rejoicing slaves.

At the old time camp-meetings, seats were provided for the colored people in the rear of the preachers' stand; and no part of the congregation was more reverent in demeanor or more attentive to the preaching of the Word. However it might be in front of him, the preacher was always sure of a sympathetic and appreciative audience in the rear. Many a timid, trembling messenger was inspirited and saved from disastrous failure by the demonstrative prayers and sympathies of the colored part of the congregation. Whatever might be the feelings of the speaker with respect to the assembly, at least the colored portion thereof were sure to be *en rapport* with the speaker.

Exclamations such as, "Help, Lord!" "Lor' bress de preachah!" "Send de powah, Lord!" with significant nods and motions, and guttural grunts peculiar to the race and impossible to represent phonographically, were sure to greet the preacher from the rear of the stand. And if the preacher "got on de rousements," as the colored patriarchs expressed it, "Amen!" and "Halleluyer!" would come rolling in from the African rearguard, and quite frequently would be echoed back again from the more impressible and enthusiastic in front, until a general shout of victory crowned the hour, and scores of awakened souls were weeping and pleading for mercy. Many a discourse, really but a moderately good exhortation, was metamorphosed into a great sermon; and many a commonplace speaker into a mighty Boanerges, by a volley of well-timed negro shouts, poured in at a critical juncture.

But sometimes the "amen" and the shout came inopportunely, as the following incident will illustrate. Rev. Henry White, an old-time Presiding Elder, was once preaching on a quarterly-meeting occasion. The gallery was crowded with colored people. His theme was the judgment of the great day, and the discourse almost overwhelmingly solemn. Becoming mightily stirred, some of the old negroes began to indulge in their favorite exclamations while the preacher was picturing the "great white throne," the "awful Judge," and the banishment of the finally disobedient. So utterly inappropriate were "amen!" and "hallelujah!" amid such solemn associations, that the effect of the sermon was thereby put in jeopardy. Mr. White paused, and explained the meaning of these exclamations to the colored people; and cautioned them against saying amen or hallelujah in the wrong place. All was quiet along the lines in the gallery, until the Elder neared the culminating climax, in which he pictured the redeemed, having passed the judgment ordeal, filing through the heavenly gates and up the gold-paved aisles of glory; when old uncle Malachi, who was ready to burst with the effort to conceal his enthusiasm, could stand it no longer. Fearful of "'sturbin' de meetin'," he sought a hurried exit by way of the steps leading down outside; but, impeded by the crowd, and the strain intensifying beyond endurance, he yelled out, as his old, grey head disappeared adown the winding retreat, "Amen, at a venter!" But the sermon was already a great success; and, besides, had reached the point where the shout appropriately came in; and old Malachi's "amen" fired the train for a general explosion and a great spiritual triumph.

Sometimes the old colored patriarchs were wont to manifest their interest in the sermon by interjecting remarks commendatory or suggestive between the preacher's sentences. Generally this habit was no annoyance, but rather helpful, to the minister who was accustomed to African peculiarities. In one well attested incident, however, it proved far otherwise.

At a camp-meeting once held at McNeal's Woods, near Easton, Md., a somewhat timid young minister of moderate ability was struggling hard to work out a sermon on the cure of Naaman the leper. "Uncle Jeems" King, an old, lame negro, whose piety and zeal were proverbial throughout Talbot County, had taken his position next the stand, where he could eye the preacher and give him the benefit of his accustomed exclamations and interjections. When the young man announced his text, Uncle Jeems spoke out: "Lor', bress de preachah!" As the brother groped and stumbled along his introduction, the old negro uttered a significant groan and said: "O, Lord! we's all pow'ful weak po' critters: help de preachah!" Getting under way finally, the young minister reached the point where Naaman, seated in his royal chariot at the Prophet's gate, awaited his response to his servant's call. "See how proud and lazy this miserable leper was!" said the preacher. "He was so dignified and conceited that he could by no means get down from his luxuriant cushions, and go in to see the man of God; but, while coming to beg a favor of a man whose lineage and whose God he despised, he must needs put the Prophet to the inconvenience of coming out to him. His vanity and impudence outraged all proprieties, and merited only defeat." A moment's pause, just at this point, enabled Uncle Jeems to put in a word of extenuation for poor Naaman's conduct; when he grunted out, so as to be heard by most of the congregation: "Umph, Lord! He was po'ly!"

This unexpected apology for the Leper was so just, and at the same time in its circumstances so ludicrous, that it upset the gravity of ministers and people all around, and effectually vanquished the unfortunate speaker, who was thrown into an embarrassment most painful to endure or even to behold. Uncle Jeems, seeing that something was wrong, without the least suspicion of his own responsibility, capped the climax by the ejaculation: "De good Lor' help de brudder! He am po'ly, too, I 'spec's!" An able exhorter came to the rescue; but his unfortunate attempt to tack on his address to the broken off sermon and the name of the "po'ly" man in the chariot, provoked a feeling of amusement that was fatal to his success. In the prayer meeting which followed among the colored people, very appropriately indeed, and quite as innocently as in the apology for Naaman, Uncle Jeems struck up the doleful chorus: "What's de matter in Zion?"

Among the most notable of the colored Methodist Episcopal ministers of the Peninsula, was Rev. Frost Pollet. He was one of the original members of the Delaware Conference, and served a term therein as Presiding Elder. Frost was nearly six feet in height, of bony and angular build; more erect than Bishop Simpson; but, except in color, not unlike him in general form and appearance. There was an admixture of about one-eighth of white blood in his veins. This seems to have given form and expression to his features which were more Anglican than African. In him, however, the negro voice and dialect were perfectly developed. His manner was marked by great simplicity, and humility was the distinguishing feature of his Christian character. He was intensely earnest and enthusiastic in his religious experience and efforts. Whenever it was known among the white residents of Princess Anne, and other Peninsular towns where he labored, that Frost Pollet was to preach, the best and most cultured of all religious persuasions flocked to hear him; and his congregations at bush meetings were ofttimes real ovations. No pen and ink portraiture can do justice to either the man or his preaching.

It was the good fortune of Rev. T. E. Martindale to hear Frost preach, on a certain occasion, in Pocomoke City, Maryland. To him I am indebted for the data out of which, in a measure, to reconstruct that discourse, and thus preserve to the world a unique specimen of African eloquence.

The text was, "Go and *shew* John agin de things which ye do heah and see. De blind receive der sight, an' de lame walk; de lipers are cleansed, an' de deaf heah, de dead is raised up, an' de poor has de Gospel preached to them."

On top of Frost's bald head was a large wen, which it was his wont frequently to rub during the delivery of his sermons—especially in the passages where he was most interested or embarrassed. On this occasion, running his hand over his head as if in thoughtful mood, he said, "Frens; what you'll heah to-night, I didn't git out'n no books; but I got it right out'n my own head." He then, by way of introduction, proceeded to give a most accurate, particular and remarkably vivid description of the circumstances, preceding and attending the utterance of these words by the Master. When this was ended, he entered upon the discussion of the old question—whether man would have reached a greater development and blessedness, had he not fallen, than that to which he might aspire under the remedial scheme of Christ's atonement and mediation. Scarcely had he propounded the problem, however, until he stopped short and called sharply to himself: "Ole Frost, you'd better come back from dar. Dem's deep waters. Don't look out, Frost, you'll git drownded!" And that was the last of that streak of speculative divinity.

Frost then took up, in order, the various characters mentioned in the text—the blind, the lame, etc.; and proceeded to discuss these physical conditions, and by them to illustrate the unhappy state and fearful exposure of "de po' sinnah." When Frost came to the discussion of the case of "de lipers," he cited the case of Naaman the Syrian. He gave the history in accurate detail, and with a strange, nervous force—a magnetism of voice and manner—indescribably beautiful. Among other things, he said: "Naaman was taken po'ly; he got wus and wus, an' nothin' done him no good. An' one day his wife couldn't help cryin' 'bout it. An' dar was a little slave gal 'bout de house. I specs dey stole her away an' tuck her down dar wrongishly. She seed her missus a cryin' an' downhearted like; an' sez she: Missus, dere's a prophet down yander in Isr'el, wher I comed from, dat can pray for Mars Naaman, an' 'buke de 'sease an' kore him. An' so his wife told Naaman, an' Naaman told de king; an' de king sent Naaman right off in a char'ot, wid a troop of hoss soldiers to 'scort him down to S'maria or sommers to find de Prophet. But he made de 'stake of goin' to de king ob Isr'el. Jest like po' sinners now-a-days. Dey goes eberywhere but to de right place fo' salvation. But as luck—by dat I means Providence—would have it, po' Naaman got to de right place at last. Sinners allers can find Jesus somehow, if dey're in right down yearnest."

Frost then described the interview with the Prophet, told about the prescription; and finally got Naaman down to the banks of Jordan, drawing on his vivid imagination for most of the interesting colloquy represented as having taken place between "Gineral Naaman and his sarvant." After getting Naaman into the water for his first bath, he represented him as saying: "I don't b'lieve in dis heah nonsense, an' I'se a gwine ter come out'n dis ole ditch." He then represented Naaman's slave standing on the shore and saying: "Master, you knows what de Prophet said. Better stay in dar an' gib de Lord a fair chance at you." As Frost represented, in most dramatic language and manner, Naaman's successive baths, the spiritual temperature in his congregation grew more and more torrid, and there were unmistakable indications of phenomenal disturbances and convulsions in that part of the religious *kosmos*. Then, changing his whole demeanor, and emphasizing his words with a measured and most impressive deliberation, he said: 'And—he—went—down—the—seventh—time!" At this juncture, clasping his hands over his head, and squatting low, as if about to spring well-nigh to the ceiling, he exclaimed: "Mighty Lord! Help ole Frost to preach de Gospel dis one time mo'!" After this invocation, he added, with effect that was irresistible: "An' he come up out'n de water, an' his flesh was jest like a sweet, little baby's!" This climax took the audience by storm; and such was the excitement, that it became necessary for the eloquent preacher to pause, while the more excitable elements cooled off sufficiently to allow him to proceed.

Under the head of raising the dead, the speaker cited the cases of Lazarus and the nobleman's daughter. The picture he drew of the sweet, Christian home at Bethany and its loving and lovely occupants, and how that home was shadowed and made desolate by the death of the beloved brother, brought tears to many eyes. At the conclusion of this description, he remarked incidentally: "Now, when de blessed Jesus was a travellin' his circuit, he used to have his puttin' up places, jest like we preachers does. An' he was allers glad to put up wid Mr. Lazarus an' Miss Mary an' Martha, 'cause dey was sich nice housekeepers, an' speshly 'cause dey all loved each other so deahly." Having completed a most graphic description of the resurrection of Lazarus, after a slight pause, in the most natural manner possible, looking over his shoulder as if to summon some person at a distance, but within hearing, he issued the imperative command: "Miss Tabitha: You come in heah, now, an' gib your testimony. We wants to know what's your 'spe'rence 'bout de resarection." And by the time he had finished his colloquy with this young lady, he again had his audience stirred by a mighty whirlwind of power.

The following specimen of his eloquence is in a different vein—not so dramatic, but perhaps even more impressive. Having selected as his text, "And, without controversy, great is the mystery of godliness," he remarked: "Bretherin' an' sisterin', dis am a great 'casion, an' I am got a great tex'. If a po' preachah take a little tex'. on a big 'casion, an' den done gone preach a po' sermont, de sembly don't git nothin'; but dis arternoon, yer shore o' de tex' anyway.

"De Possel say 'widout contivarsy great am de myst'ry of godliness;' an' if 'ligion—fo' dat's what he means—am a great myst'ry widout contivarsy, what a mighty big myst'ry it must be wid contivarsy. When ole Nick Demus went to de Mars to ax him 'bout de kingdom, he told him, 'Nick, you can't squeeze in no how widout you come like a po' little baby—got to be born agin, Nick.' Den Demus he say, 'Mars, how kin dat ar be? Dat's a great myst'ry.' Den Jesus he say, 'Nick, don't you heah dat wind? Don't you know it's a blowin'? Kin you 'splain it?' Den Nick Demus he see de pint; an' he an' de Mars war 'widout contivarsy,' and godliness war a great myst'ry.

"Fren's: I've hearn of some cullud pussuns round dese parts that go to meetin' an' shout all ober de house; an' den a goin' home dat night, dey takes a hen off'n somebody's apple-tree. Dat am a great myst'ry. But s'pose dat cullud man gits 'ligion right eend fo'most; den he leaves all de hens,—an' de Debil too—behind him. Dat am de great myst'ry ob *godliness*.

"Den dar am de myst'ry ob de Lord's keer fo' us. De Book say he count de hairs an' watch de sparrers, an' 'tend to de little baby ravens. It say also two sparrers oney fetch a fardin in de market. (I reckon a fardin am 'bout a cent.) If dat's so, one sparrer's oney wo'th a half a cent. Now den; ef de good Lord take keer ob de little sparrer what's oney wo'th one half a cent; does you think he won't take keer o' you fifteen hundred dollah niggers? No wondah de Possel say 'great am de myst'ry ob godliness.'"

The Slave code did not allow free negroes of one state to go into another. About the year 1856, Frost Pollet was so indiscreet as to cross the line and preach a sermon to the colored saints and sinners in Accomac. He was promptly arrested and thrown into prison. When the day for a hearing of the case arrived, the Court, rightly adjudging that there was no sinister purpose in his visit, released him, allowing him so many hours to leave the state of Virginia. Taking off his hat and making a polite bow, he said:

"Thank you, gentlemens; you may see *frost* down heah agin some time dis winter; but, shore es you're born, you's neber gwine to see Pollet in dese diggin's no mo'."

But "the former things have passed away." During the dark days of the war, in 1864, a State Constitutional Convention assembled in the State Capitol at Annapolis, where the subject of slavery, the question of states rights, and other great living issues of those stormy times were elaborately discussed. In that honorable body the writer, with other Unionists, pleaded the cause of the slave and of the union, on a motion that finally prevailed, to adopt into the "Bill of Rights" the following item:

"*Article* 23. Hereafter, in this State, there shall be

neither slavery nor involuntary servitude, except in punishment for crime, whereof the party shall have been duly convicted; and all persons held to service or labor, as slaves, are hereby declared free."

In that discussion, the writer took the ground that, in its aggregated existence and influence, slavery was a great moral, social and political evil, and ought to be extirpated for the following reasons: Because, it was an invasion of natural rights; could only exist in violation of the dearest and most sacred social and domestic ties; and because it ministered to the demoralization of all classes within the sphere of its influence. He held further, that slavery undermined and enervated the principles of general and individual enterprise and self-reliance forming the basis of an honorable manhood, and of all true political and material prosperity; that the legislation demanded for the protection of slavery and slaveholders, was arbitrary, unjust and oppressive to the people; and, finally, that for the above and for other reasons, the system and the code of slavery were in contravention of the principles and teachings of the Christian religion—the purest law of right and morality that had ever blessed the world; and that therefore, slavery had no right to existence and protection under the government of a professedly Christian people.

Having completed its work, that Convention adjourned in September. On the 12th and 13th days of October, 1864, an election was held for the acceptance or rejection of the Constitution framed by the Convention, and it was adopted by a majority of 375 votes. After an exciting legal contest in the State Courts, on technical points involving the validity of the vote, on the 29th day of the same month, Governor Bradford issued his proclamation declaring the new Constitution ratified by the people, to take effect on the first day of November following; and, with the midnight advent of that beautiful, frosty November morning, the shackles fell from the hands of all Maryland's bondsmen; and one hundred thousand new-made freemen walked forth into the blessings and responsibilities of personal and civil liberty.

As a rule, these bondmen came forth from their dark, sad Egypt as did Israel, recognizing the Divine Goodness that opened up a way through the bloody, red sea of war, and the madness of their unreasoning and rebellious masters. Few, indeed, were the thoughtless revelries in which even the more trifling and vicious among these unchained souls indulged. On the contrary, everywhere throughout the State on the night of the 31st of October, the freedmen assembled in their humble places of worship, or in their "quarters" and cabins; and signalled the coming of their glorious year of jubilee with appropriate, grateful, glowing watch-night services. Sermons and addresses were delivered, prayers offered, and holy songs were wafted forth on the still midnight air, until the incense of glad thanksgiving filled Heaven, and a tempest of praise swept the new, free State of Maryland. One picture will serve as an illustration; but the reader must remember it was duplicated in a thousand places that joyous night.

The scene was a newly dedicated chapel on the Eastern Shore. About 9 o'clock, on the night above indicated, the last slave having finished his last task, the colored people of the neighborhood began to assemble at the place of worship; and by 10 o'clock, almost the entire negro population of all that region was crowded into the chapel, and gathered at the door and windows in eager, expectant squads. "Uncle Jack," a patriarchal local preacher, of snowy head and most reverend mien, arose and announced from memory the hymn, beginning:

> "Blow ye the trumpet, blow
> The gladly, solemn sound," etc.

which was sung as only three hundred pairs of African lungs could sing it under the inspiration of "de year ob Jubilee" so soon to dawn. Then Uncle Jack prayed and praised and shouted by turns, until his voice was lost amid the hurricane of responsive exclamations that shook the temple. At the conclusion of his glowing invocation, the old preacher said: "Now den, chil'n, let's all dat loves de Lord, an' thanks him fo' de comin' freedom, 'main on der knees, an' be still; an' let de heart say its thanksgivin', jest in a little whisper, so nobody but de blessed Jesus kin hear."

For a little while the dropping of a pin might have been heard; then there followed a faint whisper, gradually increasing, and, at length, broken by sobs and smothered exclamations; until, finally, a "great and exceeding weight of glory" settled down like Pentecost upon the assembly. Being present with a few sympathizing white spectators, the writer was invited to address the audience. He congratulated the freedmen upon the prospect before them; and reminded them that liberty, to them, did not represent immunity from care and toil, or imply the right to live by the labor and thrift of their neighbors; but that, to be of any value, it meant liberty to work and enjoy the fruits thereof; liberty to learn to read the Bible and to have their children taught; liberty to purchase land and build houses, gathering the scattered family about the home altar; liberty to have wives and daughters defended against the bestial lust of libertines, and the unity of the family preserved against the caprice of profligate masters and the dubious exigencies of the auction block. He advised sobriety, industry, honesty and respect for manhood, whether covered by white or black skins. He told them, in a word, that the colored man who most hated the bondage of sin and the Devil, was best fitted for the new freedom now vouchsafed him by his country and his God.

Uncle Jack then added a few words of hearty approval of the above sentiments, concluding as follows: "I tells ye folkses, dis am a great day. I neber 'spected to know how a free nigger felt till I got de kingdom an' de crown up yander. But, gullory, halleluyer! In a few mo' minits, dis ole slave'll be a free man. I feels it in my bones, an' chil'n, I's a gwine ter shout!" Saying which, he suited the action to the word, and leaped for very gladness. Then, as the watch indicated·the hour of midnight, all heads were bowed in the solemn consecration of their new life of freedom to the service of Him who had so strangely broken their fetters.

"Now, chil'n, you kin sing ef ye wants to," said Uncle Jack. "You 'longs to nobody but de Lord now. Sing!" And sing they did! It was like the voice of the winds through field and forest, mingling with the chime of falling waters. Soothing cadences, swelling harmonies, gusts of praise and cyclones of "Hosanna in the highest" went rolling out from the little chapel, and floated off to hill and dale on the still, sweet breath of that November morning. It was, indeed, a jubilee anthem,—a medley of all their most joyful melodies, interluded with the voices of fervent ejaculation, and shouts of victorious praise!

Some there were who failed to live up to the glowing promises and prophecies of that thrilling hour; but, as a class, the freedmen of Maryland have made steady and rapid progress. It is absurd to judge the negro by the highest standard of Caucasian civilization, attained through centuries of development and culture. It took Jehovah forty years to educate and develop the liberated Israelites to a point where they could be trusted with the responsibilities of citizenship and self-government. In half that period, despite the disabilities arising from old prejudices and unfair proscriptions, the late slave population of Maryland are rapidly advancing to that point of civilization, where their liberation will be universally recognized as a blessing both to themselves and to the State.

The same Constitution that freed the slaves of Maryland, provided for a uniform system of public education; for a state school-tax to support the system; and required that the proceeds of said tax should be distributed *pro rata*, according to population of all races. It was the purpose of the party then in power, that, in the division of this fund, there should be no discrimination against the colored population. But, three years afterward, the opposite party came into power; and, by unfair legislation, that kindly purpose has been modified to the negro's injury. Nevertheless, some advance has been made in the direction of fair and honorable concession; and now there are indications of a growing sense of justice, that we may hope, in the near future, will insure the impartial treatment a Christian state owes to all its citizens. It ill befits a *Democracy*, claiming the principles symbolized in its name, to heap contempt on a class of its wards because of an assumed intellectual and moral inferiority; and yet, at the same time, deny that class an equal chance in the race of life. Surely if the proud Caucasian's claims to superiority be well founded, he has nought to fear from a removal of the legal obstructions from the path of his dark-skinned competitor and brother. The chivalry of the dominant knights of our grand old Maryland will be recognized and applauded in Heaven and on Earth, when they shall have obliterated the last legal vestige of the former civilization. That glorious 4th of July cannot be far distant, when Marylanders, in their jubilant celebrations, shall read the Declaration of Independence without a single mental reservation.

Poor, hide-bound little Delaware does not adequately provide for the education of even her white children. Some advance has been constrained and some concessions extorted, by the righteous clamors of the Pulpit and the Press; but, manifestly, the governing politicians of that State are more afraid of education for the masses than they are of the direful ravages of a wide-spread intemperance and the onerous burdens of an alarming pauperism. The Legislature has, at last, conceded to the proscribed, disfranchised and politically helpless negro race, a pittance for education proportioned to the relative amount of their taxes for general public purposes. This small amount would be considerably increased if the "cunningly devised" "Act for the Collection of Revenue," so called, were not purposely designed to obstruct and prevent the collection of the poll tax from negroes; the payment of which is a prerequisite to the exercise of the rights of the elective franchise. But, although "The mills of the gods grind slowly," they do keep on grinding, and they "grind exceeding fine;" and, little by little, Christianity and education will so accomplish their work, even in Delaware, as to constrain fairness and justice at the hands of an honest, Democratic manhood; and will make such disgraceful and humiliating statutes thenceforth an impossibility.

In the light of the future, the children of Delaware politicians of to-day will stand and look back at the legislation of their fathers, as we now look at the revolting wrongs of the old slave-code; and wonder how such legal abominations and monstrosities could ever exist in free America and in the last quarter of the nineteenth century.

CHAPTER VIII.

UNCLE STEPHEN, THE SLAVE PREACHER.

AWAY down in Somerset County, Maryland, not far from where the waters of the Great Annamessex mingle with those of the Tangier Sound, dwelt Mrs. Priscilla W——, an aristocratic widow of olden times, with her sons and daughters, together with their numerous slaves. The widow and her children lived in elegant ease and luxury; while the negroes tilled the generous soil, and gathered the abundant harvests. In addition to these resources, there was a shipyard on the plantation, where workmen were continually busy building or repairing bay and river craft for purposes of travel and traffic, between that part of the Eastern Shore and the great city of Baltimore. Such of the slaves as were not needed on the plantation, were either hired out to other farmers in the surrounding regions, or, if they gave evidence of any mechanical turn, were put to the trade of ship-building.

"Uncle" Stephen, the subject of this sketch, first opened his infantile eyes to the light on this plantation, on the 2d day of March, 1814. He was born in a little cabin on the banks of the river, the murmur of whose rippling waves upon the pebbly strand oft served as his lullaby, when his mother was too busy cooking for the shipbuilders to sing him to sleep. Here, amid the caroling of birds and the dancing of the sunlight on grassy sward and rolling wave, little "Steve," with all the swarming nest-full of brother and sister picaninnies, romped, yelled and gamboled.

It is customary in biography to consult the tables of genealogy, in order to account for the career of the hero by the extraction or achievements of his ancestry. Stephen, his father, was an American Indian, descended, for many generations, of wild but noble freemen; whose great boast was their tall, straight, graceful stature, and their agility, endurance and bravery. His mother's name was Sarah. Her father was a native African warrior, who suffered the misfortune to become a prisoner of war, and finally a Maryland slave. He had been torn from a young bride in his native jungles, whose loss he had mourned with aching and sometimes almost breaking heart.

Every new invoice of slaves, arriving in that part of the colony for many years, was eagerly searched by "Wycongo," with the vague hope that his beloved "Manona" might be among the exiles, but in vain. At length he committed the last hope to the grave, and resigned himself to his cruel fate. About this time his master brought from Baltimore, in one of his schooners, several female slaves purchased in that city, one of whom was a comely Asiatic. In figure and feature she strongly resembled Manona, the bride of his youth, though of lighter hue; and Wycongo very soon laid his heart at her feet—the *hand* was not his to offer—and sued earnestly and eloquently for her love, at least in *action;* for their speech was so dissimilar as to make any verbal communication exceedingly difficult. After repeated efforts, by the employment of signs and a few English words she had been able to pick up, Altona, the Asiatic maiden, succeeded in making Wycongo understand that she also had been torn away from a lover she could not forget. Thenceforth Wycongo's love was deepened and intensified by the sympathy of a fellow feeling, which for some time he vainly tried to make her understand. In order to succeed in telling Altona his story, Wycongo devoted all his spare hours and Sundays to giving her verbal lessons in his English; and having finally made her acquainted with his sorrowful history, he was rewarded by the assurance of both her sympathy and her affection. At Wycongo's request, and with her and her master's consent, Altona's name was thenceforth changed to Manona. "It is so purty, an' soun's so nat'ral like," explained her husband.

"Congo" and "Nona," as they were thenceforth called upon the plantation, were at once settled by the master in the aforementioned little cabin, down by the shipyard on the shore of the Annamessex. Congo became so expert as a mechanic, that he soon reached the honorable distinction of being appointed one of the foremen among the slave laborers; and Nona was constituted cook for such of the negro workmen as were unmarried.

Here, in due course of time, Sarah, our hero's mother, was born and raised. Here, as the wife of Stephen the Aborigine, she succeeded her mother in the simple arts of slave housekeeping; and here her son, whom she called by his father's name, grew up and learned his trade, becoming like Wycongo, his grandfather, an experienced hand and foreman.

In Stephen's veins flowed the red current formed by a confluence of blood from three continents; and, as the reader would naturally suppose, he was somewhat *sui generis*. While he was growing up, his mother treated his antics and idiosyncracies from the Asiatic standpoint. His father applied the Indian code. And his master meted out to him the kind and measure of discipline usually considered, by the statesmen of that day, most effectual in keeping the noble red man of the forest in his appropriate place. Thus the Asiatic rod; the American policy, and the Indian tactics for the preservation of the domestic peace were applied by turns, or all at once, in poor Steve's case; and, very naturally, the graduate from such a juvenile university was an exceptionally unique character. Equatorial restfulness and oriental imagination and dreaming, ofttimes made Steve seem, like the cat in the chimney corner, fast asleep; but only let some mouse of possible mischief or daring deviltry attempt to steal abroad, and he was instantly wide awake and off for the "scrimmage." None of his exploits however were malicious; they were rather the outcroppings of irrepressible mischief. Hilarity and inquisitiveness were his besetting sins, leading him into heedlessness, and once nearly costing him his life. Having received a commission one day from "young Mars," but little older than himself, his jolly mood led him to such antics in the performance of the duty, as to occasion his tumbling over a steep bank into the river; whence he was finally rescued, more dead than alive, by some of the men at the shipyard, attracted to the spot by the vigorous yelling and tearful lamentations of his playmate master. When he sufficiently recovered to appreciate the lesson, his mother laid him across her lap; said to him: "De Lord must a sporn yer life fo' some good eend;" and then emphasized and impressed the oracular declaration by about twenty well aimed blows with the sole of one of her old shoes. The expression on poor little Steve's countenance, when he at last resumed an upright position, gave ample evidence that the impressive lesson had taken due effect.

The following incident will illustrate Steve's peculiar propensity for juvenile investigation. His young Mars "Jeems" having grown old enough to feel an interest in his mother's welfare—his father having meantime died—was entrusted with the duty of the general supervision of the shipyard, and took possession of the office his father had previously occupied. He carefully imitated his father's movements and habits, even to the retention of the little brown whiskey-jug, which was replenished weekly, and statedly tested three times a day; and was then put back into the corner of the desk as he had seen his father do before him.

"Mars Jeems, what's dat ye got in dat jug?" inquired Steve one day, strolling in at the office door just in time to see the vessel removed from his master's lips to its accustomed corner.

"G'long, you fool," replied the young master. "Yer always pokin' yer nose into other people's business. It's only a little medicine."

"Is ye sick, Mars Jeems? What ye take 'em for?"

"Its none o' yer bis'ness, nigger," replied Mars Jeems. "But sometimes I don't feel right, and then I take a little medicine."

"Make ye feel good, Mars?"

"Yes, all over in spots, as big as a blanket. Now, you Injin nigger, if you don't git out, I'll kick you out."

Steve vanished; but he didn't feel well. The more he thought about his condition the worse he imagined he felt, until he concluded he must die if he couldn't find opportunity to test Mars Jeems' medicine. The young master's departure to dinner finally afforded Steve the coveted chance; and when his master returned he found him indulging in all possible antics, the office in utter confusion and the jug nearly emptied of its precious contents. Steve thus explained: "Golly, M–Mars; wuz zo –zo bad wid a pain, tried yer me'cine. 'Spec' I took spoo–oonfull mor'n 'nuff. Mars; feels spo's–spots 's big 's two 'r tree bla–blank's. Whoop!" Saying which he gave a kick which overturned his master's desk, spilled the ink on his books and papers and broke the precious jug; and seemed bent on a general wreck of the office, meanwhile laughing and yelling and tearing around like one possessed. As in Steve's blood three continents were represented, so the most reckless and grotesque features of the African, the Asiatic and the Indian "drunk" seem to have been combined in this exhibition; and it took all the forces of the shipyard to bring him into subjection. Fortunately for Steve, when the hilarious effects of the "me'cine" began to subside, the "Spoo-oonfull more'n 'nuff" of the poison he had taken produced a reaction that made him deathly sick, and left him prostrate. He did not need the flogging he received next morning to strengthen his determination never to take any more of that kind of medicine. Pity it was "Mars Jeems" did not join in the promise he exacted from Steve, and take it no longer. But then Steve was only a "nigger" slave; the master was a free American gentleman, and an Eastern Shore aristocrat! And in that day and country, the wealthy young planter who failed to drink whisky, gamble, "go a fox huntin'," and

"Dance all night till broad day light,
An' go home with the gals in the mornin',"

was hardly considered eligible for admission into first-class society. This phase of southern opinion has, however, been materially changed, or greatly modified by the mutations of the last quarter of a century—especially the transition. from slavery to freedom. Gambling, rum-selling and drunkenness are now generally considered disreputable; and labor is beginning to grow respectable. In fact, much of what was once the upper stratum of Eastern Shore society has settled to the bottom; while the industrious, non-slaveholding whites, taking advantage of their opportunity, have arisen to the vacant place. Not infrequently the son of the plantation overseer of a few years ago, now gives employment to the son of the former aristocratic planter and slave-owner. It is supposed to have been an Eastern Shore aristocrat of broken fortunes, who, just after the war, for a whole year, kept the following advertisement in a New York newspaper: "*Wanted*—A situation for a gentleman's son." At the end of this time, the family being about to starve, the genteel father and his darling boy pulled off their old kid gloves, rolled up their sleeves and went to work. The healthful exercise has improved their brain power and manly independence as much as it has their muscle.

Just after the incident above narrated occurred, Steve's old mistress died; and by her will he, the human tripartite of Africa, Asia and America, became the property of her son James. A human being *property!* A mind, the vehicle of independent thought and determination— "a living soul," with the stamp of creative Infinity upon it—*property!* A son of God—crowned by his Maker to reign in the realm of never-ceasing being—transmuted into a machine, to be circumscribed, owned, domineered, manipulated, valued and sold for rags and dust, as the property of his brother man! "The days of this ignorance" and wrong "God winked at." The world was a great infant, and the Father of Lights drew the curtains and let in his sunshine only as its unaccustomed eyes could bear it. The removal of the last vestige of those curtains by his red, right hand of bloody war caused much weeping to mercenary eyes; but joy came with the further opening of the new, bright morning of freedom; and now, while there may be a few who *would*, the vast majority of Maryland's former slaveholders *would not if they could*, resume the rights of ownership over their former bondmen. Verily the intelligent man whose life spans the stirring events of the last half century, has lived longer than Methuselah.

About this time an event occurred that formed an important epoch in Steve's life. In fact it completely revolutionized his nature, and gave new impulse and direction to those invisible forces of his being that were least fettered by the chains of his bondage. We will relate the story as nearly as possible in Stephen's own quaint dialect. Said he:

"When I was 'bout twenty years old—dat wus a gwine on well nigh to fifty years ago—dere was a camp-meetin' in one o' Mars Jeemses woodses, 'bout two miles from the shipyard. An' dem times de cullud folkses dey camped wid de white folkses, an' had dere part o' de 'campment to de rare ob de preachin' stan', wid a fence atween dem an' de white people. Dat was all right I reckons; but I used to set dare on a plank to hear de preachin', an' fogit what de preachah was a sayin', a thinkin' an' a wonderin' whedder in de place de Master was a preparin' up yander, dere was any 'tition fence to keep de niggers in dere own part of de great camp-meetin'; an' wedder de great Mars an' de mighty angels, when dey gits up to preach a great 'scourse to de 'deemed 'sembly, turns der backs all de time to de po' darkeys; but dat was when I wus young an' thoughtless.

"Well, as I was a goin' to say, says I to Mars Jeems one day—dat was afo' I'd eber seed a camp-meetin'— says I: 'Mars Jeems, please sah, kin I go to de camp-meetin' to-night, arter I git done dis task o' hewin' you done gone gib me dis mornin'?' Sez he to me, sez he: 'Wot you want to go dar fur, nigger?' Sez I to him, sez I: 'Jes fo' a little fun, Mars; I's comin' back afo day, in time to feed de hosses an' git ready for de day's work.' An' den Mars Jeems he say: 'Yes, you rascal, an' den be too sleepy to work termorry? Well, go dis time, but you need'nt ax no mo' afore Sat'day night.'

"Well, sir, ef eber you seed a darkey make chips fly, dis chile did from dat time till sundown, when I finished up de last stick. Den Mammy she had my pone an' herrin' all ready, an' when I slid inter a clean shirt, wid a herrin' in one hand an' a hunk o' corn pone in de udder, dis chile cut stick down de road fo' de 'campment. When I got dar, de pine knots was a blazin' on de fire stan's; an' two pow'ful big men was a blowin' de trumpets; an' somehow it kind o' made me feel like de judgment day was a comin'. Howsomever de great 'Sidin' Elder he got up in de stan', an' call all de people out to preachin'; an' aldo I didn't see no cullud folkses about where I was, an' was kind o' skeered an' trimblin', I 'cluded I'd better go up to de stan' wid de rest. An' bless yo' sould, honeys, when I got dar, I was de only nigger in de 'sembly. Dreckly a gemman he come an' say: 'You black rascal, what you a doin' on dis side de fence?'" An' I say: 'I didn't know as dey was any udder side de fence.' An' den he say: 'I'll show you der is;' an' wid' dat, he grab me by de arm, an' led me through de crowd to a high plank fence, an' say: 'Now, nigger, git out'n dis.' I 'cepted de invitation in sich a hurry dat I fell'd ober, 'kase I was afeered he wus a gwine ter kick me. Some o' de folkses, white an' cullud, was considerable tickled at de way I tumbled; but I got up, an' went' an' sot down 'mongst de cullud 'sembly. Dreckly de preachah denounce de hime an' de meetin' begun.

"When de preachah tuck his tex' 'bout de sheep an' de goats, some on one side an' some on de udder, thinks I to myself dat mus' be me he's talkin' 'bout: 'spec I's one ob de goats. Anyhow, I's 'vided off on dis side de fence. An' den when he tell 'bout de great judgment day, an' 'bout de King 'vidin' de good from de bad, an' drivin' de wicked down to 'dition, I begun to feel pow'ful bad; so I tried to think 'bout suffin' else, an' put my head down, an' stuck my fingers inter my years. But jes' den de preachah he call out mighty loud: 'Him dat has years to heah, let 'im heah;' an' all to onct it seem to me de Debil war about to put de han'-

cuffs onter me, an' I hearn de chains jingle, an' I begun to go down; an' den I look up an' seed Heaben a flyin' away like a clowd, all full ob de saints wid snow-white wings an' golden harps. An' den I hearn der singing, away furder an' furder off, like a echo dies away 'mong de woodses 'long de riber shore; an' de same time I hearn a mighty rumlin' 'way down, dat comed nearer an' nearer, till de groun' begin to shake under whar I sot; an' dat's de las' I knowed till I comed to an' found myself a hollerin' for mercy, a rollin' on de groun', an' de cullud folkses a singin' an' a shoutin' all roun' me.

'Bout dat time I look up, an' seed de same clowd dat went away comin' down agin from Heaben; but it was a pow'ful distance off. An' I seed de great Marster, in de form ob a lamb, a standin' on de edge ob de clowd an' a lookin' right down to whar I was. An' 'bout dat time de people seemed to see him too, for dey struck up de hime:

"Oh, de bleedin' Lamb! He was found worthy;"

an' den, chil'n, I cried, 'O! dow blessed Lamb, do please ride down on di clowdy chariot to dis awful pit an' help dis po' sinkin' sinner!' An' den I sced dat de Lamb was all bloody, an' I 'membered de ole song:

'Oh, he died fo' you an' he died fo' me;'

an' de nex' thing I knowed he knocked off my han'cuffs, an' pulled me outen de mire, an' washed me clean, an' put a white robe onter me, an' tuck me up on de cloud on a 'scursion through all de Paradises ob de halleluyer regions. I tells ye, chil'n, I neber 'membered to tell Jesus 'bout promisin' Mars Jeems to be home afo' day to feed de hosses; an' when he landed me agin on de yearth at de blessed ole camp-groun', de mornin' sun was up an' a-shinin'! 'Dere now!' sez I to myself, 'I done gone forgot all 'bout Mars Jeems an' de hosses; but neber mind, I'll go tell him 'bout de 'scursion, an' as how I couldn't git back no sooner, an' what a good nigger I's agoin to be, an' may be he'll let me off. So off I goes, runnin' an' jumpin' an' a hollerin' glory down de road, till I meets Mars Jeems a comin' out de gate on his hoss, a gwine to look for me. Sez he:

"'You crazy fool! whar you bin?'

"'O, glory! Mars Jeems,' sez I, 'I's bin on a heb'nly 'scursion, an' I wants you to go dar too.'

"'Yes, you black rascal!' sez he, 'I'll take you on a yarthly 'scursion. Take that!'

"Jes' den he brought me a wipe ober de shoulder wid his cowhide, dat a'most lifted me off'n my feet; but I hollered 'Glory, halleluyer!' an' started a runnin' for de house, an' he a runnin' his hoss alongside o' me, an' a puttin' de cowskin onter me wid all his might, an' I a hollerin' glory ebery time till I made harbor in de stables. By dat time he got tired o' fightin' an' I'd got sobered down so I could 'splain matters. So I told him all 'bout bein 'saved by de bleedin' Lamb, an' how much I love him, an' how happy I was, an' how good an' faithful I was a goin' to be ef he'd let me jine de meetin'; an' den he say: 'You black rascal, you oughter come home when you promise to. I'll teach you to mind what's said to you;' an' den he turned and walked away to de office, an' I seed de tears a runnin' down his face as he turned to go in at de door. Bime by, when I was a hewin' off by myself, Mars Jeems he come out to me, an' sez he: 'Steve, how does ye feel?' Sez I: 'Bress de Lord, Mars Jeems, I feels mighty sore on de back, but pow'ful gladsome in de heart.' Den Mars Jeems go to de office agin, an' dreckly he comed out wid some wheel-grease on a oster shell, an' say: 'Steve, I speck I struck you harder nor I 'tended dis mornin'. Lem'me 'noint yer back wid some o' dis.' So I strip down my shirt, an' Mars Jeems greased my back whar it was cut an' welted; an', sez he: 'Steve, I hope I shall never have to whip you agin;' an' dem was de las' licks he eber struck me. Chil'n, dat blessed day was, as I said, long time ago; but I's neber forgot it. I's still on de 'scursion to de New Jeruserlam; but sometimes de passage am bery stormy, an' de waves roll high an' de heabens git dark; but de ole ship o' Zion mighty safe boat; de Cap'n he know de sea an' he bridle de storm; an', bime by, I specs to heave de anker overboard in de harbor ob de kingdom!"

I have thus given Uncle Stephen's experiences as nearly as possible, as detailed by himself, in an exhortation delivered at a camp-meeting many years ago. The effect was most thrilling. Smiles and tears came and went like April sunshine and showers; and, at the close, a tempest of divine power burst upon the assembly; and many, like the boy of fifty years before to whose experience they had listened, were crying for mercy.

To a philosophic observer Steve's sudden conversion —unexpected to himself, and unheralded by a single sober thought or serious reflection—might have given little promise of permanency. But "God's ways are not as our ways." He who formed the mind and fashioned the heart, knows more than one door of possible ingress; and, in this instance, as in that of the Philippian Jailer, he seems to have loosened the bars and bolts with the wrench of an earthquake and a hammer of thunder. So real was the moral revolution, in this case, and so completely was the prisoner of Satan set free, that the vicissitudes and exposures of fifty years, varying all the way from the humiliation of slavery to the honor and responsibility of the Christian pastorate, have never moved him from his steadfastness. "Uncle Stephen," the patriarch of seventy years, and an honored superannuate of the Delaware Conference, still lives to take his occasional turn as lookout on board "de ole ship," but says he is "roundin' de cape an' nearin' de port."

Very soon after his conversion, Steve graduated to his position as one of the foremen in the shipyard and upon the plantation. When he was twenty-five years old, his mother died; and soon after, Rachel, a dusky maid of the plantation, by consent of the master and the kindly office of the senior preacher of Annamessex circuit, was taken to the cabin by the riverside to be the partner of his joys and sorrows. Here, in the course of a few years, three little slaves, they called their children, were added to "Mars Jeems'" estate.

At length an irrepressible longing for freedom moved Steve to make a proposition to his master to purchase his liberty. Could he but get free, he thought he could, in course of time, also "buy the time" of his wife and children, and thus leave to his descendants a heritage of manhood. His master would not consent to an absolute sale, but said: "Steve, I shall not probably live very long: pay me eighty dollars a year while I live; and at my death my will will make you free." He accepted the offer, and immediately hired himself to another party, who, at this time, was managing the ship-yard; and, besides meeting his obligations to his master, laid by a considerable sum every year as the nucleus of his future fortune. With these accumulations, he finally purchased a lot of his master, and built himself a comfortable cabin. Under the slave code, no title to property could be given to a bondman; but the instrument that was to make him a freeman was also to secure to him his little home.

Said Stephen to his master one Christmas day: "Mars Jeems, has ye eber fixed dat bisness of our'n?"

"No, Steve," said his master, "but I'm going to do it on New Year's day. Come, take a little Christmas apple toddy with me."

"No, thankee, Mars Jeems," said he; "ye knows I got 'nuff dat stuff dat day in yer office, when I was a boy. I promist you, an' I promist de Lord, I'd neber do so no more. An' furdermore, ye knows I's a 'zorter in de church now, an how'd dat look—de brown jug in de pulpit! Hyah, hyah, hyah! No, Mars; ye must 'scuse me."

"Mars Jeems"—rarely sober of late years at any time—entered, that Christmas day, upon a prolonged debauch from which he never recovered. *Delirium-tremens* ensued; but, at length, after weeks of anxiety on the part of his family, he seemed about to regain his health. Finally, one March night, he retired, apparently in full possession of his normal faculties, to awake next morning a raving maniac, in which hopeless condition, after a few weeks, he left this world.

Stephen was a sincere mourner at his master's grave. They had been playmates in childhood, and companions in youth. With the exception of a few instances of cruelty, for which no doubt the master was afterwards sorry, his bearing and conduct had been considerate and kindly. But, alas! that master was himself a slave to evil habits and died a prisoner in hopeless chains. To Stephen, however, there was one consolation. He was now a freeman and a freeholder! His master had secured the presence of an attorney at his home, on New Year's day; and, it was generally supposed, had made suitable disposition of his business affairs. At length, however, one of the heirs assured Stephen that his master had left no will and no papers or memoranda whatever touching his case; that the attorney who was present on New Year's day found him mentally disqualified for business; and that it would be the sworn duty of the Administrator to return him in the schedule of appraisement as a part of the personal estate.

Poor Stephen's heart sank within him. From the summit of manhood's royalty, in which for a brief day he had rejoiced; from the heights of a glowing expectancy irradiating all his future, he went down, down to the uttermost depths of a helpless and hopeless bondage! In the sixteen years his master had lived after selling him his time, he had paid him thirteen hundred dollars for his promised freedom; and had invested besides about four hundred dollars in the lot he had purchased and its improvements. By the absence of a will with the promised title, all this too reverted to the estate. A correct estimate of justice would have induced Christian heirs to have carried out the contract; to have said to the disappointed and sorrowful man: "Go in peace;" but the descendants of the honorable house of W—— gauged their notions of equity and justice by what the frigid technicalities of the law permitted. In this decision they were greatly strengthened, the following Sunday, by a sermon from the Rector of the parish church on the text: "All things whatsoever ye would that men should do unto you, do ye even so to them." The learned divine was himself a slave-owner. In his exegesis, he applied the rule to all the relations of life on this wise: "Whatsoever ye, being in the lawful condition of slaves, would that men should do unto you, *as subjects of a lawful servitude*, so do ye, as slaves, to those younger or less influential servants over whom, for the time, ye are appointed by your masters as overseers! And so do ye, as masters, to your slaves!" Of course, this was simply saying, The law of might, that makes some men slaves and some others masters, is right; the entire slave code is right because it is law. If a man is under that law he ought to be satisfied with his condition. He ought to want to be dealt with according to the laws and usages of slavery. His interpretation meant that because a human being had been wrongfully deprived of his kingdom of manhood, he ought to smother his instincts, trample on his crown of royalty, and obliterate God's image from his soul! As well might one say that the flame shall cease to ascend or gravitation lay aside its forces! The reputation of the Rector, however, was thenceforth assured; and these lawful heirs of poor Stephen's life and labors, "in love and charity with their neighbors, and following God's commandments," could, with one hand, take the holy communion, and with the other appropriate the property and the soul and body of a defenceless brother, redeemed by the same Sacrifice whose shed blood they were celebrating.

The heirs to the estate explained both the Law and the Gospel, bearing on the case, to Stephen, in justification of their course; and the poor negro was utterly bewildered. He, however, as he said, "left it all wid de Lord," and resolved if possible to retrieve his broken fortunes. Being put up for sale, at the vendue of the personal estate, for the term of one year, with the privilege to extend the term; by permission of the Administrator, he bid himself off at one hundred and twenty dollars a year for life. He then rented of the heirs his own house and lot, and was permitted to take his wife and children with him, on condition that he would support them; and thus, while rearing a family of slaves for the market, relieve the owners of the expense of their maintenance. It took very hard work, almost night and day, on the part of both Stephen and Rachel, to pay the price of their precarious liberty and support the family; but the obligations were all faithfully met, and something accumulated towards another effort for real freedom.

This condition of affairs lasted for three years. Meantime, while two other souls were born into slavery in the little cabin, the three elder children had grown to be valuable. Very strangely the W——— estate had so dwindled in the interim, and the farming had been so unremunerative, that in order to keep up their accustomed style, the family found it necessary to dispose of some property in exchange for ready cash. Stephen's wife and three elder children were singled out as the victims. While eating their frugal meal, one day, two men came to the cabin and notified Rachel that she could have a half hour to bundle up such clothing as she thought necessary for her and the three children; and that then, in obedience to orders received from the family, they must separate her and the older children from her husband and the two little ones, and take them to the slave pen at Princess Anne, to be inspected by the traders preparatory to the day of sale. From the scene that ensued, angels must have turned away their sympathetic eyes. The prayers and wailings of the stricken parents and children were heart-rending. For a few moments wife and children, clinging to husband and father, begged the protection the law of nature and of God would seem to have placed in his keeping. And then, when rudely thrust away by the interposing "officers," the poor mother, with streaming eyes, fell on her knees; and, wringing her hands in the anguish of despair, cried out: "Oh, Jesus! pity an' help dis po' slave wife an' mudder, an' her lone 'panion an' 'stressed chil'n. Oh, Lord! how kin I go 'way from my po' little babies!" Heaven and earth seemed to be deaf to her wail. In a little while, she and the three older children, tied together and hurried on before the men, who were on horseback, passed out of sight of the desolate cabin and the heart-broken man at the door. Gathering the two little ones in his arms, Stephen fell on his knees by the rough stand, whereon lay his old Bible, and cried out: "O, dou God ob dis Book—dou whom I trust an' love,— why has dou fo'saken me!" And then, obeying a sudden impulse, and taking the little motherless waifs with him, he sped to the plantation mansion to intercede for his wife and children. His entreaties, however, were in vain. In fact, the family, incensed at what they called his "impudence," threatened that they would "turn him into money too," if he didn't behave more respectfully.

Having obtained permission to leave the two little ones in the care of old Aunt Dinah at the "Quarters," Stephen returned to his cheerless home; secured his few possessions as best he could; took the one hundred and fifty dollars he had saved in three years from its hiding-place, and went forth praying God to help him in the rescue of his wife and children. Before the night of the day following, he found three kind-hearted men, who agreed to purchase the children, so as to keep them in the neighborhood; and a fourth, who promised to lend him a sum sufficient to enable him to become the redeemer of his wife from bondage. The sale was to take place in Princess Anne the following Tuesday. Stephen was there at an early hour, vainly seeking an interview with his distressed wife. He was rejoiced, however, in due time, to meet all the gentlemen who had promised to aid him. At length the ringing of the auction-bell announced the hour of sale; and, in a little while Stephen's wife and children, with some other slaves, emerged from the prison and were led to the auction-block. Poor Rachel scarcely lifted her dejected eyes, from which the tears of an unutterable agony were silently falling; and the distressed children sent forth their plaintive wailings. The scene was so pathetic that some of the spectators were constrained to retire from the locality, and the eyes of some who remained were moistened with sympathetic tears.

Stephen stood a little in the rear of the group, and was unobserved by his heart-broken family. He shall tell the story in his own way:

"While I was a standin' dar a prayin' fo' de good Lord to stan' by me in dis hour ob need; an' while de auctioneer was a tellin' 'bout de age ob my wife, an' a braggin' on her counastution an' fine qualitycations; one o' dem 'bruited, red-nosed nigger-buyers as was dar, he come up to my wife an' takes her by de chin an' nose to open her mouth so he could 'zamine her teeth, like she was an ole hoss or mule, de same time sayin' 'Well, ole mare, le's look at yer teeth ;' an' I tells ye, folkes, it was more'n dis chile could stan'. I got mad; I felt de bery Debil all through my blood an' bones; an' I took one step to hit him wid de heavy club I had; when the Marster he speak to de ragin' storm in my sould an' it come calm in a minit. An' right den an' dar de Lord saved me more'n I'd eber bin saved before, an' I foun' myself a whisperin' to myself, 'Dou shill keep dem in perfeck peace, whose heart am stayed on dee.'

"Well; den dey went to biddin'—the Georgia men an' my friend; an' dey run'd her up from two hundred dollars to five hundred—dat was Mars Neddy Payne's bid fo' me—an' den de trader he come up an' slap my po' wife on de shoulder, an' poke her in de sides an' breast, an' feel her mussel; an den he put on another twenty-five dollah bid, an' Mars Neddy he made it thirty. Den de trader wait some time; but bime bye he say five hundred an' thirty-three dollahs, an' Mars Neddy say 'five thirty-five.' Den de trader he say suffin' 'bout fools an' went off; an' a little while arter, de auctioneer he say, 'goin'–goin'–goin', three times; and——gone!' an' de nex' moment, honeys, I had Rachel in my arms, an' we bofe forgot we wasn't in de meetin'-house, an' begun to shout an praise de Lord. But de crier ob de sale fetch me a whack wid his stick, an' say, 'Hold on ole man; dis my meetin'.' Den de chil'n was sold. De boy fotch four hundred; de oldest girl three fifty, an' de little one three hundred dollahs; an' de gemmens was all true to dere words an' bought 'em; an' dey lem'me take 'em home wid me, same as afore.

"Mars Neddy he paid de four hundred an' I paid de hundred an' thirty-five dollahs, an' den I gibs him my wife till I could pay 'im de four hundred. Rachel went out washin'; I worked in de shipyard all day, an' cotch oysters or made an' 'paired shoes half de night; an' in four years time I had Mars Neddy nearly paid off. 'Bout den de family needed some mo' funs', an' dey makes up der minds to sell me. When I hearn about it I wus in a mighty trouble; but de Lord he'd allers helped me, an' so Sat'day night I went out inter de pine thicket, 'way off, an' prayed an' wrasseled all night dat de Lord would help me dis one time mo'. 'Bout de break ob day, jes as I seed a little streak o' light 'way off in de east, it seem to me mighty strong arms got under me, an' a voice whisper 'Cast di burden on de Lord an' he will 'stain dee;' an' chil'n, when I waked up de sun was 'way up an' a shinin' right down in my face! Den I went to de cabin kind o' peaceful like, an' Rachel she say, 'Steve, where's ye bin?' 'Ise bin a prayin,' to git the vict'ry,' sez I; for I didn't want Rachel to know de trouble afo' de time. 'Well,' sez she, 'I thinks ye'd better git de victory in de day time heresomeafter;' but she didn't know how dark dat night was, and how much I needed de victr'y right den.

"Well, dat mornin' me an' Rachel went to meetin' at de ole Saint Peter's Church down by Mr. Coulburn's creek. De preachah's tex war, 'Light am sowed fo' de righteous, an' joy fo' de upright in heart;' an' it seem to me de clouds got thinner, but I couln't see yit which way de sun was a goin' to come through at; but I was a watchin an' a prayin'. After meetin' a gem'man by de name of William R——, —a nigger trader's agent— he call me one side an' say, 'Steve, do you know you've got to be sold?' Sez I, 'Yes, sir, I've hearn so.' 'Well," sez he, 'what ye doin' fo' yourself?' An' sez I, 'I don' know what to do.' An' den sez he, 'You come over an' see me to-night.' So dat night I goes over, an' Mr. R—— gib me a 'greement in writin' fo' me to git gem'men to sign, bindin' 'em to help me buy myself; 'an' now,' sez he, 'you go an' see how many you kin git to sign it.'

"So den I started. I had two weeks afo' de sale. I went as fur as I could o' nights, an' got a few to sign it. When Sunday come, it was a dark rainy day, an' I walked all day from one to anudder till I was bout gib out; but I got sev'el mo' signers; an' dey all promist to keep it secret; for de family wanted to git me out'n de way; 'cause while I was dar, dey was all de time 'minded 'bout der treatment o' me; an' 'sides when de neighbors seed me, dey gen'ly had somethin' to say 'bout de treatment. Ef de fam'ly 'd a knowed what I was a doin', dey'd a sold me right off, or a put me in de pen.

"Fine'ly I got all de names but one. Dar was a near neighbor ob de family dat was one o' der 'tickler frien's. His son was a grown up young man an' had money, an' wanted to help me, but his father wouldn't agree to it. But de young man he say to me one night, 'Stephen; ef ye do all ye kin, an' jest lack one man to 'scribe twenty-five or fifty dollahs, you come to me, an' I'll stan' by you; but I don' want de ole gemman to know it.'

"Well, it turn out I couldn't git along widout his name. It was de las' night I had to work afo' de sale. Dere was three great ferocial dogs, dat was mighty dangersome, an' it war a'most wo'th a man's life to go dar in de night. But I went a prayin' de Lord to 'tect me. Dere was anudder difficulty: I didn't know what room de young gem'man slep' in, an' it wouldn't do to wake de ole man. So I prayed, 'O, Lord, take charge o' de dogs' mouths, an' 'rect my steps, an' keep ole Mars Ward fast asleep.' Den I went to de eend ob de house, under a upper winder, an' give three thumps on de weatherboardin'; an' de nex' minit here come one o' de dogs a trottin' roun' de corner! I was terrible skeered; but I chirup'd to him, an' he come a waggin' his tail an' begun to lick my hand. Jes' den de winder raised, an' young Mars Tommy Ward put his head out an' kind o' whispered, 'Dat you, Uncle Stephen? All right; I'll be dar in a minit.' So he come out, wid a pencil, an' put de paper up agin de house an' writ his name; an' den I jes' cotch de boy in my arms an' cried fo' joy, an' said, 'Lord, bress an' 'ward dis deah boy fo' his kindness to a po' slave.' Afo' I left, I had it all 'ranged wid him dat he was to 'tend de sale an' bid me off, an' also collec' de 'scribed money an' fix all de business, de which he done so.

"Well, when de day 'rived, de officer come 'bout light, when I was a eatin' my pone an lasses; an', sez he, 'Ole man, I'se got orders to take you an' de two little niggers to Princess Anne.'

"'What fo', mars?' sez I. 'You've got to be sold,' sez he. 'Oh!' sez I, 'not the po' babies, I hope! Dey won't fetch any money hardly.' 'Can't help it,' sez he. 'I've got de orders from de family.'

"An' den Rachel, she begun to take on fo' sartin, an' pray an' beg; but it warn't no use. She had to go to de little trunnel bed, an' pull de po' babies out an' put on der close, afo' dey got wide awake; an' wid her tears a rainin' down on der po' little, 'stonished faces, Rachel gived 'em a mudder's last kiss ob 'fection an' a hunk o' co'n pone; an' den we was tore away from her 'stracted clingin', an' hurried off down de path to de road.

"Ef it hadn't a bin fo' de po' little chil'n, I should a told Rachel I 'spected to git back to her; but I was so 'stracted 'bout dem,—'cause not knowin' de 'tentions o' de family, I'd made no 'vision to save 'em,—dat I neber thought 'bout myself. Fact is, ef I'd a bin sure we'd all a gone to de same neighborhood in Georgy or Caroliner, I'd a give up buyin' myself, an' gone wid 'em, to take keer o' de po' little things; but dere was no chance fo' dat; an', 'sides, de good Lord had helped me in de plan to buy myself, an' I reckoned it was best to carry it out, an' trust him to take keer ob de dear little babies in de strange land.

"Well; when de boy was sold a gemman from de Souf bought him; an' den I begun to pray de Lord dat he might 'duce him to buy de little sister; fo' he was a nice lookin' man. So I cotch his eye an' beckon to him, an' he come to me; an' I told him to please to buy de little girl an' keep 'em togedder an' teach em to be good, an' dat I would pray fo' him an' dem as long as I lived. Den he promist me, an' told me he was tryin' to sarve de same Marster, an' dat he would try to bring 'em up right; an' aldo de tears run'd down my face, I felt a mighty comfort. I knowed po' Rachel would feel better too on dat resurance. Shore 'nuff de gemman bought de sister; an' den de auctioneer call me to de block. Mr. R—— had 'vised me not to shave, so dat de white in my beard would make me look old an' I wouldn't sell so high; de which I done so. 'Cept fo' dis, I 'spec' I'd a fotch a thousan' dollahs. But young Mars Tommy Ward was dar as he promist, an' he bid me off fo' six hundred an' eighty dollahs. Mr. R—— told me after de sale dat he 'swaded de traders dat was a biddin', not to go bery high fo' a old nigger like me.

"When I got de matters all fixed up by de help o' Mars Tommy, it war about night. I wanted to see de little chil'n afo' I left; so I went to de hotel, an' de gemman dat bought dem gim'me a note to de keeper, an' when I went in de po' little things was a playin' wid some ole blocks on de floor. Little Neddy he say, 'Pappy; is ye gwine ter take us home to mammy now?' An' dem words a most broke my heart. I'd a give up my life dat moment to a sent de dear babies back to der mudder's arms! But it warn't no use; so I knelt down an' took 'em to my 'stressed heart fo' de las' time. Den I prayed fo' strength; an' 'mitted de po' little slave orphans to de Lord; an' said, 'Be good Neddy; be good Rachie, an' de blessed Jesus, he'll be yer friend; an' bime bye yo'll git free an' come home to pappy an' mammy in Heaven. When ye git tired a playin', lay down togedder dere in de corner on dat ole bed kiver, an' go to sleep; an' ter-morry a nice gemman will come an' take you to live wid him in a purty house all full of nice things. Den dey axed: 'Is you an' mammy comin' too?' I kissed dem fo' de answer, an' tore myself away. It was de last kiss—de last sight ob der little wonderin' faces. I have neber laid my eyes on 'em since dat night; an' never got any tidins'. When de wah was ober, I went down to de Caroliners an' Georgy, an' 'quired an' wrote eberywhere, but I had to come home widout any tidins'. Der mudder was den gone to de better lan', an' maybe dey an' she'd got togedder agin, where der's 'no mo' tears, neider sorry nor cryin', kase de former things is passed away.'"

"Well, den I started to walk home, some twelve or fifteen miles. I'd had no dinner nor supper 'cept two ginger-cakes. Fact is, my grief fo' de po' chil'n made me almost forgit de wants ob natur; an' now, as I trudged along through de mud and de dark, I felt pow'ful weak like, and begun to think I should give out; but I kep' a prayin' an' a trudgin' until at last, 'bout midnight, I got home. All was dark in de cabin, an' it never looked so awful gloomy afore since de day dey took Rachel an' de udder chil'n away. I stopped and lisened. All was still at fust; den I heared a groan, an' dreckly anudder. It seem like de dyin' groan ob despair; an' I knowed jest what it meant. It was my po' heart-broken Rachel's all-night wrastle wid de angel, in de dreary land ob de inemy. So I steps up softly to de door an' tapped on it. Den all was still, an' I tapped agin. 'Who's dar?' sez a faint voice. 'It's me, Rachel,' sez I; an' de nex' minit de door was opened an' Rachel swooned away on de floor. When, at last, I got her fotched to, she 'turned her thanks to de Lord fo' bringin' me back to her, an' den axed about de babies. So I had to tell her all about de whole transaction, an' 'bout de partin' an' all; an' den we talked, an' prayed, an' cried, an' tried to say somethin' to comfort each udder all night long; an' in de mornin' —thank God fo' de mornin', it always comes sometime, somehow—in de mornin' we started on one mo' struggle fo' freedom an' de kingdom. Seven years from dat time I paid back de las' dollah fo' myself, an' it all 'mounted, wid de interest counted in, to 'bout twelve hundred dollahs."

Just after Stephen had paid the last dollar of the above obligation, the War of the Rebellion broke out; and in 1864, by the voluntary action of her loyal citizens, the chains of slavery were all broken, and Maryland became a free state. This event gave Stephen his three children, who had served in the neighborhood, all of whom were now about grown up; and, in the general rejoicing that ensued among the colored people, this Christian family, come up out of great tribulation, took a prominent part. Stephen had meantime graduated into the local ministry; and, by reason of accumulated years that rendered him venerable, he now began to receive the designation by which the colored people at that time were wont universally to express their reverential appreciation: he received the honorary degree of "Uncle." On the great watch-night occasion of Maryland emancipation, more fully described in another chapter, Uncle Stephen, it is said, selected the Jewish year of Jubilee as the foundation of his address, and ' 'livered a pow'ful 'scourse,' concluding after the following manner:

"Now, chil'n; some o' ye was born free; some o' ye was sot free; some o' ye God an' de 'Publicans has jest 'mancipated free; but, like de ole gineral said to de

'Postle, 'wid a great sum 'tained I dis freedom.' But, bress de Lord! anyhow, we's now all ob us got free. P'raps some feller say, 'Now I'm gwine ter do es I please.' But ye haint got no right to do es you please, onless ye please to do right. 'Mancipation don't turn you loose an' shet udder peoples up; nor put you bosses an' de ole owners slaves. Ef we all do de right way, de time will come bime-bye, when de chil'n an' gran'chil'n ob de ole marsters 'll jine our chil'n an' gran'chil'n in celeberatin' dis day same as de 4th o' July. Fo' dey'll find out arter awhile dis day 'mancipates dem same de which it do us.

"But, chil'n, I wants ter tell ye:—Der's a wosser bondage nor slavery ob de body. Dere am de bondage ob de sould to sin an' de Debil; an' some ob ye's a sarvin' old Satin, a doin' de dirtiest work in his kitchen an' hog-pen, an' not a gittin' nothin' but lyin' promises an' promisin' lies. De blessed Jesus, he 'mended de ole constitution an' sine an' seal it wid his blood; an' he open de do' an' say come forth to de juberlee; an' he bring along de Gospel train to take yer all to de heabenly land, wher we'll all be free an' happy, an' sing an' shout de juberlee forever; bress de Lord!"

Then, being himself a fine singer, Uncle Stephen led the assembly in the following song:

> "De Gospel train am a comin';
>   I hears her jest at hand;
> I hears de car wheels a movin' on;
>   Dey're a rumblin' through de land.
>   *Chorus.*—Git on board, childring;
>   Dere's room fo' many mo'.

"I thinks she'll halt a minit;
　She'll wood up on dis line;
She'll give ye time to step on board;
　An' yit she'll make her time.
　　Chorus.—Git on board, etc.

"I sees de injine banner,
　A flutt'rin' in de breeze;
It's a drippin' wid de Saviour's blood,
　And yit it floats wid ease.
　　Chorus.—Git on board, etc.

"De 'spences am not heavy;
　De rich an' po' are dare:
No second class on board dis train;
　No diff'rence in de fare.
　　Chorus.—Git on board, etc.

"Dere's Abraham an' Noah,
　An' all de prophets too;
An' all de saints from ebery land;—
　An' oh, what a heav'nly crew!
　　Chorus.—Git on board, etc.

"Bime-bye she'll climb de mountain,
　An' roun' de curve she'll fly;
An' blow de final toot, an' halt
　At de mansions in de sky.
　　Chorus.—Git on board, etc."

And during the remainder of that memorable night, Uncle Stephen and his fellow-servants in Christ celebrated their emancipation, as a race, from human bondage; while some there were of the bondmen of sin, who accepted the invitation of his exhortation and song; paid the fare in the surrender of self to Christ; were by him made "free indeed," and took passage for the heavenly city.

Not long after this event, a circus exhibited in Princess Anne. So universally did the laboring class patronize shows, that it was deemed impossible to do anything in the ship-yard; and a holiday was declared in order that all might feel free to avail themselves of the opportunity to see the circus. Uncle Stephen, believing that such exhibitions were injurious to his race, called together the ship-yard hands and others within reach; and proposed that, instead of visiting the circus, they hold an all-day meeting at the little chapel near Coulbourne's Creek. The invitation was accepted by a few, who, like those of old in the upper room, "continued with one accord in prayer and supplication," and with a similar result. A revival of remarkable power followed, in which a moral revolution was wrought among the colored people of that region, the good effects of which are still visible.

When toiling to pay for his own body, Stephen covenanted with the Lord that, if he would bless him with prosperity and help him finish the unnatural and wearisome task, he would then give himself wholly to the work of the Lord for the religious instruction and elevation of his race. But his success in business, for the accomplishment of the above purpose, caused him to lose sight of his promise. Money began to be attractive; and he set his heart on its accumulation. His faithful Rachel had meantime gone up to her reward, and a young wife had come to supply the vacant place. "Why," thought he, "can't I remain here, and lay up something for a rainy day, and do what I can for the salvation and elevation of my people in this neighborhood?"

The General Conference of the Methodist Episcopal Church, held in 1864, took the preliminary steps for the organization of the Delaware Conference; and when the plans were finally matured, and the list of local preachers, who were to form the nucleus, was published, the name of Uncle Stephen was among the number. Notice of this fact and of the place of meeting for organization was duly communicated to him, causing him great uneasiness. Everything was in the way: his business engagements and attractions; his young wife and child,—how could he take them out into a work so unpromising? And, besides, he was growing old—couldn't work long; and who was going to feed him and his family when he was worn out? Finally one Sunday, as the time neared for the conference meeting, Stephen stole forth from the cabin to a solitary walk, in which he hoped so to adjust the matter with his conscience, that he could remain where he was; when, suddenly, the hand of his young wife, who had softly stolen up behind him, was laid upon his shoulder. Addressing him, she said: "Stephen, when I 'cepted your 'posal an' married you, suffin' seem to whisper to me dat you'd become a trav'ler fo' de Lord; an', mind wot I tells you, man, cf de Lord calls you, you'd better pull up stakes an' go. Wherever he takes you to, I'm willin' to go wid you."

This message and assurance from his wife broke the chains of the world's influence; took the burden of anxiety off his heart, and started him out with joy upon his career as a Methodist itinerant. Though beginning late in life, and without even the rudiments of literary culture, Stephen made good use of his opportunities; and, in his present conversation little of the Negro dialect of his former bondage can now be detected. Full of interest indeed has that career been; and great is the temptation to still further pursue the interesting annals of this humble life; but having started with the simple design to chronicle the struggles of an enslaved unfortunate for freedom, and the reward that finally, after great discouragements, crowned his efforts, I must go to glean in other inviting fields of Peninsular history.

As the old soldier oft gathers his grandchildren about him, and tells the thrilling story of his exploits in the Indian or Mexican battles of long ago; so Uncle Stephen, leaning on his well-worn staff, and looking back over the eventful field in which he has demonstrated his heroic manhood, loves to recall and relate in detail the incidents of his humble but victorious life. But his toilsome journey is nearly ended, and the wayworn traveller expects, ere long, to lay him down to peaceful rest. May his eventide be as serene and blessed as his morning and midday were stormy and sorrowful.

CHAPTER IX.

OLD TIME SCHOOLS AND SCHOOLMASTERS.

HOW time flies! A single flash of memory illumines all the intervening chasm. One single step of thought, and I stand again on the strand of childhood's orient, looking forward with inquiring vision into the gorgeously tinted and promising, yet mysterious and wonderful future. Forty-eight years ago, leaving my little four-year-old, playmate sister, Sadie, in the old farm homestead with mother, I, the only brother, trudged bravely by the side of my two older sisters, to the newly opened country school, in the new neighborhood, in Caroline County, Maryland, where my honored father had recently settled. How big I felt! I was no longer a baby; I was a boy—a big boy! Long time ago—a whole year before—I had graduated from frocks to pantaloons! I wore a brand new pair of red-topped, long boots, with my pantaloons legs tucked into them, so that the fancy tops would be visible, and impart to the wearer an aristocratic air. And now I was big enough to start to school! "Bully for me!" thought I.

The school was but a quarter of a mile distant from home; but to our childish fancies it was so far, that mother—dear, sweet mother—gratified us by putting up our dinners in a little basket. There was some nicely fried chicken on a little plate; then eight or ten large Maryland biscuit; then, nestling at one side carefully, a cup of nice, clear, strained honey, with paper tied over it to prevent spilling in case of accident; and a knife and spoon, topped off with three large gingercakes; and over all was tucked a snowy napkin. Only big sister Retta could be entrusted with that precious basket; and Emma and I cast many interested glances towards it, as, hand in hand, and bearing the books, slates and inkstand, with goose quills to make pens, we proudly marched along the winding highway, under the leafless branches of the great white oaks which bordered the farther side.

At last, with a gathering group of expectant children and youth of from five to twenty-one years of age, we stood before the open door of the new school-house. Not that the word *new* describes the house: very far from it; but the *school* was new; the school-master was a new arrival in the neighborhood; and the house was newly and for the first time used for so noble a purpose. Will the reader believe it? The house was really a deserted negro cabin, that stood by the highway-side near Townsend's Cross Roads, three miles from Denton, the county town. For an area of twenty-five square miles between that town and the Delaware line, this was the only school; and this was started by a private subscription managed by my father. The Maryland law, at that time, liberally provided that if the people of a neighborhood would subscribe for the tuition of twelve scholars at five dollars each, then the State would furnish a like amount for the education of the same number of "charity scholars." There were no public provisions for school houses; and whether there was house or school, depended altogether upon the character of the population that, amid rural mutations, might happen to gather in any given neighborhood.

This new school and every school in that region for several years, was in a rented house. This particular house was built of logs, the interstices being filled with clay to keep out wind and rain. It was eighteen or twenty feet square, and about eight feet to the eaves; with a door front and back, each opening outwards. Midway between the doors and the north end where stood the chimney, at a convenient height, part of a log was sawed out, the aperture being filled with a three-light hanging window, which, as occasion required, could be propped up for ventilation.

Where the chimney stood, was an aperture six feet wide and four feet high, into which the stone and mud walls of the fire-place were built, to a height above where the blaze of the great log fire would usually reach; and, above that point, the flue was made of logs and sticks, liberally daubed within of clay. Though not one of the wonders of the world like the "Tower of Pisa," this chimney had yielded to northerly attractions, until its centre of gravity had become endangered; and its former sable proprietor had prudently interposed the safeguard of a stout prop, thus holding the discouraged chimney to the performance of its duty. At the south end of the house, in order to adapt it to its use as a literary institution, almost an entire log had been removed. This aperture was covered by a wide board, fastened by hinges to the log above, and secured to that below by staple and hook. Like the sash before mentioned, this board was propped up to admit needed light and fresh air. Just below this aperture was the writing desk, extending across the room against the wall. Here, alternately, the girls and boys made "pot-hooks and hangers" with their goose-quill pens, after the pattern set by the teacher; and finally graduated to the distinguished accomplishment of being able to draw a note of hand or receipt for "ten dollars, good and lawful money of the United States of America," and to affix thereto their own, real, written signatures. The teacher "set the copies" during the noon hour; but made and mended pens at all hours, when they happened to be presented for that purpose. Hence the name still so commonly applied to the pocket knife. It was not unusual to see the teacher dividing his time and attention between a page of Comly's Spelling-book, where some sweating pupil was painfully struggling with the problems of orthography, and the quill he was slitting and whittling; meanwhile, stealing an occasional moment for a furtive glance about the school-room, to see that there was no pinching, or pin-sticking, or snickering behind books or slates, going on among the unruly urchins.

In addition to the so-called writing-desk, the furniture of this school-room consisted of a desk and chair for the teacher, and three or four slab benches across the end of the room, next the writing-desk. In cold weather, a bench was set near the great fireplace, and was occupied by alternate platoons of the shivering scholars to thaw themselves out. Three formidable hickory rods, of varying size and length, adapted to the sex and size of the culprits; and a pretty, little, red maple switch, suited to the æsthetic tastes and tender sensibilities of the smaller urchins, completed the outfit. In addition to this, however, in this particular school, were the few personal effects of the teacher and family—a table, a few broken chairs; a pot, kettle, oven and frying-pan; and last of all, but first in importance, his worthy but grunting spouse and equally grunting pig. The good dame tried hard, but in vain, to impress upon the mind of his swineship, that his proper sphere, during school hours, was outside, making nasal investigations in the swamp near by the back door. But, contrary to the usual proclivities of his species, his preferences were decidedly for association with the *literati;* and, when excluded, his persistent song of reproachful complaint, rendered feelingly in O sharp and Y minor, quite often necessitated his readmission; when he would stretch himself before the fire and grunt his satisfied assent to all his master's edicts. Tom, the teacher's son, was enrolled among the advanced pupils. He could spell most of Comley's hard words "by heart," and was equally well versed in the *classic* vocabulary of the denizens of the thickets and swamps, who gathered at John Jones' at the Cross Roads every Saturday afternoon, to hold shooting-matches and drink hard cider. He could work problems in compound multiplication, either in the Arithmetic, or in trouble and embarrassment in his mother's domestic arrangements. In a word, Tom played the leading part in the school exercises and recreations, and played—the mischief generally.

Well; in this one-roomed kingdom, our enthroned master lived and wielded the rod; gave his orders; heard the reading and spelling lessons, and looked over the examples worked or attempted by the advanced scholars; and, at the same time, his good wife baked the "johnnie-cake" and fried the bacon for dinner, or washed up the dishes and did her darning and patching. She was an antiquated and demure matron, who wore a white cap and spectacles, gliding almost noiselessly about the school-room kitchen, except when, occasionally, she came into collision with the pig, or with Tom, when detailed by her for some temporary domestic service; such as fetching wood or water, or, perchance, paring potatoes and turnips.

Mr. Marshall, the schoolmaster, was the fitting counterpart of such a spouse. He bore his distinguished honors meekly, yet with becoming dignity. He was evidently impressed with the importance of his office to the neighborhood and to himself; and to see him, as, at 9 A. M., he assumed the throne and issued his peremptory command to cease the games and resume studies in the emphatic pronunciamento — "Books!" and then supplemented it with an explosive "Silence!" that fairly made the cabin tremble, would have impressed the beholder that our teacher was consciously one of the main pillars of the American Republic. And so he was—in that corner.

Mr. Marshall's clean shaven face—for only rowdies wore beards in those good old times—was furrowed over with many wrinkles of benevolence and care; and the friction of many anxious years had polished his bald head until it had become a favorite skating rink for the festive house fly. One little patch of iron grey hair remained in front above his pug nose, which was combed up and carefully trained into a sort of drake-tail ornament; and the little remaining on either side above his ears, was twisted into little tufts, sticking out at right angles, and giving him somewhat of the appearance of a nondescript animal of the baboon persuasion with three horns. The grotesque effect was heightened by the presence of an immense pair of brass-bowed spectacles which alternately bestrid his nose, and adorned his bald and glistening pate—all fit index to the vast library of knowledge entombed within that venerable skull.

The entire curriculum of our school was covered by the three cabalistic letters, R. R. R., understood to represent the three great sciences, "Readin', Ritin' and Rithmetic." The three G's—Grammar, G'ography and

G'ometry, had then scarcely been dreamed of as ever possible to be taught in a country school. It was not until several years after—not indeed until the renowned "Chinquepin" school-house had been built, over a mile away on the road to "Punch Hall"—that we ever heard of such a study as English Grammar, or Geography.

The Primer or rather *a* primer—for it mattered not what it was, so there were A, B, Cs in it—was the text book most in demand in Mr. Marshall's log-cabin school. Mine had a red cover, and grotesque wood cuts, that, in my juvenile eyes were wonderful. As there were no two primers alike, the large class in first principles was heard one at a time, occupying nearly one-half of the master's time. His method of teaching A, B, Cs, was to point, with a little stick he kept for the purpose, to each letter in regular order, call its name, and require us to pronounce the name after him. As his time was divided between pointing to the letters and watching Billy Wadman, Dick Sorden, Bill Dan'l Roe, Sally Price, *et al.*, it not infrequently happened that the urchin reciting was looking anywhere else than at the alphabetical forms pointed out, and called in turn, by the master himself. It required most of the winter for many of us to learn to distinguish these different signs of sound. My great trouble was with the first letter; but I soon became such a scholar, that when Mr. Marshall, out of all patience with the ever-recurring hitch at the beginning of my recitation, would stamp his foot and yell "*A!*", I would repeat the provoking name, and then go right on, with the precision of clockwork, to the close at Z.

Finally, at the end of three weeks, he concluded I was sufficiently well drilled in first principles to proceed to "my a, b—abs." But, lo! when he pointed to A, on the new page, there was the same old hitch. Again he yelled "A!" Again I repeated A, and followed it with B, from force of habit; when my patient teacher arrested me with the inquiry: "What's A B spell?" "C," answered I, supposing the next letter in the old routine was the proper thing in the new regime. Then, to my disgust, Mr. Marshall turned me back to the old page, and began pointing at the letters promiscuously; when he at last discovered his promising pupil had wasted his time learning the names of the letters in rotation, whose forms he was utterly unable to distinguish. Having thus at last discovered his own faulty method, my teacher continued the promiscuous exercise, until, in a few days thereafter, he had the satisfaction of graduating his pupil to the next page; he having mastered all the alphabetical forms and names, even to that of letter A.

The following dialogue, literally correct to the best of my memory, will illustrate our schoolmaster's method of teaching spelling:

"Come here, John Linsey Breeding. Where's your lesson, sir?"

"Them's 'em."

"Well, go on, sir."

"A, B."

"That's not B, you numskull—D!"

"A, D, Izzard."

"Izzard, the—dog's foot! Where were you born? Some fool must have been your teacher—who was it?"

"Daddy teached me my A, B, C's; and Mammy——"

"Yes—ah—well, that's not Izzard. Call that letter Zedd or Zee. Now, go on, sir."

"A, D, Zedd or Zee—"

"Haint you got no sense, John Linsey? I didn't tell you to call that letter two names; but one or the other—Zedd or Zee. Call it Zee, dunce; and hurry up with it."

"A, D, Zee, dunce."

"Well—well! Don't you beat the—the Injins?"

"Don' no—spect so."

"Call that letter *Zee!* Now, go on."

"A, D, Z, E—A, D, Z, E—"

"Well?"

"A, D, Z, E, well."

"It isn't *well* at all, you goose! I meant to ask you what A, D, Z, E, spells."

"I don' know; d'you?"

"What does your daddy dig out his pig trough with? Now spell it."

"A, D, Z, E, grubbin-hoe!"

In the roar of laughter that ensued, kind-hearted Master Marshall was compelled to join.

As a general rule, scholars were not permitted to attempt reading until they had mastered the spelling-book, even to the long words, like "concatenation, hieroglyphically," etc.; and our next teacher invented a test word, it was necessary for the pupil to master, before he could take up the initial reading lessons about the Wren, the Robin Redbreast and the Lion. This test word was —*Honorifticabilitudeanditatibusque!* When the pupil could repeat and spell this huge medley of nonsense, going back, at each syllable, and pronouncing up to and including the last syllable spelled in regular order, without a hitch or blunder until he reached the towering conclusion, he was graduated to reading.

After mastering the few reading lessons in the Speller, the next book in order was the "Introduction to the English Reader," and after that the "English Reader," provided the pupil could conveniently secure them. In Mr. Marshall's school, however, and for years afterwards in that neighborhood, the pupil brought whatever book he could secure from the meagre library of his humble home—not infrequently the New Testament. It was absolutely impossible for the teacher to arrange his pupils in classes; and consequently each one must needs be heard separately. The time being limited and the books generally of a grade too difficult for beginners, to facilitate matters Master Marshall usually read along ahead of the scholar, sentence by sentence, or a few words at a time; the pupil repeating after him, in drawling style, as correctly as a parrot. Of course, learning to read, or learning anything else, under circumstances like these, was incidental, if not accidental. In like manner, the beginner in mathematics was plunged headlong into the profundities of Pike's Arithmetic; two-thirds of whose examples, involving money values, were stated in pounds, shillings and pence. I have never ceased to have a most painful recollection of how, after I had mastered a few examples in the four cardinal rules in simple numbers, I was left to struggle bewildered amid the mazes of compound problems in English money, until I utterly lost faith in the utility of the science. Mr. Marshall, it was said, could "do all the sums in the 'Rithmetic." He was reputed to be a veritable Pythagoras at "figgerin'." He was, withal, very obliging to show his scholars how by "*doing* the sum," but he never explained it. It is doubtful indeed whether he could, having learned arithmetic as he taught it—simply by rote.

When Master Marshall's time expired he moved away; and, alas! I never saw him more. A colored woman moved into the classic hall; and father hired another deserted hut, a few hundred yards farther from our home, which was a little more sightly and comfortable than that above described. As to capacity, our new teacher, Mr. Nathan Wilson, was likewise a link in the ascending series. He was a Quaker, a quiet bachelor of about fifty years of age. Consequently he was peculiar —very peculiar, so people said. I only remember that he stipulated for but two meals a day at Samuel Dunning's where he boarded, to save a discount of one-fourth on the cost; and also that he did his own washing, ironing, patching and darning on Saturdays, and at other odd hours, from the same economical motives. He had had but one suit of clothes within the memory of his acquaintances. This suit was of grey Cassinette. When any portion of a garment belonging to this suit became threadbare, forthwith Master Wilson purchased a new piece of goods as nearly as possible of the same quality and shade; and removing the underneath side of the sleeve, the fronts of the pants, or the—any other part, he neatly inserted the new material. I remember well that the collar and lapels of his coat were thus renewed; and that when a rent, from a tussel hereafter described, occurred in one side of the skirt of his swallow-tailed coat, it was taken off and a piece much darker in shade substituted; and, as some part was continually giving way and being replaced, there came to be finally every imaginable shade of grey and every possible texture of Cassinette in that unique suit.

While Master Marshall's hickory rods were generally innocent ornaments, except as to poor mischievous Tom, and a few kindred spirits; Mr. Wilson's furniture, in that interesting line, was brought into constant requisition, and needed to be almost daily replenished. Neither nationality, age, sex or "previous condition of servitude" exempted any scholar, who was thought to have forgotten or disobeyed some rule; but I really believe his liberal use of the rod was inspired by conscientious convictions of duty. When the old Dutchman flogged his boy, Hans, he said, "Now, vot you dinks?" Hans replied,

"I don't gone dinks notin', sir." "Yaw, you do—you dinks cuss words, and I whips you agin." Perhaps, like Hans' devoted parent, our new teacher set himself to discover the ratiocinations of the average young American, in certain apparent states of abstraction or provocation; and thrashed him for the naughty thoughts he imagined would naturally come into his mind in any such given condition. Be that as it may, I solemnly aver, that for many of the floggings I received from this devoted friend and teacher—averaging nearly one *per diem* for a year—I found it impossible to discover any cause; and he was too quiet and dignified to explain. Again and again, as I sat unconscious of violating any of Master Wilson's rules; the hickory, pitched with the unerring aim of an aborigine, would roll from my person rattling down upon the floor. That performance meant a notification that it was now my interesting duty to take that switch back to the teacher's desk, and stand to receive the chastisement supposed to be needed for my intellectual development. Sometimes my next neighbor on the slab, being involved in the misdemeanor, real or imaginary; we were both required for the service of returning the projectile to the battery—one at each end; but, on arrival, the handle end was relinquished to Master Wilson, and we twain became active partners at the other end. Many solemn vows were made to have a settlement with Mr. Nathan Wilson, should we live to manhood's estate; but when that time arrived, we unanimously reconsidered and rescinded the resolution, esteeming it dishonorable to thrash a "non-combatant!"

Our teacher generally had it all his own way, and quietly enjoyed his favorite pastime; but I remember one exception, in which a regular set-to was the result of his attempt to inflict the penalty for breaking one of his rules upon the seventeen year old son of the old Quaker who boarded him; and who, so far forgot his pacific training as to resist the teacher's onslaught. The battle lasted fully five minutes.

All the slab benches, with the master's desk and chair, were overturned. Books, slates, ink-stands, hats and dinner-baskets were promiscuously scattered in beautiful confusion. The screaming girls and small boys mounted the writing desks for safety. When, finally, hostilities ceased, the rod had drawn blood from the Quaker boy's face and hands; and his teeth had drawn blood from the calf of our Quaker teacher's leg. The final scene in the tragedy exhibited George Fox Dunning lying discouraged under a bench; Nathan Wilson sunk down exhausted and panting into his chair, with trowsers nearly torn from his person, and minus one swallow-tail; and, alas! both teacher and pupil utterly back-slidden from the "testimony" of the Hicksite fathers. This battle took place in the morning, and so demoralized both belligerents and spectators, that during the entire day the school failed to recover its normal "*status quo ante bellum.*"

Master Wilson's curriculum was the same as that of

my first teacher; but his methods were better, and there could be no skulking. The pupil must know his lesson or take the consequences; and as, of the two evils, lessons gotten were preferable to consequences taken, we all learned "right smart" during the year we were subjected to his regimen. But, being deemed a little too warlike in his methods of preserving the peace in his domain, the trustees, at the end of one year, excused him from further service, and employed in his stead Mr. Elisha M——. This gentleman was not a Quaker. In fact he was, ecclesiastically, not anything in particular. But he was very kindly disposed towards his scholars. In avoiding the mistake of his predecessor, he swung to the other extreme, and thus saved himself, as well as his pupils, a world of worriment. Many a good, jolly time did he have, joking with the larger pupils and romping with the small boy, in the little log hut a mile from my father's house, on the road to "Punch Hall."

Master Elisha was not a man of one work. He was "handy with tools." He was a famous huntsman, capturing many a raccoon and opossum; and was equally renowned among the herring and shad fisheries of the Choptank, in whose activities he generally bore an important part. Furthermore, he was a professional politician; a loyal worker in his party; an excellent judge of brandy and rum, having tested about all the samples falling under his observation for the past twenty years; and now, for his distinguished services to his party, cooping and inspiring voters the night before the election, he had been recently appointed an honorable Justice of the Peace. His literary qualifications, however, were below even those of Master Marshall; and, worse than all, his intellectual perceptions were often befuddled by imbibing too freely of the contents of a mysterious bottle of "medicine" always gracing his lunch-basket, and used, he said, "to keep off the Ager." He used the rod occasionally, but in a benevolent and good-natured sort of way.

Although not more than eight or nine years old at the time of Master Elisha's reign, as to correct spelling and rapid reading, I was the most advanced scholar in the school, and could "do" most of the "sums" up to the Rule of Three; so that when, on Tuesdays, he went to hold Justice's Court in Denton, he left me in charge of the department of instruction, with one of the big boys, as secretary of war, to aid me in preserving the peace. Strange to say, the exercises usually proceeded in regular order, and the stammering recitations of boys and girls of all ages were faithfully heard and corrected by the juvenile and conscientious teacher; who was too profoundly impressed by a sense of the honor and responsibility, thus conferred, to betray his trust.

On such occasions, the behavior of the school was surprisingly good. Occasionally, however, the secretary of war for the time being, would enter into a conspiracy with some of his companions to get up a row, "just for fun, you know;" and a lively time was the result. It usually ended with a verdict from the extemporized jury in the case, that Bill Cahall, or Ned Sweedling, or Wes. Stafford was to blame for the deviltry, and must be flogged by the little teacher. Forthwith the secretary of war handed me the rod, hauled the offender before me, and I gave him the "ten lashes well laid on," according to the sentence of the regent. It was difficult to determine which was most amused—the school, the teacher, or the suffering convict.

A little after this time the school house at Chinquepin was completed. We thought it very fine in appearance and comfortable in its appointments. It was furnished with a writing desk on either side, instead of but one as heretofore; so that both boys and girls could write at the same time. There were six nice slab benches, three each for boys and girls; but all so high from the floor that the smaller children literally went to roost on a perch, whenever they *sat down*. Many a time when thus perched, trying in vain to shoot an ideal arrow athwart some mathematical chasm, my helplessly dangling feet, by reason of obstructed circulation, would feel as if pricked by a thousand needles; and the constant effort, by twisting and squirming, to relieve my discomfort, made my dear, patient mother an expert at patchwork. This new school house was furnished with a large ten-plate stove in the centre of the room. Altogether it was so very fine that there was much competition among country professors, as to who should have the distinguished honor of presiding at Chinquepin. The Trustees were really embarrassed with applications; and hit upon the happy expedient of settling the question of a teacher for the new school, by appointing Messrs. R., G., and S. a committee to examine the several candidates as to their fitness and qualifications. After several candidates had been disposed of by these erudite gentlemen, Mr. Samuel Wiseman, of Queen Anne County, whose name and appearance did well befit each other, presented himself, and profoundly impressed them. He introduced himself in a wonderful flow of high-sounding words; complimented the Trustees for "the profundity of their prudential philosophy, in requiring teachers to submit to a submission of their professional qualifications to the intellectual scrutinizations of gentlemen of your (their) distinguished cultivation and urbanity." He said he was glad "a new and ponderous epoch had dawned; and was rolling its triumphal car of Juggernaut along the ages." He believed they would "project a discrimination into their official prerogatives, that would lead to the broadest altitude of the mundane prosperity of their sectional advancement." He concluded with: "Here, gentlemen, is my certifickit, from the Trustees where I teached last year, of my literal capacity."

At this point Mr. G., with a dazed sort of demeanor, ventured the inquiry:

"Mr. Wiseman, what sort o' books kin you teach?"

His reply satisfied the entire Board. Said he:

"Gentlemen: I don't profess to be *compos omnium vincibus*—that is, like a quack doctor, to do everything better than everybody else; but what I do I *do*. I teach all the common branches, commonly teached in common schools; and, in addition, gentlemen, I teach G'ography, English Grammar, Orthography, Etymology, Syntax and Prosody!"

The Board was profoundly satisfied, and Mr. Wiseman was at once engaged. Notwithstanding his attainments and capacity, equalled only by his towering egotism, I do not remember that any of his fortunate pupils have ever reached any great distinction. Great privileges and opportunities do not usually long continue. It was so in this case. Mr. Wiseman's departure from Queen Anne County had so seriously affected some of her citizens, that a constable came one day and persuaded him to return; and, when last heard from, an appreciative public had provided him with entertainment and employment, better suited to his versatile talents, in a celebrated institution in Baltimore.

Our next teacher at Chinquepin was Mr. Marion Dawson—a really accomplished teacher for his day. In addition to the usual primary branches, he taught History, Geography, Grammar, and higher Arithmetic with Bookkeeping; and by the time his principalship was ended I was ready for graduation. Being now large enough to be very useful on the farm, I attended school only during the winter months; following the plow, and wielding the hoe and axe, or driving a team, during the remainder of the year. But when I was fifteen or sixteen years old, my father sent me to the Academy in

Denton, at such times as I could be spared, where I learned something further of the mysteries of literature; and completed my preparation for introduction to College life.

Let me assure the incredulous reader, these pictures of my school-boy environments and experiences are not overdrawn. Thousands now on life's western slope, who fifty years ago were Eastern-Shore-Maryland boys, can bear witness to the substantial correctness of this sketch. But the times have wonderfully changed; and similar facts and experiences are now impossible.

The boy who, from 1837 to 1844, struggled amid such difficulties, to open the windows of his being to God's and nature's light; twenty years thereafter, with like-minded compeers and compatriots, in State Constitutional Convention assembled at Annapolis, pleaded and voted successfully for a requirement in Maryland organic law, providing the means of liberal common-school education for all the State's children. Our constituents sent us there to make freemen of a hundred thousand slaves. We counted nearly three times that number of our fellow-citizens enchained by the bondage of ignorance; and among the proudest achievements of any representative body, was that bold stroke by which the Maryland Convention of 1864 opened the prison doors to the wronged bondmen; and, at the same time, opened the temple of knowledge to the admission of rich and poor at the expense of the commonwealth. No man or party has dared, or will ever dare that door to close. Through the valiant Union-men of that convention, God said, "Let there be light;" and, amid the brightening hours of our waning century, that light "shineth more and more unto the perfect day."

CHAPTER X.

HUMORS OF A MODERN ITINERANT.

ADDRESS TO BISHOP FOSTER.

IT is held by some that the pun is the lowest grade of wit; and, by dignified worthies, the punster is regarded as an intolerable nuisance, to be carefully avoided and scathingly denounced. Let the reader holding to this view skip the next few pages.

In 1878, the Wilmington Conference was held at Chestertown, Md., Bishop Foster presiding. The business of the session had closed; and the Bishop was about to address the Conference, preparatory to announcing the appointments, when one of the preachers arose; and, with an air of ominous solemnity, began an address. Under the impression that some unheralded storm was brewing, Bishop Foster knitted his brows, suspiciously watched the speaker, and prepared himself for a prompt and vigorous use of the gavel, should the rising storm threaten the peace and harmony of the conference. The transition in the Bishop's features, from sternness to a smile, and thence on to hilarity, was like the gradual blossoming of the distant dawning into the full-orbed day. The speaker's rebuke to the Conference for its unseemly merriment and his appeal to the President for the preservation of order, in conjunction with the spicy and humorous character of the address, were a little too much for the self-possession of the dignified *Episcopos;* and, freely unbending, he heartily echoed back from the platform the mirth of the ecclesiastical body before him. Meeting the author the following morning, he warmly thanked him for the address; said it had relieved him of a great burden, and requested its publication. It afterwards appeared in the *Christian Advocate.* The address was as follows:

"*Mr. President*: While doubtless you have received much light from your cabinet reflectors, I deem it proper at this deeply interesting point in our conference proceedings, to say some things to you that I think you ought to know, concerning our Peninsula, and the laborious and self-sacrificing ministers who occupy its territory. I trust I shall wound no brother's feelings; and if, in anything I may say, I shall seem to you to transgress the rules of propriety, you have only to call me to order, and I promise to be an obedient son in the Gospel.

"Our conference territory, Bishop, from the northern *McFar-lane* to the extreme southern *Towns-end*, is the garden spot of America. Except where our fields are already *White* unto the harvest, our pastures are *Green* and flowery, and our *Sheppard* is tender and kindly. The opportunities for *ministerial* usefulness are most inviting to our chief *Gardner* and our *Foreman*; while the *Lay-field* is also unsurpassed. There is no stagnant

Poole in all our bounds. Our healthful streams and broad, *Bryan*-y bays invite our *Fisher*-man; while our noble old camp forests afford ample scope for the dexterous cunning of our stalwart *Hunter*.

"The Southern portion of our territory is mostly a beautiful and fruitful plain. The upper half is varied by the *Ridge-way*, while still beyond rise the towering *Hills*, that ofttimes 'Skip like lambs,' and 'rejoice together.' Nestled between these, and smiling in its summer sweetness, is the *Martin-dale* where our conference warblers *Carroll*, and our C sharp *Bell* peals forth its joyous melody.

"We have a good *Mil-by* the Delaware Railroad, at Harrington, and our enterprising *Millers* grind and bolt the finest flour. Our *Smiths* are experts, and always 'strike while the iron is hot;'" not infrequently causing the *Sparks* to fly around, especially on Missionary Anniversary occasions.

"We repudiate the insinuation that we are an un-*Kemp*-t assembly. No conference craft is more gracefully *Rigg*-ed, or more ably *Mann*-ed. Besides, we are celebrated for *Prettymen;* and I assure you it is no paste *Jewell* that sparkles on our bosom. Our greatest *Bain* is a heavenly blessing; and he who most puts on *Ayres* is *A-very* modest man. Our milkman is a *Creamer;* and the supplies furnished by the *Chandler* of our conference yacht, are always done up *Browne*.

"We seldom get into a *Hough* about either our appointments or disappointments; but '*Dare* to do right,' and *Al-dred* to do wrong in every emergency. We transact our ecclesiastical business on the one *Price* principle, and have *Syphred* up our profits to the full amount of one English *Shilling*. Although lately we somewhat lost *Hart*, and are sometimes unable to see clearly our *Way*, at critical junctures; we have thus far managed to 'hoe our own *Roe*,' cheered by the assurance that both *England* and *France* will remain our unflinching allies. Whenever we see dangers threatening the Church, we always *Warner* to stick down her *Pegg* and *Barrett* bravely, until our noble *Redman* of the forest, tomahawk in hand, shall come to her rescue.

"The casks of our skillful *Cooper* are never used for beer at *Brewington;* but although we are a distinctly pronounced temperance organization, we always keep on hand for legitimate use a little *Todd*-y, which—should your arduous labors in the council require—shall be cheerfully placed at your disposal.

"I looked over our Conference roll, *Andrew* from the names therein these reflections; but regret my inability to weave the name of my friend *Hutch-in*, as well as those of many others, on account of their not being *Called-well*. I sincerely hope, that in consideration of our *Gray* heads, this little ebullition of impertinence shall be allowed to go *Scott*-free. In conclusion, Bishop, we hope ever to *Merritt* and enjoy your *Foster*-ing care."

OUR SENIOR BISHOP'S CANE.

At the session of the Wilmington Conference, held at Middletown, Delaware, under the presidency of Bishop Hurst, a committee, of which the writer was a member, was appointed to convey to Bishop Scott, then confined to his home a few miles distant by age and feebleness, the fraternal greetings of the Conference. During that visit I presented to our venerable Father in Israel, a cane I had made of wood taken from old Barratt's Chapel. It was inscribed, "To the Senior Bishop;" and it was the donor's intention that it should pass, as an heir-loom, down the venerable and apostolic line, until the last Methodist Episcopal Bishop shall be called home and crowned in the heavenly kingdom. The cane is now in the possession of our honored Bishop Bowman. May he retain it for many years, and, like Moses, never need its support, even in going up the heights of Pisgah to his ascension.

Accompanying the presentation of the cane to the veteran Bishop was the following address:

"*Bishop Scott:* It may be considered a very indecorous thing to assault a Bishop,—dastardly, indeed, when that Bishop, by reason of infirmity, is unable to defend himself. But, sir, I have come to-day to give you a good *caning;* and for this I claim ample justification.

"You well know, sir, that, many times, you have 'laid hands' on inoffensive brethren. You once laid hands on me; and why should I not, now that I have a good opportunity, retaliate? Let me assure you, you richly deserve what you are about to suffer at my hands, and the verdict of this committee and these visitors will sustain my conduct. As you are no ordinary offender, it is no ordinary caning I propose to give you.

"This cane, like the Wilmington Conference, is mostly a Peninsular production; but, like the said conference, it has enough imported material in its composition to symbolize the cosmopolitan character of Methodism.

"It is a plain, unpainted cane. In this it harmonizes with certain old-fashioned notions of our fathers against moral or social shams and veneers; the conviction that character is essentially real, unpainted—'most adorned when unadorned the most.' It is not, in itself, a very nice or valuable cane; but to me it is nice, and pretty, and of great worth. It is partly because God made us, I think, that he finds so much in us to interest him. So I like this cane, for one reason, because my own hands shaped and polished it.

"This cane is taken from a Methodist Episcopal Church building that has stood one hundred and two years, and that probably will continue to stand until the 'Gospel of this kingdom shall be preached in all the world as a witness unto all nations;' and therefore it may be interpreted to point to the conclusion that Methodism has come into the world to stay throughout all the centuries.

"From its position in that old Church, this cane helped echo the voice of the first Methodist Bishop who ever proclaimed salvation in America. It is intended that the last one in that line of honorable succession shall lean upon it, as, bending with age, he looks up from the last hour of the last day of the last century to behold Messiah's glorious coming.

"In our version of the Scriptures, we read that Jacob, the aged Patriarch, 'worshipped, leaning on the top of his staff.' Our Roman Catholic friends translated it: 'Jacob worshipped the top of his staff.' If a Methodist Patriarch should reverently uncover his head and cross himself before this relic, more holy than any in the Vatican, who shall find fault of his Methodist high-churchism, when it is explained that this staff is *made of timber from old Barratt's Chapel?*

"There is an inscription on this silver band. By a singular coincidence, that inscription was engraved by a Presbyterian brother, who, more than fifty years ago, was wont, sometimes, to run away from his own church home to seek a little genial warming at the good Methodist fire you were, at that time, accustomed to enkindle in the pulpit of old Ebenezer Church in Philadelphia.

"The inscription hereon is, 'To the Senior Bishop;' and when you shall at last go up to possess the land where patriarchs get young again and where pilgrims have wings, you will leave it as a legacy to the next Senior in office; and thus it is to support, in turn, the grandest line of 'apostolic succession' the world has ever known. Honored and beloved Bishop and Father in Israel, accept this tribute and consider yourself duly caned!"

At the closing session of the same Conference, a similar cane was presented, on behalf of the body, to the junior Bishop, *in fee simple.* So that should he live to be the senior in office, and his body grow old and feeble, he may be enabled to bear himself gently adown the sunset slope to his resting place, grasping in either hand a material staff descended from the days and hallowed by the touch of Coke and Asbury. A striking coincidence of this pleasant episode was that both the Senior and Junior Bishops—Levi Scott and John F. Hurst—were products of Peninsular Methodism. When our haughty neighbors ask doubtingly, whether any good can come out of this "Nazareth," we point proudly to these noble Sons of the Peninsula, whose names and fame have reached the outer boundaries of the Methodistic world, and will be honored through all time.

THE OLD TIME PRESIDING ELDER.

When the Peninsula constituted a single District, as in the days of Chandler and Bœhm, the Presiding Elder was "a man in authority," and regarded as almost the equal of the Bishop in official dignity and responsibility. As in those days, frequent change in spiritual grazing was considered necessary to the symmetrical development of both pastor and people, it was deemed advisable to change the preachers every four or six months. In the absence of the Bishop, this work devolved on the Elder. Furthermore, the circuits being ofttimes larger than a county, the official gatherings at Quarterly Conference were often almost equal in numbers to an Annual Conference; and the Sunday congregations of such occasions were immense. All this tended to clothe the office of Presiding Elder with great dignity and importance. It was doubtless an exaggerated ideal of the Elder of the Peninsular District, in the days of the Fathers, that "Paul Picturemaker" painted, in his poem published years ago in the *Conference Worker*. His description was as follows:

OUR 'SIDIN' ELDER.

'Twas in the days of yore—the good old times
When men were simple-minded, and the lines
'Twixt worldly vanities and Christian livin'
Were closely drawn; each state its bound'ries givin'
With mathematical precision, so that
By cut of coat or trowsers, you could know that
A man had "got religion"—had the leaven
To "rise" his nature to the state of Heaven.

As Uncle Samuel's fightin' men all dress
In fightin' clothin'; so, a man might guess
With certainty, before these days of evil,
Whether a man was 'listed 'gainst the Devil.
But modern style, with its enormities
Hath blasted Christian *uniform*ities;
And, these days, should you go to shoot Philistines,
You'd, like as not, destroy a lot of Christians.

But, had you known our 'sidin' Elder, you would
Have thought him for this mundane station too good.
His frame was tall and stalwart—awe-impressing;
And, by his *uniform*-ity of dressing,
He was a live epistle, read of all men;
His old clothes even e'er did loudly call men
To quick repentance. 'Twas an inspiration—

So many thought—that gave the information
To Elder Jones, and taught him to prepare them
And wear his clothes as holy angels wear them.
And some there were who held, when he ascended
To Zion's heights, by angel guides attended,
The clothes he had on earth and wore to meetin'
Were just the thing to walk the golden street in.

In those good days, before we'd heard of "Station"
A *circuit* would have made a "right smart" nation;
And Quart'ly Conf'rence was its parliament,
And Elder Jones its august president.
The preachers and officials gathered round him,
And, with their solemn homage, meekly crowned him;
For he portentous questions thus propounded—
"Any complaints? Appeals? Reports?"—then bounded
Off to the finances—'twas kind o' funny:
His questionin' was sure to end on money!
And, when his twenty dollars down they paid him,
A peaceful smile his face was e'er arrayed in.
True, some there were who'd sometimes make suggestions,—
"Why can't our preacher ask these quart'ly questions,
And preach the quart'ly sermons? *Cui bono?*"
But our wise Elder always answered, "no, no!"

Jones preached, on Saturdays, an exhortation
Proportioned to his little congregation.
He thought it vain to aim his longest arrows,
Or fire a cannon, at a few cock sparrows.
But people thronged from near and far for Sunday,

And sang and shouted, oftentimes, till Monday.
On these occasions, Elder Jones would load up
His preachin' gun until it nearly blowed up
In firin' off; and when he got good aim
Upon the crowd, he always brought down game.
He measured six feet high and weighed two hundred;
And, with the "rousements" up, he fairly thundered,
And thundered on, till multitudes, by littles,
Convicted were of their great need for—victuals;
Nor did he cease till many hundred sinners
Were penitently prayin' for their—dinners!

And when at last the "Amen" came, the meetin'
Doxologied, and made tracks for the eatin'.
The Elder led the way to Brother Pickens',
Where he was sure to find the best fat chickens,
And other things to suit—all to his notion;
And here, for full an hour, he paid devotion
At Epicurus' shrine, till nature, too full
For comfort was; and then, with visage rueful,
He left the scene, a sad and vanquished hero,—
Enthusiasm and zeal all gone to Zero,—
And smoked his pipe, and dozed the time away
Before the big, log fire the live-long day.
Sometimes between his naps, if it were handy,
For stomach's sake, he'd take a little brandy.

Our Elder was a gentleman polite;
And, oftentimes, it was a jolly sight
At Conference, to see him shakin' hands;—
Gath'rin' the preachers into little bands,

To while away a leisure hour in smokin',
Meanwhile amusin' them with drollest jokin',
Until they all a noble fellow thought him,
And generous obeisance gladly brought him;
They said "Amen" to all his views and notions,
And voted "aye" on all his Conf'rence motions.

The Gen'ral Conf'rence year was the occasion
Of our good Elder's highest animation
And most polite attentions. Bowin', smilin',
He captured all, with winsome ways beguilin'
But on the Conf'rence floor, our Elder rose
Resplendent, in the sight of friends and foes;
And represented all his territory,
And told the tale of his own fame and glory
With glowing tongue. And when the Bishop called
The names upon his District list enrolled;
He answer made in eulogy most glowin',
Until, if heroes might be made by blowin',
Not Paul or Peter e'er were half the wonder
As Elder Jones' modern sons of thunder:—
Not one but ought the Church to represent,
And to the Gen'ral Conference be sent.
But, gen'rous souls! while conscious of their merit,
Each hoped he would the Eldership inherit;
And waited patiently to pick these bones
When he should wear the crown of Brother Jones.
Thus, our good Elder's sugar-coated talkin'
Sent him the streets of New York town to walkin',
While all his glorious preachers took their stations,
And starved along on deferred expectations.

"THE QUART'LY CONF'RENCE,"

Paul Picturemaker described in one of his characteristic productions, was probably held by Elder Jones, or by one of his cotemporaries. The reader will possibly recognize, in the description, some delineations near akin to scenes he may have witnessed in Quarterly Conferences of much more recent date. It is not impossible some modern official, by looking closely, may discover some faint traces of personal resemblance. If so, it is hoped he will not fail to recognize the likeness; or, like a certain New Testament character, "go his way and forthwith forget what manner of man he is." The description appeared some years since, in the *Christian Advocate*, and may bear repetition here. It is as follows:

"Please come to order," our good Elder said;
Then called to prayer, and reverently led
In our devotions. Loudly did he call
On Heaven to bless the Church, the Pastor—all;
And to his invocations, twelve chief laymen
Gave fit response in one united 'Amen!'

"The Pastor listened gladly. Recently
He'd come to Frogtown; fixed up decently;
Gone round the circuit preaching to the people—
In Frogtown Church 'twas said he shook the steeple—
Bartholomew could not have louder thundered;
And saint and sinner oped their eyes and wondered
How W—— Conf'rence could retain such men,
When Bishop timber was so scarce, and when

Great men were needed for the high positions
Of Editors, and other such fruitions.
 "But here he was, with wife, and children nine,
To tug and toil, and spend his precious time
In striving for the good of saint and sinner;
To do God's work and trust God for his dinner.
As when Elijah by the brook was fed;—
The raven bringing daily meat and bread—
Though he were neither epicure nor glutton,
Must oft have wondered whether beef or mutton
Would be the next invoice the good bird brought him;
So, this itinerant sat there and thought him
Of hungry mouths—of breakfast, dinner, supper,
And cyphered mentally of bread and butter.
 "'Any complaints?—Appeals?' the Elder said—
'Reports?' Then the good pastor raised his head;
And, drawing forth his foolscap, written o'er
With kind and hopeful utt'rance, took the floor,
And read his first report; while wink and nod,
'Twixt high officials, told the man of God,
More plain than words could tell the cheering story,
That Frogtown Circuit was next door to glory!
With saints so gen'rous—so appreciative;
In whom all noble impulses were native,
He'd feast on chicken broiled, and lamb and peas,
And dream of Heav'n 'on flowery beds of ease!'
 "Scarce was he seated, when old Brother Jones
Rose to his feet, and said in nasal tones:
'I, Mister President, do make the motion

That that 'ere paper's 'zactly to our notion.
Frogtown's ne'er had so good and great a teacher;
And, for my part, I say, God bless our preacher!'
'Amen! Amen!' resounded from all quarters.
'God bless him, and his wife, and sons and daughters!'
Again the pastor thought, 'Such hearty praying
Can only be the twin to gen'rous paying.'

"The rev'rend Elder, glancing toward the gallery,
Said: 'Now we'll hear report on Pastor's salary.
Be lib'ral, brethren; let your preacher see
That you appreciate his ministry.'

"With long-drawn sigh—with sanctimonious mien,
Well suited to a solemn funeral scene,
The Chairman of the Stewards, Brother Leecher,
Made their report on how they'd feed the preacher.
'The times is hard,' he said, 'and gittin' tougher;
But Frogtown ne'er will let her preacher suffer.
We've calkerlated things down to a fraction,
And vote four hundred by unan'mous action.
Our figgers was three hundred sev'nty-seven;
But we've resolved to make the hundreds even.
The twenty-three that's over, Brother Sower
Can use to aid our school and help the poor.
We've counted up, and made the sal'ry ample
So Brother Sower might set a lib'ral 'zample.'
'Amen! Amen!' arose from sev'ral voices;
'In generosity Frogtown rejoices!'

"The pastor stared around with startled seeming,
Like one too soon awaked from reckless dreaming;

And, at the Elder's question: "Has the pastor
A word or two to say?"—he popped up faster
Than hare from humble, homestead brush-heap kicked
    out,
And said: "Dear Brethren; I'm completely whipped out!
Do you suppose three hundred sev'nty-seven
Is going to feed, and clothe and school eleven?
And keep a horse and buggy, and pay car fare
While I am striking for you in this warfare?
Let's see;—thirty to each—a fraction over,
Counting the old mare one. The sacred clover
Grows very short, my brethren: we can't live on't,
Much less adopt your plans and give on't.
It ill consists with good propriety
To tease your preacher with anxiety;
And keep him all the season wond'ring whether
He'll able be to bring both ends together.
To what extent your narrow paying pinches
Your pastor, sirs; be sure so many inches,
Mentally, will drop off from your teaching:
Starvation paying makes starvation preaching!
This *verbum sapienti* my speech closes;
And, if you're wise, you'll look beyond your noses.'

"'I call the man to order!' quoth a brother.
'Our preacher, Mister Elder, nor no other,
Hain't got no right to git up and abuse us
For what the facts, in these hard times, excuse us.
We're '*verdant sapheads*,' are we? Guess we'll show him
We see beyant our noses where we go in!

I tell you, sir, we've done the best we can
In our report; and now let every man
Make calkerlation of his own expenses,
And see if 'tis not time to put up fences,
To keep his charity on proper grounds, sir,
As well as keep its *object* in good bounds, sir.
To keep our preachers poor will keep 'em humble,
And save 'em, sir, from many a dangerous tumble.'

"'I think so, too,' said worthy brother Farmer,
And 'said his piece,' each moment growing warmer.
His dozen farms, he said, were so expensive,
His charity henceforth must be defensive.
His store-bill, yearly, was not quite three hundred;
And at the preacher's wastefulness he wondered.
With salary, and presents oft received,
He said, with him it couldn't be believed
But that the preacher fared as well as any,
And he would vote him *not another penny!*

"Then brother Bondholder arose, and said:
'To vote big salaries I'm sore afraid.
My state and county taxes are so heavy,
That, when you add the Church and preacher levy,
I've little money left to lay away,
In surplus bonds, to cheer the 'rainy day.'
Besides all this, the working men all live,
And get along, and have a bit to give,
Receiving by the day one dollar fifty;
And, if the preacher and his wife are shifty,
And pinch along, I think they'll come out even

Quite easy on three hundred seventy-seven.
Men who dependent are on *Christian charity*,
Should eat roast turkey only for a rarity:
To often fast, or eat not to satiety,
Is good for health, and ministers to piety.
In olden times, when preachers were not greedy,
But shared the hardships of the poor and needy,
They preached for *souls*, and therein was their pay
That sent them oft rejoicing on their way.
If Brother Sower would be good and wise, sir,
Let him win souls, and he will win the prize, sir.'

"Again the pastor rose. His weary heart
Was wounded deeply by the cruel dart
Thrust at him; and again he warmly spoke:
The great Apostle to the Gentiles wrote,—
'The laborer is worthy of his wages;'
But, by the verdict of our modern sages,
He should have said *unworthy*. Now I ask,
How can a preacher execute his task,
And keep up with the age, in all its capers,
Unless he read the latest books and papers?
Why, on four hundred, it is plain to see
The brains or stomach must fare scantily;
But as the stomach makes the louder claims,
It gobbles all, and leaves nought for the brains.
The miracle of making bread of stones,
Or savory soup of old, dry, barren bones,
Is forced upon your preacher; so, no wonder
The people leave, as well as come in hunger.

These extra needs, sirs—how am I to meet them?
I 'preach for souls;' but, bless you, I can't eat them.
But could I thus my table spread with dinners,
I'd much prefer a fatter class of sinners!'

"'Order!' the Elder cried; 'I put the motion:
All who're in favor of the Steward's motion,
Say aye.' And forthwith, without hesitation
They voted 'aye' for mutual starvation!

*   *   *   *   *   *

Truth often stranger is than any fiction:—
The Conf'rence closed with Sower's *benediction!*"

THE CONSERVATIVE MULE.

Among the animals honored by notice in Scripture history, is the mule. His value to the human race, as a *puller*, before the invention of steam engines, it is now difficult to estimate. He works with equal facility with his machinery reversed, and either end foremost; pulling backward nearly as well as forward. Accidentally and occasionally, he has proven useful as an obstructionist; but, sometimes, at critical junctures, he is liable to become a little too *conservative*. He is the most magnificent *backer* in the world; but, his eyes not being completely reversible, his locomotion in that direction has often precipitated catastrophe, resulting in mutual disaster to animal and driver. This useful but dangerous animal is a striking type of some specimens of the *genus homo*, occasionally encountered among Church officials.

"Paul Picturemaker," like most Methodist ministers, has had some experience in church building. Some of his experiences along this line have been a little grotesque notwithstanding their annoying features. It is not generally a popular thing, *per se*, in the Wilmington Conference, to oppose building a new church, where it is generally conceded one is needed. All the members usually—Bros. Skinflint and Clinchemtight included— loudly favor the proposal. But when the time comes for definite action, these two dear brethren, and others whom they have influenced, manage, by some well planned diversion, to precipitate a new issue that creates factions and necessitates a postponement. At the same time, their loud protestations of what they will do and how much they will contribute, in certain contingencies that are always well nigh impossible in a progressive community, helps them to a reputation of exceptional liberality and devotion. If the new church can be located on the old cemetery on a back street; if it can be of a certain style that outrages architectural decency; or if it shall be stipulated in the deed that no organ, or other musical instrument, shall ever be used therein; or if it can be located on the suburbs, where brother Clinchemtight has twenty town lots for sale, he will give five hundred or a thousand dollars—otherwise *not one red cent!* Having thus issued his manifesto, and laid down his ultimatum, he significantly and complaisantly pats his wallet pocket, and says, "Now take your own course, and build your church—if you can!" If by a nearly unanimous vote it has been decided to build a church and chapel on the least objectionable location named by him, his mind suddenly undergoes a radical revolution as to the *style* of the building all had agreed upon; and he declares in favor of a church fifty feet square, with galleries on three sides, or he cannot conscientiously contribute. About this time, the pastor and those really desiring a new church discover that the question with Brother Clinchemtight is "how *not* to do it;" and they go ahead in the fear of God, and "build a house unto the Lord" without his assistance.

It was during Paul Picturemaker's successful struggle to build, amid such untoward circumstances, that the poem found below was suggested and produced. Being read in manuscript before the Church Lyceum, although the statement was honestly made that the character therein delineated was purely imaginary, certain parties who heard of it took offense, and claimed that the design of the author was to hold them up to ridicule. Calling attention to it the following Sunday morning, Mr. Picturemaker gave utterance to a sincere and kindly disclaimer; told the congregation he would have the production published the following week, so that all could inspect it; and promised to make a present of ten dollars to any man who, after reading it, would aver his belief that any part he might select was intended to represent his case. The poem was accordingly printed, but no one claimed the proffered ten dollars; and thenceforth all was quiet on the Broadkiln. The production was the following:

ODE TO YE OLDE MEETIN' 'OUSE.

A relic of the past—the good old days
Our fathers knew, before the evil ways
Of these last times had lured so many feet—
The old house stands, in solemn silence meet.

'Tis hoary now with near a century's storms.
The lights and shades alternate nights and morns
Have heralded, have plowed its wooden brow
With honorable wrinkles; and the boards
That close it in, like once well brightened swords
Ornate with rust, are painted sombre hues
By oft-returning storms and gathering dews;—
Perchance in mourning for the Saints' economy,
That finds whitewash forbid in Deuteronomy.

'Tis on a quiet street—near out of town,
Walled in with stone,—with willows waving down
Their graceful branches. Our good fathers thought
It was not meet their worship should be brought
To profane notice; and, to "gather in
The wand'rings of their minds" from earth and sin,
They built their churches on some lane or alley
Where Satan might not his chief forces rally.

The village graveyard, where the silent dead
Sleep side by side—each in his lowly bed,—
Lies spread around. Our sires, so good and brave,
Were wont to pray and worship near the grave.

"Hark! From the tombs, the doleful sound," they said,
Was more impressive, sung amid the dead.
  As John the New Jerusalem describes,
Must I this house of prayer. Its equal sides
Lie four-square. Breadth and depth and length and height
Show forth its praise in geometric light.
Three sides are galleried—the wise design
Of some famed architect of olden time—
A man of Pythagorean ways, and skill
To utilize his travels, and fulfill
His mission. Journeying o'er Peninsular sands,
Alert t' appreciate the time's demands,
He spied, hard by some thrifty farmer's barn,
A house well-ordered for its num'rous swarm.
On three sides ranged, were rows and rows of sticks,
And on these nodded twenty dozen chicks.
So, this itinerant, without *chick-en-ery*,
His church erected like an old-time hennery.
  The end, ungalleried, was set apart
To holy use. It was the precious mart
To which was brought the Methodistic wares
That current were in olden-time church fairs.
The towering "preach-pen," with its winding stair,
Lifts high the preacher into middle air.
'Twixt heav'n and earth suspended, it was thought
His meditations for his flock were brought
In hearing distance towards the open door,
Where white-winged mercy-angels hover o'er
The portal. But the poor man ne'er received

The Lord's attention to his plea aggrieved,
Until, with toilsome journey down that steep,
He bended low, with Mary, at the feet
That nails were driven through, and lisped the name
That lustered Bethl'hem's manger with its fame.

In preaching, too, the fathers gravely thought,
If lifted high, the parson would be brought
So very near the Lord, he'd catch the Spirit,
And so his preaching have the greater merit.
But ofttimes it hath happened, from this height
While shouting down to men in earth's dark night,
The facts have shown, alas! too near Heav'n's portals
The preacher was to waken drowsy mortals.

The ventilation question, was a theme
Deemed idle nonsense, modern fogies green
Had thrust upon the Church. What need was there
For any more of breath, in praise and prayer
Than a big meetin' house would hold? And, then,
Long prayers and sermons would be uttered; when
A moderate supply, to him who spoke, ah!
Would haste the Amen, or the scamp would choke, ah!
Besides, 'twould many cords of wood require,
Beyond the needed pile, to raise a fire
To warm "all out o'doors," if holes were made
To let in outside air,—the old folks said.
And so, they built this church around a hole,
And closed it in, and warmed it up with coal,
And kept it there all seasons, 'round above 'm—
Themselves for God's use meet—roast in an oven!

The congregation all—from parson down,
Were cooked and smoked and dried, and done up brown!
 An aged pilgrim, late I've heard complain;
Soliloquizing in the foll'wing strain:—
"Ah! Times has sadly changed: high-fangled notions
Has crept into the church; and our devotions,
That onc't was hot and steamin' in all weather,
Has 'vaporated out and altogether.
Schools, colleges and cultur' kills us dead, ah!
We've died of rush of brains onto the head, ah!
The Conference has made the wretched blunder,—
Thinks brains is requisite to pulpit thunder;
And sends her fledgelin's off to Drew and Boston;
And this is one thing puts such extra cost on.
The time was onc't, when sermonts was so cheap,
A 'quarter' paid up for a three months' heap,
But now envelops—fifty-two a year—
Annoys and keeps our souls in mortal fear!
Pshaw! There was brother Burley, our good preacher,
Was worth a dozen moderns as a teacher.
He wasn't school larn't, but could stamp and holler,
And preach two hours, and then the sermont foller
With song, and invitation to the sinner;
And things would git so high we'd git no dinner!
Why, haint I seen him give one mighty jump,
And spring down to the altar place, kerthump?
And couldn't he bang the Book, and hold it high,
And shake it at 'em till they'd almost die?
That's how I come to seek religion early—
Was skeerd into't, and saved by brother Burley.

"But now, alas! these venerated walls
Are soon to ring no more with holy calls.
A preacher come, who said to our young people,
Let's build a church and put on it a steeple;
And make one room above and three below,
And have an organ and a bell, you know;
And stained glass, gothic windows, and a cross,
In token that we've 'counted all but loss.'

"And now the new church lifts before our eyes
Its 'bominable steeple tow'rd the skies.
Ere many Sundays, they'll be movin' in;
Raisin' the mischief with that music thing,
And grindin' out their worship to their notion—
Pleasin' the Devil with their sham devotion:—
It's awful, shameful, mean, irrcv'rent, wicked!
The self-willed rascals ought to be well kick-ed.

"And then agin, behold what money needless
Is spent upon this house by persons heedless.
'Tis true, it's not my money—'tain't my way
To waste my substance for 'a rainy day'
On worldly vanities, when Christian charity
Begins at home, and goes out for a rarity.

"Why all this waste? I ask. Was not our sires,
Who built this old house—watched its altar fires—
As good as us their childring, and our brats
That swing long coats and wear two-story hats?
'Tis wicked pride this precious ile to waste
To feed weak vanity and sinful taste—
To build, on false pretenee of motive holy,
A costly temple to the 'Meek and Lowly.'

"Ah, me! Our Methodism has so come down,
I think I'll jine another church, up town:
It's fine and costly—can't see what 'twas made for;
But, never mind; there's one good thought—'tis paid for.
The preacher there prates not of givin' money
To Heaven's cause, but feeds on milk and honey.
I'm tired of hearin' here, to all tarnation,
This everlastin' cry of consecration!"
Thus spake he; and, with one spasmodic lurch,
He landed, boots and breeches, out the church.

Farewell, old man! Farewell, old church, together!
You're both exposed to drear and stormy weather;
But, dear old fold; 'twas not thy fault or fraud,
That led poor Dives to forsake his God.
Thy lessons had he heeded 'gainst vile pelf,
He'd not, like Judas, gone and hanged himself.
Farewell, old centenarian, tried and true!
Ring, ring the bells! Ring out the old! Ring in the new!

FUN IN THE PARSONAGE.

"What? Fun in a minister's house?" exclaims dear, pious, old brother Drearygroans. "What is the church coming to? No wonder there's no revival? Ah, me! It wasn't so in the good old times!"

"Now, Brother Drearygroans, didn't you and all your family laugh most heartily the other day, when the dog, trying to steal the soap-grease, got his head in the keg, and cut such comical antics vainly trying to extricate himself?—When, to release him, you had to knock the top hoops off? Why were you guilty of conduct so unbecoming an exhorter?"

"Well, it was so funny, I couldn't help laughing."

"Just so, brother; and why shouldn't you have laughed? And was a good, hearty laugh any more innocent in your back yard than it would have been in my house? For what purpose did our kind Creator put the laugh power in us? Now, Brother Drearygroans: if you always bend a tree in one direction, it will grow crooked. But if you bend it equally in all directions, it will strike an average and grow about right. So with human moods. They should change with circumstances. The Book says there is 'a time to laugh;' and, if a good laugh don't happen to meet us accidentally, as that met you the other day, we should put on our spectacles and go out to hunt one. Now, there wasn't any laugh in the parsonage study that day; nor at the ironing table; nor in the cook-stove; nor in the sewing machine; nor in the children's hard lessons; so we just made up our minds to open the parsonage parlor that evening, invite a few good-natured friends, and send Fun word to come along with his metaphorical monkey, and help us have a jolly good time."

It was our big boy's seventeenth birth-day anniversary. So at half-past seven o'clock that evening, when the children had finished their lessons and the friends had gathered, Rob and his brothers and sister were called to the parlor. Evergreen letters on the walls revealed the significance of the occasion. And then followed sparkling conversation, wit and humor, jokes, games and "lots of fun," during which "that boy" was made to feel he was a personage of some importance in that parsonage. Finally, the parson and *pater familias* produced and read the following appropriate personal reminiscence:

WHEN I WAS SEVENTEEN.

Though many years have come and gone
   Since youth's fair bloom was on my cheek,
Though minstrels sing no more the song
   They used to sing, young hope to greet;
Yet well do I remember now
   The mystic, silvery sheen
That shone about my boyish brow
   When I was seventeen.

There were no shadows o'er the morn;
   No spots upon my rising sun;
No cloud foretold the distant storm—
   Sad prelude of the days to come.
All things were bright as bright could be,
   And verdant things were green;
And verdant glory mantled me
   When I was seventeen.

The downy morn grew into day,
   And downy beard grew on my face.
The Grecian Cupid was my lay
   And goose-grease did my *caput* grace.

Sweet peppermint its perfume gave
    To aid the witching scene;
And love's weird wand did o'er me wave
    When I was seventeen.

High were the hopes that swelled my breast,
    And high the collar which I bore;
A golden glory graced my crest,
    And golden nankin tights I wore.
And then, where gathered maidens fair,
    Might I be often seen.
What wondrous visions filled the air
    When I was seventeen!

I live again in days of yore;
    And now I think me of the night
When, trembling at the old Church door,
    I bowed, and stammered in my fright:—
"Shall I—the—pleasure have,—Miss Stout,
    To see?"—Alas! How mean!
A bigger gallant "cut me out"
    When I was seventeen!

I loved, of course—yes loved and dreamed,
    That she whose smile my being thrilled;
Whose face in queenly beauty gleamed;
    Whose light my world with glory filled,
Would, one day, be my wife; but, Sir,
    A slip came in between:—
A naughty preacher married her
    When I was seventeen!

ANNIVERSARIES.

Many anniversaries have been recognized in that parson's home. Two specimens will serve as samples. The first is of

A WOODEN WEDDING EXTRAORDINARY.

The husband himself read the ritual, which was brand new, and made to order for the occasion. Of course he pocketed the fee. At the appropriate place in the ceremony, the parson joined himself and his bride together with a pair of wooden handcuffs; put a wooden ring upon her finger, and crowned her with a decidedly unique and showy head-dress, made of pine shavings. This was followed by a graceful passage over the hymeneal broom-stick; and the kiss to the bride was responded to by a switch on the parson's back at the hands of an outraged spectator. The following was the *ritual* used:

> Five cycles fulfilled now—
>   Their tournaments tilted;—
> Since the parson said, "Wilt thou?"
>   And both of us—*wilted!*
> And now, ere we start on,
>   Let's understand whether
> There's a plan we can part on,
>   Or still hold together.
> Shall we take a license stronger,
> And wear the handcuffs five years longer?

These years have been sunny,
    With clouds intermingled.
Sometimes little money
    In our pockets has jingled.
But despite all the snatching
    Our love-cords to sever,
Our biting and scratching
    Ties us closer together.
Shall we pass another ring
And lengthen out your apron-string?

We're, both of us, older,
    And much better looking;
And you're a brave soldier;—
    I, a good judge of cooking.
Your exploits in warfare
    Are all written down, ma'am,
In the sad, lonely, short hair
    On the top of my crown, ma'am.
Should we 'list as new recruits,
Will you spare the stumps and roots?

Once there were two of us,
    While we were free of us;
Then there was one of us:—
    Now there are three of us!
Baby arms round us twining,
    Binding either to other;

Angel sweetness enshrining :—
  She takes after her—f—mother!
Shall we jump the broomstick o'er,
And trudge along for five years more?

I've "popped;"—wilt thou keep me
  "For worse or for better?"
Come now, I entreat thee,
  Accept of this fetter.
Is silence consenting?
  Then put on this ring, ma'am;
And, never repenting,
  We'll e'er gaily sing, ma'am:
Come on, my partner in distress,
And don this wooden-wedding tress.

Now, friends; we're before you
  In our blushes and beauty;
Make haste, we implore you,
  To render your duty.
Once more we're to "go it"
  Adown life's swift tide:
A switch for the poet—
  A kiss for his bride!

TIN WEDDING.

On the 5th of February, 1884, the Methodist Parsonage at North East, Md., was crowded with about one hundred guests, to celebrate the *tinth* anniversary of the marriage of the pastor and his wife. While the festivities, usual to such an occasion in a Christian home, were at their height, a unique and unexpected ceremony was performed by Rev. C. F. Sheppard, who read to the bride and groom the following ritual in verse, composed by Hon. L. A. C. Gerry of Port Deposit; on behalf of many friends of that town:

"1874. REV. AND MRS. ROBT. W. TODD. 1884.

The 'bell, book and candle' ye need not be dreading,
   Nor *black-pig-tailed* music drummed out of tin pans;
We wish you great joy at your shining, *tin* wedding:
   Be *soldered* the tongues which oppose the blest bans.
Your home may be neither a mansion nor palace,
   It may be a cottage both lowly and plain;
But blest 'neath the sway of the true-hearted Alice,
   'Tis richer than many a more lordly domain.
Nor can the dark shadows of old melancholy
   E'er wither the leaves of the family tree,
Where the 'Quaint and the Humorous,' pleasant and jolly,
   Diffuses his ecclesiastical glee.
Besides, for your joy this decade hath modelings
   Of miniature 'Robbies' and 'Allies,' I ween.
This day is the brighter because of the *Todd*-lings—
   The tiptopest *Todd*-lings that ever were seen.
May the *cup* of your blessing be large as a *basin;*
   And *grater* your bliss than to all would be *safe:*
Your sorrows so little that never a trace in
   Your faces could show that the *tin*-iest waif
Of the wickedest fairy had caused you a sorrow.

May *spoons*-ful, aye, *ladles*-ful, *pails*-ful of bliss
Now flood you with gladness, so great you must borrow
　The *cans* of your neighbors, lest oceans you miss.
May griefs pass away just like water in *colanders*—
　Vanish like whiskey down true Irish throats;
Or krout before famishing, big-bellied Hollanders;
　Or pence in the pockets of Johnnie O'Groats.
We cannot be with you at this festive meeting,
　Which grieveth our hearts, and our stomachs far more;
We long for the hand-shakes, good words and good eating;
　But doubt not our absence will add to your store.
This night, while friends gather, and joys round you thicken,
　Oh, think of the absent and drop us a tear;
Then solace your souls with the leg of a chicken—
　(You'd be minus that solace could we but be there)
Yet we'll not be envious, though not at the party;
　Fate grant you a banquet would flatter the gods!
We wish you all joy with the wish true and hearty:
　Long live th' i-*tin*-erating *tin*-wedded Todds!"

This "ceremony" was greatly enjoyed and "brought down the house." The presents con-*tin*-gent on this celebration numbered nearly two hundred, and came from all points of the compass, in addition to the *North East* point. While all were useful or ornamental, many were elegant and some were unique. Among the latter was a special package from three good matrons of Dover, Delaware, containing a half-pint of beans, a slice of evaporated apple, a diminutive smoked herring, and two *tin*-y *tin* plates, on which to serve these dainties. Like the Snow Hill poem mentioned hereafter, this kind remembrance was doubtless " *owed*."

The musical propensities of the household were not forgotten. A distinguished divine, whose name perhaps it were as *well* should not be *Cald*, in this connection, on account of his modesty, sent a fine-looking cornet. The tone of the instrument was a striking mixture between the reedy and the wheezy. It was not quite apparent whether the kind donor had tested its tone qualities by the explosive passages in his own impassioned utterances, or had considerately sought to adjust it to the wheezings of the *asthmatic* recipient. Had the gentle brother who selected the second instrument been accustomed to the eloquent and melodious utterances of the renowned *Burke* of the old English Parliament, he could scarcely have selected a cornet of more splendid tone qualities. Another instrument came from the *Hill* of *Snow*. Its tone was heraldic and prophetic; a transfusion of the jubilant spirit of the brave, bachelor knight who sent it. It was interpreted to herald his early departure from the dreary, *Snow*-y *hill* of celibacy to the sunny and blossoming verdure of the tropics of love and wedlock. It was accompanied by the following lines from his graceful muse:

"*OWED*
TO THE REV. R. W. TODD,
ON HIS *TINTH* WEDDING DAY.

The matrimonial sea—and the thought oft appalls—
Like the Cape of Good Hope, is notorious for *squalls*,
At least, so 'tis said; and be sure 'tis a sin
Not to blow the *fog-horn*—so I send it within.
But if 'tis all false, none the less do I say,
You should blow all the fog from this subject away.
Then blow, trumpet, blow; and please, Gabriel, be still
Till the actor arouse an old *Bach* at Snow Hill.

ENVOY.

If ten years of *Toddy* has started no spree,
Then women are angels—may there be one for me;
But if sweet figs don't grow on th' hymeneal thistle,
Surely ten years for a *horn* is paying dear for your whistle."

On this production the recipient ventured the following *critique* in the *Peninsula Methodist:*

"Some allowance must be made on the ground of 'poetic license;' but it is a brand new idea to notify the mariner of *squalls* by sounding a *fog-horn*, or to disperse a *fog* by the blast of a trumpet. For the former the sailor must 'look out;' and *squalls* are the best possible agencies for dispersing the latter. It must be candidly confessed, however, that usually the matrimonial sea is rippled by *squalls*, and beset with *rocks;* and the *cradle* of' this deep' quite often disturbs, rather than promotes 'peaceful sleep.' However, let the timid Snow Hill bachelor be encouraged by the remembrance that, in our case, the fogs of doubt have given way before our little *breezes* of experience; and that, after a ten years' voyage, amid *squalls* and *rocks*, the craft starts out again for another cruise, as good as new, and with three romping little sailors on board, who were not present at the original launch."

The wedding cake for the above interes*tin'* anniversary was supplied from Green Hill, the residence of Rev. T. S. Thomas. Certain innocent-looking young maidens from that region con*tin*uously and per*tin*aciously demanded that the bridegroom cut them a few slices therefrom; but as they had forgotten to furnish him with a pair of tinners' shears, he imper*tin*ently declined. The cake contained an *entire service of tin dishes!*

Professor John G. Robinson, now of Baltimore, is an old Eastern-Shoreman; and, by reason of his business relations with that part of the State, and his frequent presence at our Conferences and other gatherings, he seems still to belong to the Peninsula. A notification to the writer, an old pastor, of the approach of the twenty-fifth anniversary of the marriage of Mr. and Mrs. Robinson, occurring November 14th, 1879, called forth a congratulatory poem; which, at the appropriate point in the festivities, was most effectively read by Rev. Dr. Poulson, calling forth the enthusiastic applause of the two hundred guests crowding the spacious parlors. The Professor had the poem printed in silver letters; and, mounted in a silver frame, it hangs in his best parlor. It is as follows:

TO PROFESSOR AND MRS. JOHN G. ROBINSON, ON THE OCCASION OF THEIR SILVER WEDDING.

O, ring the bells! yes, ring the silver bells!
A joyous eve their melody foretells.
Turn on the lights; stir up the grate right cheerily;
All voices—joining in the chorus merrily—
Send the glad music forth in happy greeting,
And shout the welcome to our festal meeting!

>O, say; do you remember
>The fourteenth of November,
>Eighteen hundred fifty-four,
>When, before the bridal door,
>Stood a youthful couple, knocking,
>While the very earth seemed rocking
>'Neath their heart-throbs? Then the portals
>Opened to these longing mortals:
>John and 'Liza then went through, sir;—
>Thenceforth *one—no longer two*, sir.

>>Plodding along
>>Amid the throng;
>>'Twixt smiles and tears,
>>Through rolling years,

The happy pair have reached the silvery line,—
November fourteenth, Eighteen-seventy-nine.
Queriest thou, "Doth John regret his venture—eh?"
The *answer's* in this quarter of a century.

Once there were *two*—then only *one* of them;
But *now*, great guns! you see there are *some of them!*
    Ida, Helen, Eva, Charlie,
    Inglis, Howard, May and John G.,
    Jennie, Jessie, Clyde and Grace,
    And Willie—goodness! What a race
    Of Robin's daughters, Robin's sons!
    How the human torrent runs!—
    Enough to form a congregation,
    Run a school, or stock a nation:
    "Quiver full of arrows" chosen;
    "Olive plants"—a baker's dozen!

    Fathers, Mothers, Sisters, Brothers,
    Friends, acquaintances and others
    Gathered in this festive meeting,
    Take again our kindly greeting!
    *   *   *   *   *   *

    Slowly, rapidly, the years
    Passing by, 'twixt smiles and tears,
    Have their episodes been making—
    New experiences creating—
    Until five and twenty winters,
    With their usual season *inters*,
    Have their silvery threads been knitting—
    Bride and bridegroom well befitting—
    Through their locks the white frost spreading:
    Graceful flowers to deck this wedding.

> Let every guest
> Now do his best.
> While bells are ringing,
> Let joyous singing—
> Your salutations—
> Congratulations—
> Best kind wishes,
> And silver dishes—
> A gala wedding avalanche
> Overwhelm this jolly ranche!

And now, adieu. May bride and bridegroom live on
With bread to eat and something left, to give on,
> 'Mid kind caressing
> And Heaven's blessing,
Until another wedding glee is holden,
Whose sunshine, love and presents shall be *golden*.

WASH-DAY.

Moving day and the season of house cleaning, have been immortalized by painters and poets as periods of special interest in the domestic world. But for relaxations and recreations of this sort, homes would stagnate and humanity become torpid. Instinct teaches the eagle to "stir up her nest" for the benefit of her household, who, without it, would settle into inert and finally helpless imbecility. So moving day and house cleaning do their part towards making heroes and martyrs. But justice has never been done to the humble wash-day, which is as prolific of clean, healthful saintliness, as house cleaning is of noble heroism. The following humble effort to rescue this most interesting day from its obscurity and neglect, is given for what it is worth; and, it is hoped, it will be appreciated by the lovers of fair play and justice:

"WASH-DAY"—A POME.

Ho! all ye parsons, young and old,
List, as the story I unfold;
Though half the glory can't be told
    Of wash-day.

The Sunday strain has laid you low:
Blue Monday shadows cloud your brow;
And clouds oft robe your saintly *frow*
    On wash-day.

A pain, perchance, is in your head;
And you would longer keep your bed;
But—hustle out! For, hark, she said:
    "'Tis wash-day!"

You're washed and dressed, and down the stair;
You've read the lesson—said the prayer;
And now you try the bill of fare
    For wash-day.

The scraps from Sunday meals—the trash—
Is stewed and stirred and turned to hash.
"Refuse to eat it?" 'Twould be rash,
    On wash-day.

Yes; gulp it down, and ask no questions;
Don't criticise—make no suggestions;
Some *frows* do *splode*,—yes, e'en the best ones,—
    On wash-day.

The garments soiled are strewn around;
Tubs, pots and wash-boards take the grouud,
And things go splashing, slopping round
    Through wash-day.

The baby, in his meditations,
Scolds the perverse concatenations,
That leave him to the sad mutations
    Of wash-day.

The older urchins join, and do
Their "level best" to "put you through:"—
"Blue Monday," thus, is doubly blue
    On wash-day.

If, from this steam and suds and bustle,
Out from the parsonage you hustle,
To exercise your mind and muscle
    On wash-day;

You dare not, howsoever brave you
Are, make a call. A fool or knave you
Will be esteemed. "Soft soap" won't save you
    On wash-day.

If to your study you would hie,
And sermons make, 'tis vain to try;
They're blued, wrung, starched, and stiff and dry
    On wash-day.

"Pray for relief?"—A vain petition;
Your pouting vain—your fretting, wishing;
You'd best, like Peter, "go a fishing,"
    On wash-day.

To prove my wisdom in this matter,—
This *pome* was writ amid the clatter,
And steam, and suds, and dash and spatter
    Of wash-day.

CHURCH ANNIVERSARY.

The first Sunday in June of the Centenary year of organized Methodism in America—1884—was the 89th anniversary of the dedication of the first Methodist Episcopal Church at North East, Maryland. The day was appropriately celebrated with memorial services befitting the occasion; and with a thanksgiving offering that cleared the new and beautiful church of debt. The following commemorative poem was read by the pastor, the author of this volume:

SABBATH, JUNE 6TH, 1795.

As dawned this hallowed morn in sweet repose,
  Opening its gentle eyes to drink the light
Of day's bright orb, as o'er yon hill he rose;
  So waked that Sabbath, from the tomb of night,

We come to celebrate. In joyous strain
    The birds poured forth their carols, and the flowers
Exhaled their sweet perfumes; while hill and plain,
    Enrobed in Summer verdure, filled the hours
With holy thoughts, and reverent emotions,
Fit prelude to the holy day's devotions.
On yonder hill, where sleeps the sacred dust
    Of your forefathers; stood, in meek array,
Their humble temple—symbol of their trust
    And unpretending piety. That day,—
Floorless, unplastered still—its naked walls
    Were, the first time, to echo back the song
Of joyous worshipers; the trumpet calls
    Of Heaven's heraldry. As those who long
For home and rest, these Methodistic sires
Had longed to light their sacred altar fires.

Now the glad day had come. At yester-noon
    On sober steed, along the highway came
A manly form, with classic face, abloom
    With healthful glow, and radiant with the flame
That love enkindles; while his mild, meek eyes
    Shed benedictions on the school-house swarm,
Who looked up from their play in blank surprise
    At the strange spectacle. His noble form
Was clad in *reverend* black, close buttoned; while
    A low-crowned, broad-rimmed hat shaded his face,
Holding the grey-streaked hair, that, in the style
    Of olden times, flowed down, in wavy grace,

Upon his shoulders. Breeches, fitting close,
  Reached to his knees, while leggings buttoned down
His limbs, for most part hid his faultless hose.
  Buckles of silver graced his shoes. From crown
To foot, quaint neatness reigned in grace supreme,
As Asbury on North East road was seen.
A second steed brought up the rear, to carry
Needed supplies, and his good man, black Harry.

The news soon spread around; and, pell-mell, came
From farmhouse, cottage, mansion, shop and lane
Their denizens, with welcome words of greeting,
Who forthwith voted for an extra meeting.
The pastors, Benny Abbot, Frederick Carp,
With Elder Richard Whatcoat, made the start;
And numerous laymen, with the Trustee board:
Hart, Jones, George, Sweasey, Howell, Aldridge, Ford,
With the good Bishop, holding consultation,
At once extemporized a dedication.
Couriers went forth, to bear the news abroad
Through all the region—"Come, and worship God!"

So, on this 6th of June in '95,
  As hour of eight draws near, an eager throng
Swarms up the Back Street road, unto the hive
  For Love Feast. Tho' no clam'rous bell's ding-dong
To worship calls, the spirit's quickened ear
Obeys love's heart-beats with a glad good cheer.
Each comer bears a ticket to the feast,

And sentries at the door admit the guest,
If plainly clad; for neither flower nor feather;
No ruffled skirts; no jewelled form whatever
Can enter there. To-day, in looking o'er
A village congregation, rich or poor,
Imperfect vision might mistake it for
A garden, full of fruits and flowers; or
A museum of birds and feathers rare;
But, in "ye olden times," the places where
Our sires and matrons gathered, much resembled
The growing wheat; while, here and there, dissembled
In beauteous green, deceitful tares were growing,
Despite the Master's careful toil and sowing.

Well, that fair morn, all seated on the sleepers,
On sills and boards, the sowers and the reapers
Of '95, in reverent devotion,
Mused, sang and prayed, while flowed the glad emotion
Of holy joy. The pilgrim, toiling up
The rugged mountain steeps, refilled his cup
From Calvary's spring. The weeping penitent
  From miry slough below, in joyous bound,
Leaped to the Rock. The traveler, who went
  That morn by dry and thorny road, now found
The land of Beulah, rich with Eden's bloom;
  While he who, from the lofty mountain top,
Surveyed the scene, amid the light of noon,
  Shouted to all below, "Come up! come up!"

The hour of ten arrived. The Bishop rose
And read, " O, for a thousand tongues !" As flows
Niagara adown its rapids, so
The sweep of holy song—now high, now low,
To tune of "Northfield" flowed. Like ocean's roar,
As joyous billows break along the shore;
So, in deep cadences, up to yon height,
And out, o'er all the vale, in glad delight
Rolled the refrain: " Your loosened tongues employ ;
Ye blind, behold, and leap ye lame for joy !"

And then black Harry prayed. In homely phrase,
In figure rude, but redolent with praise;
His simple thoughts took wings; and up the steep,
To where the cherubim their vigil keep,
In Christ's own holy place, they entrance found,
Till saint and sinner felt " 'tis holy ground
Whereon we kneel." And when "Amen" was said,
In stillness tremulous, on every head
Rested a " cloven tongue, like as of fire !"
And then, once more, the joyous vocal lyre
Gave forth its melody of song. And now
Again arose the Bishop. On his brow
Great thoughts had traced their lines: his beaming eye
Gave forth the light, that once on Sinai,
Illumined Moses' face; and as he read
The sacred Book, where the Great Teacher said,
" Upon this rock I build my Church, and hell
Shall not 'gainst it prevail ;" a holy spell

Of reverent silence seized the list'ning throng,
As for two hours,—nor did the time seem long,—
The apostolic herald preached salvation,—
The heritage of every tribe and nation:
Extolled the mighty strength of Judah's lion;
And pledged that strength for the defence of Zion.

The Gospel bread that day was good—not better
Than men are wont to eat in ages later;
But in these busy times, men live so fast;
So push and crowd and cram at life's repast,
That they have little time or inclination
To linger at the feast of free salvation.
If, to hear Twain or Perkins, they a shilling
Pay; then, for ninety minutes, they are willing
To swelter through the ordeal, and esteem it
Too short. But the same audience will deem it
A heartless outrage, if the Heav'n-sent legate
Intent on saving them, should, by this, belate
Their dinners fifteen minutes. Thus, we see
That what men please to call the great disparity
'Tween preaching old and modern, is the rarity
Of old-time appetites, and old-time charity.

Well, on that Summer day, as climbed the sun
To zenith height, and poured in flood of noon
His fiery torrent down; love's holy flame,
From yonder pristine temple's sacred fane,
Went up to Heaven, till glory crowned the hour,—
Till saint and sinner felt the wondrous power

Of Pentecost; and, in North East, that day
Our Church " moved in " her home, and came to stay.
Let us, her sons and daughters, gather round
Her altar fires to-day. 'Tis holy ground
Whereon we tread. With rev'rent mien
We own our fathers' God; and, 'mid the scene
Where dead and living mingle, seal our vows
To join their anthem in the upper house.

A CENTENNIAL SERVICE,

Commemorative of the one hundredth anniversary of the organization of the Methodist Episcopal Church, was held in August, 1884, at the Woodlawn camp-meeting, in Cecil county, Maryland. On the invitation of Rev. Jos. France, the minister in charge of the meeting, the writer composed, on the camp-ground, and read as a part of the programme the following commemorative poem:

1784. EPISCOPAL METHODIST CENTENARY. 1884.

In Southern Wales, in Sev'nteen forty-seven,
An infant voice floats on the breath of even,
Which Destiny Divine ordains shall tell the story,
Of free Salvation and Messiah's glory
To eager multitudes in many lands;
Till ocean, breaking on her nether strands,
Shall sound the requiem 'long time's vast billow,
Of him who sleeps upon her coral pillow.

I sing of Thomas Coke, the noble son—
Wealthy and cultured—who the prize had won

Of worldly ease and fame; but who, like Moses,
Forsook the sweetness of Egyptian roses
For Sinai's thorns:—who like his loving Lord,
Obedient to his holy will and word,
Gave labor, wealth, and life itself, to win
To Heaven trophies from the field of sin.
Ordained in his young manhood, faithfully and well
He offered Heaven and forwarned of Hell:
Proclaimed a Saviour whom he had not known;
Till, as he one day preached him, Heav'n's light shone
In his dark heart; and then exultant faith,
Leaving the tedious, torturous mountain path,
Soared up to heights where manuscript was lost,
And words leaped from his heart; and Heaven's host
Was present, witnessing the truth, till men
Grew penitent and turned from sin; and then,
For Christly faithfulness his Bishop hurled
Him forth to the cathedral of the world.
His tongue of fire, unquenched by tyrant flood,
Flamed on in burning words. The cleansing blood
He still proclaimed, till popular demand
Reversed the edict; and the sexton's hand
That rang the bells of Petherton, to tell
Of Coke's disgrace, once more rang loud and well
And joyously, to call him home again
To preach salvation in the Saviour's name.

But Coke had tasted liberty. The stale,
Dry bread of formalism, did thenceforth fail

To feed his noble soul. The narrow bounds
Of legal parish; and the stated rounds
Of parish work, reined in his panting heart;
Till, breaking churchly bit, he made the start
For diocesan empire, wide as earth;
And, in his apostolic life, gave birth
To our Episcopacy, universal,
Honored, victorious and without reversal.

Four years, o'er England's darkened fields, he flew—
A fiery herald. Then he plumed anew
His Gospel pinions for our waiting wild;
And, at his coming, freedom's empire smiled
Him welcome. Like the trained ambassador,
Charged with a mission fraught with vast import; or
A shepherd with good news to sheep, untended
In the wilderness; with haste Coke wended
His way from great New York, over the hills
And valleys; through the towns and villages; by mills,
And through the cities full;—resting alone
The Holy Day,—till gladly he should come
To that dear spot of which his ears had heard
As Israel heard of Horeb, and the Word
Who said to Moses:—" Be thy shoes unbound;
The place whereon thou stand'st is holy ground!"

Favored Peninsula! When He who made
The earth and sea, finished his work, and said
" 'Tis very good;" turning away, his last,

Best smile upon thy sleeping face was cast,
And there has ever lingered. And so, when,
In later years, our Saviour smiled again
On our sad world, it brought forth Methodism—
The rainbow glory of the Gospel prism!
And thou, sweet spot! of all the world most favored,
Hast most of Methodism; nor hast thou wavered
In thy allegiance. A hundred years
Of toil and struggle—heroism and tears
But makes thy glory brighter; and thy fame,
Like that of Eden, 'lumines with its flame
The wide, wide world of Methodistic name.

Hither the Heav'n-appointed Bishop sped;
And, by this rising morning star, is led
Unto the holy place where Barratt's altar
Glows with the sacred fire. No legal halter
Hampers the great commission of his Lord:—
"Go ye in all the world, and preach the Word"—
But free as mountain stream, the message flows
From tongues set free by sturdy freemen's blows
In revolutionary strife. And here,
That day, the multitudes from far and near
Were gathered. 'Twas a holy Sabbath morn
In Indian summer. Fields of ripened corn
Waited the reapers—symbol of the day
Of God's great harvest, where extended lay
The whitened fields, awaiting Heaven's reapers:—
Where scattered flocks were bleating for their keepers.

Now the glad day had come. The shepherd chief
Entered the waiting fold. Turning a leaf
In the great Book, he read the blessed Psalm—
"The Lord my shepherd is;" and holy calm,
Still as the breath of eve, came o'er the place:
And throbbing hearts grew still; and peace, and grace
And holy joy came on the gathered saints
Who graced the Love-feast. As the artist paints
Alternate lights and shades, in beauty blending;
So in this scene, the Holy Ghost descending,
Inspired and led the service, blending song
And prayer and utterance; until along
Each heart's warm current flowed the glad emotion
Of Love Divine in saintly, warm devotion.

And then the unbarred doors were opened wide,
And the great throng poured in, a surging tide
That overflowed the house, and gathered near
Each open door and window, glad to hear,
E'en from the outer courts, the joyful news
That came that day, alike to Greeks and Jews,
And unnamed wanderers of every nation—
The joyful news of full and free salvation!

Opening again the Book, the preacher read
Where his great prototype, St. Paul, had said:—
"Christ Jesus; who, to us, is made of God
Our wisdom and redemption, cleansing blood
And righteousness." With logic like the granite,

He broad foundation laid, deep in the planet
Of conscious verities. Then, on this base
He placed a sculptured stone, on every face
Of which stood out, in startling, bold relief
Some chiseled form of human woe or grief:
A captive bound—a wand'rer lost—a soul
Exposed to Sinai's bolt—a leper foul
Wailing "Unclean! unclean!"—true symbols all
Of human helplessness—that threw the pall
Of hopeless night o'er many a waking heart:
That, as at Philippi, caused men to start
From quaking hell beneath; and, anxious, cry
"What must I do?" The preacher's eagle eye
The scene surveyed. He saw the time had come
To ope the darkened skies, and let the Sun
Of Hope shine down. And, as the welcome light
Came in, there stood, revealed to human sight—
Crowning the monument the preacher builded—
A form Divine, with God's own glory gilded.
"See! see!" he cried; "Behold the man who frees us!"—
They oped their tearful eyes, and looked on Jesus.

The preacher paused, but lingered, looking o'er
The weeping multitude; when, through the door,
Pushed in a manly form, whose saintly face
Was calm and thoughtful—radiant with the grace
That came of deep communion with his God.
It was Coke's Aaron—bearer of the rod
Of Israel's guidance through the wilderness

Of early struggle, tow'rd the hoped-for place
Of Churchly empire Prophecy foretold;
Where deserts smile—where Heaven's flowers unfold
Their beauty, and exhale their sweetness o'er
The goodly land. Till that hour, ne'er before
Had these men met, save as they met in spirit,
Around the common altar, where the merit
Of Jesus' blood unites in one all stations,
And makes one family of all earth's nations.
Thus Francis Asbury first looked on Coke.
For thirteen years, while revolution's smoke
Obscured the sun of peace, this son of peace
Had published the good news, that Righteousness
And Peace had met, embraced and kissed each other:—
Each looked in other's face, and each said, "*Brother!*"

As these two stranger brethren met, the flow
Of love fraternal came. The tender glow
Of mutual sacrifice for human weal,
As if by holy instinct, fixed the seal
Of spirit brotherhood; and, in that place,
With loving kiss—with brotherhood's embrace—
Two Christly hearts were joined in wedlock holy,
To nobly dare and perish for the lowly.

Three other manly forms the tableau grace:
One born near Havre, Maryland;—the place
Of Christian Freedom's birth—and "born again"
On horseback, while a boy, amid the flame

Of sev'nteen sev'nty-five, making the wildwood
Ring back the echoes of his joyous childhood,
Made free and innocent:—who, when he came
To manhood's heritage, bearing the name
Of *slaveholder*—he who had been redeemed—
Heard, whispering in his soul a voice that seemed
To say: "My son; let the oppressed go free!"
And, pausing in the fam'ly prayer, he said:
"Lord; the oppressed shall go!" Then, while he prayed,
A world of slaves to sin before him stood;
And o'er him bended low the Son of God,
And said: "Whom shall I send, and who will go
To bear my message 'mid this scene of woe?"
Then Freeborn Garrettson—God's son, born free—
Joined Heav'n's own unrestricted embassy;
And, ere he gave to Methodism his hand,
Had gathered thirty converts to her band.

With humble, rev'rent mien, there stood near by
A man untutored, but with rich supply
Of inborn eloquence:—a white-souled man,
Done up in colored envelope,—who ran
On Asbury's errands; listened to his teaching;
Polished his boots; and, sometimes, beat him preaching!

Whatcoat was there; and, seven other preachers
Of name unknown,—but whose fair fame as teachers
Is writ in Heaven,—were gathered there that day
To lift the cross, and swell the joyful lay.

HUMORS OF A MODERN ITINERANT. 317

The tableau, thus complete, let us still carry—
Coke, Garrettson, Whatcoat, Asbury, Harry—
To widow Barratt's home, where willing hands
And loving hearts attended the demands
Of tired and hungry nature. There, that day,
The Bishop's council met. Before it lay
The whole, broad land. King George's Bishops, moved
By hate of liberty, and lucre—loved
Better than they loved souls—forsook their sheep,
And left to Methodism the watch to keep,
While battle-storms, in fury, rent the fold;
And Judases their God and country sold!

No Church *Episcopal* then set up claim
To being or authority. The *name*—
"Episcopal"—was captured by our sires,
And held as contraband, till altar fires
Should be enkindled, that would burn on fanes
Of Christian liberty. And then, the names
Of Asbury and Coke, on the first page
Of the great history, of the great age
Of our great Church, Episcopal, were writ
Ere *other* name, Episcopal, the lip
Of priest had passed, in all our new domain
Conquered for freedom. Thus, in freedom's name
Our Mother Church, first coming to baptism,
"Episcopal" affixed to Methodism.

Well, that day Coke his council called at Barratt;
And, after prayer, it was determined thereat,

To call, at Baltimore, a conference
Of ministers, on Christmas Eve. And thence
They sent forth Garrettson, like the swift arrow,
The glad, good news from north to south to carry;
And call the heralds forth, from vale and mountain,
To Lovely Lane, to ope the churchly fountain
Of governmental rule, and power and rod;
To vanquish Hell, and take the world for God!

Then joyous Christmas came, and brought three-score
Itinerants. Weary, unkempt and sore
With the campaign, and long and wintry tramp,
They file down Light Street, to the place of camp.
Each soldier counts his trophies—tells his story;
And each to Jesus gives the praise and glory.
The vet'ran with white locks, the stripling youth,
The middle-aged—all champions for the Truth—
Gathered about their leaders; heard and spoke,
Debated, counselled, pending the great vote
That stamped with favor Bishop Wesley's plans:—
That unchained Methodism—that broke her bands,
And turned her legions loose upon the field
Of the wide world, the sword of God to wield;
Till watchman on to watchman shouts the song
The earth around—her hills and vales along:—
"One Methodism o'erspreads the world's vast plains;
All hallelujah! Christ Messiah reigns!"

The century now rolls away. The story
Of Methodism's exploits, misfortunes, glory

Is written in earth's archives—in the Heaven—
In angel memories—in all the leaven
Of modern progress—through all her sister churches—
Through all the fields where science makes researches;
And, hand in hand, with God and all good men,
She marches tow'rd the blessed era, when;
With all her saintly sisters, of all names
And climes—with angel band that flames
About the Throne;—she and they all shall come
Around the grave where death shall find his doom,
And bury all contentions with their foe.
Then, from the ransomed host, shall ever flow
The glad, sweet song:—"To Him who us hath loved;
And, in his precious blood, all stains removed,
And made us Kings and Priests unto our God;
To Him be wisdom, power, dominion's rod
And glory, through the happy, endless day, when
All tribes and worlds shall shout eternal 'Amen!'"

THE ELDERSHIP, AND THE HARMONIOUS QUARTET.

In 1876, while stationed at Easton, Maryland, the writer drew up a memorial to the Wilmington Conference, on the subject of the Presiding Eldership; which was signed by the entire male membership of the charge, and, at the proper time, presented to the conference. The memorial asked that the Wilmington Conference petition the General Conference, to so modify the Presiding Eldership, as that, while retaining its most valuable features, the office would be divested of its expensiveness.

This, it was held, could be effected by reducing the Districts to ten or a less number of charges; at the same time relieving the Elder of holding the Quarterly Conferences, and appointing him to the pastorate of one of the charges in his District. About one-fourth of the conferences voted in favor of the resolution to so petition the General Conference. Whether this minority embodied the wisdom of the Conference on that question, it is not the purpose of the author to discuss. Minorities are sometimes right.

A day or two after presenting the memorial and advocating the resolution, the writer was appointed by a meeting of the Easton District preachers to present the name of Rev. C. Hill to the Bishop as their choice for Presiding Elder. After representing to the Council the wishes of the meeting, the genial President, Bishop Scott, jocosely remarked that he felt somewhat disposed to ignore the request, and appoint the bearer of the message himself to that position; as, by serving a term in the Presiding Eldership, he would be likely to be cured of his unfortunate heresy on that great question of church polity. His good-natured threat, however, was not executed, and the wishes of the brethren were duly respected.

Three years afterward, on the death of Rev. John Hough, of precious memory, for some reason unknown to the writer, Bishop Simpson sent him a commission to assume, forthwith, the duties and responsibilities of the vacant Dover District.

As to his experience in the sub-episcopal office, he may say, that if he ever entertained a query as to whether a Bishop's Council, like the average corporation, is a body without a heart and soul, that questioning was thus speedily settled by a most emphatic negative.

The first Council was composed of Lucius C. Matlack, Charles Hill, Thomas S. Williams, and Robt. W. Todd. Afterwards Thos. E. Martindale filled the place vacated by Chas. Hill. The presiding Bishops were, in order, Edward G. Andrews, Thomas Bowman, John F. Hurst, and Matthew Simpson.

In these council sessions such was the harmony; the brotherly courtesy; the entire willingness to consult the general good of work and workers; and the mutual voluntary concessions and helpful suggestions and adjustments; that two of the Bishops were prompted to remark that the exhibition, in its degree, was both anomalous and most grateful. To the existence of this pleasant state of affairs, none contributed more, if indeed so much, as Lucius C. Matlack.

The following tribute of love to the memory of this great and good soldier of Jesus Christ was delivered by the author of this volume, on the occasion of the memorial services held by his bereaved flock, in the Methodist Episcopal Church, at Cambridge, Maryland, July 3d, 1883:

REV. LUCIUS COLUMBUS MATLACK, D. D.

Sixty-seven years ago, the infant cry of a child they called Lucius, was borne to the world on the silent breath of the morning. In the early moments of

Sabbath morning, June 24th, 1883, the same voice was heard, for the last time on earth, saying: "God's holy will be done: I am not surprised;" and then the tired breast of Lucius C. Matlack rested from its laborious struggle; and his manly form laid down to rest, and listen for the trump and the voice that shall herald the eternal morning.

On the following day, the precious dust, which had been hallowed by his blood-washed spirit, attended by his bereaved and stricken companion and orphaned boy, and by a deputation of the sorrowing Church bereft of his holy ministry, was conveyed to Port Deposit, and to the house that had been the former home of Mrs. Matlack. A little over ten years before, our brother and sister, a happily wedded twain, had gone out from this little home to the blessed experiences of a most fitting and congenial matrimonial union; and to the equally congenial life-work of winning jewels for their Master's crown.

On this sad return to the bridal scene, it was fitting the casket containing his manly frame, should be deposited on the precise spot, where he and his bridal partner had stood and taken the mutual vows that made them one till death. Thence we bore his body to the village Church, whose walls had so frequently echoed with his eloquent words, and placed it in the chancel so often graced by his manly presence; where glowing tribute was paid to his worth, and fitting expression given to our sense of loss and bereavement. Then, amid the peltings of a furious rain-storm, the sad funeral cortege wended its way to the beautiful hills of Hopewell, the place of interment. On leaving the church, the lips of her who sorrowed most whispered her heart's desire that the falling floods might be stayed while we laid our precious burden in its last resting place; and Heaven heard her prayer. While all around, in sight, copious showers were deluging the valleys, not a drop disturbed the farewell service at the grave, or hastened the departure of sadly-lingering footsteps.

Hopewell never received a treasure of more precious dust than the sleeping form of Lucius C. Matlack. And no more fitting location and name could be found as his place of sepulture. Topographically about the highest point of land in our conference territory, it is appropriate that he, who, in his physical stature, form and feature, was most noble and courtly amongst us, should there lie down to his rest. It is fitting that his consecrated body should sleep at our nearest point to the heavens. And if, from Christ's Paradise, a white-robed and white-winged soul is ever permitted to visit the spot where his dust reposes; from the heights of Hopewell, to the vision of our departed brother, God may sometimes reveal the old Peninsular battle-field, over which, as a Christian soldier, he fought, gladdening his redeemed spirit with the assurance of the cumulative and culminating victories of the cross.

"Hopewell." How suggestive the name! A well-grounded, well-assured hope of resurrection and immortality cheered him through life and as he entered the valley; and cheered us for him, as we turned sorrowfully away from the holy spot where we laid him down to his peaceful slumber. Sleep on, Lucius, among the beautiful, green hills of Cecil! Shout on, Lucius, from the mountain peaks of glory! We are hearkening; and, by God's help, will try to follow the shining pathway that leads up to where thou art standing!

Where shall I begin in the task these loving brethren have invited me to undertake? And how shall I fitly perform this work of love? The greatest obstacle I encounter is the greatness of my affection for the—to me—more than friend and brother whose life and virtues we here and now commemorate. The poverty of my words, as compared with my impulses of love and sorrow, is an embarrassment I may not hope to surmount.

To Lucius C. Matlack, nature was generous—even lavish of her gifts. To a physique noble, kingly, beautiful; and a face and feature in striking harmony therewith; with every curve, lineament and expression instinct with the health and force of the most robust and manly vigor; she added the splendid endowments of a strong, careful, discriminating intellect, furnishing all the attributes of a possible commanding greatness, in any field of attainment or achievement he might have chosen for the exercise of his powers.

Mingled with these great elements of natural strength, however, was a native modesty that held him in check from self-assertion, and led him to esteem others as better and more capable than himself. Such were his natural endowments of humility and modesty, that he scarcely had need of the Apostolic admonition, not to "think of himself more highly than he ought to think." Indeed there were times in his life when this inherent timidity and self-abnegation became so nearly excessive, as to prevent his doing full justice to his manhood and his mission. Although one of the leading spirits in the great anti-slavery agitation, and the author of an ably written history of the events leading to emancipation, his part in the stirring drama is modestly kept in the back-ground. But, on the whole, these were doubtless to be numbered among the endowments that gave strength to his character, and attracted the profoundest respect of those who best knew him. It was his native modesty, together with the embarrassment incident to a defective vision, that occasioned the apparent reserve sometimes calling forth unfavorable criticism, and led some to suppose him cold and indifferent, or even haughty. Those, however, so fortunate as to come near enough to Dr. Matlack to understand him, and feel the pulsations of his great, manly, but loving, gentle heart, found a cheerful, genial friend, whose affectionate attentions attracted the most unreserved and respectful confidence. His was a nature to lean on and tie to, and never find our reasonable expectations disappointed.

These adornments of nature were carefully polished by a culture none the less genuine that it was obtained, for the most part, outside the schools. Laying the foundation in the common schools, and in the literary and theological course prescribed by the Church for young ministers; he succeeded, by his native power and industry, in reaching a scholarly eminence that merited and won for him the honorary degree of Doctor of Divinity; and that commanded the respect of the most cultured of his fellows. To these natural endowments and adornments polished by industrious study, grace added her charms, until it was no exaggeration to apply to him the glowing words in which the Apostle expressed his wish for the attainment of Timothy, and call him "a man of God * * * perfect; thoroughly furnished unto all good works."

As to religious attainment, experience and profession, Dr. Matlack was exceedingly cautious in his steps and careful in his utterances. At every stage of the journey from the City of Destruction to Beulah Land, the ground was critically examined; and no steps were counted or relied upon that were not consciously felt to rest upon the solid granite of God's Revelation, as interpreted by the dual and harmonizing utterances of reason and experience. But all these conscious steps were taken; and, as a general, strong in his victories and resources, he held and occupied every advanced position taken; until the foe, pressed to the very verge of manhood's empire, was hurled over the battlements; and Lucius C. Matlack was anointed a king and constituted a priest unto God, to rule over and minister in the realm of his own redeemed nature. With him, God's will was not only supreme, as authority to be respected; but as a blessing to be enjoyed—a delight and a luxury to be eagerly coveted. It was no new thing, superinduced by the exhaustion of the last struggle, for him to say, "God's holy will be done." It was the established habit of his daily being. It was the language and poesy of his holy psalm of life; and, in these words, he was but epitomizing hurriedly, with breath too precious for extended speech, the last paragraph and experience of that psalm. Amid the last conflict, so unexpectedly precipitated, and the gathering darkness of the night of death, the dying victor was enabled to gasp, "I am not surprised!" The last foe found him armed and ready.

After eleven years of intimate association and fellowship, in all the varied relations in which it was my great honor and privilege to come into contact with Dr. Matlack, I am proud, without qualification or reservation, to declare it as my profound conviction that the will of God was the rule of all his actions, words and thoughts.

Dr. Matlack more perfectly obeyed the Golden Rule—"Whatsoever ye would that men should do to you, do ye even so to them,"—than any person I have ever known. I have known him grievously misrepresented and injured, not only without being excited to retaliate, but without even a word of complaint. In all the years of our intimate and confidential association, there never fell from his lips a word of bitterness, or an insinuation that reflected unkindly upon any of his fellows. His pure nature was transparent; he had no covert, selfish purposes to subserve; and I would as soon suspect the highest Archangel of being the head of a proposed sinister combination in Heaven, as to have thought Lucius C. Matlack capable of being complicated with any similar ring or clique on earth. But he not only possessed the negative but also the positive form of Christian charity. He would not only do no harm to any; but, to the utmost of his ability, he would do good to all—to foe as well as friend.

In the council sessions, in which it was my lot to serve with him, his consideration and love for his brethren, shone with a steady and undimmed beauty. When,—as must always and necessarily be the case,—some one was about to be pressed into an undesirable place, our dear brother's kind heart always prompted him to co-operate in any measures that might promise relief. When any member of the Council was distressed by untoward complications, in his relations to the appointments and preachers, this unselfish man of God was always ready to adjust himself and his work to the exigency, and aid in the happy solution of the problem. At the last conference, during the fourth session of the Council, when most of the preachers except the outgoing Presiding Elders had been stationed, Bishop Simpson inquired of Dr. Matlack as to his wishes for himself. The answer was characteristic. It was, in substance: "You know, Bishop, what I told you thirteen years ago. It is not for me to choose. I have one thing to say, however: I want no appointment for myself, until we provide suitably for all the brethren on my District."

As a counsellor and administrator, our departed brother was eminently wise and prudent. I doubt whether any person or interest was ever harmed by his counsels. These valuable qualities were recognized by the chiefest powers in our Church, in his appointment to superintend our work in Louisiana; and also in the very complimentary vote he received, in the General Conference of 1872, for the Episcopacy. For similar reasons he was selected to represent the Louisiana Conference in the General Conference of the same year, and the Wilmington Conference in the years 1876 and 1880.

Dr. Matlack was an able preacher of the Gospel. He attempted no lofty flights. He made no pedantic displays. He never amused and entertained his hearers with any scientific, metaphysical or theological speculations. He proclaimed no new and liberal theories (so called) of the Gospel. But he honored the Law. He gloried in the Cross. He exalted Christ as a Prince and Saviour. He proclaimed salvation—full, complete, present, for all who would receive it. He was a meek but confident professor and possessor of the "like precious faith;" and, with becoming modesty, he did not shun to declare publicly and often, in his sermons, what his Saviour had done for him. As the result, his preaching was plain and simple. A child could understand it. It was profitable. It was not confections and flowers, but bread. It always fed the hungry; and, not infrequently, created a hunger that it also satisfied. In the pulpit he was not always equal to himself and his highest efforts and attainments. Sometimes the current reached a valley, where it was almost provokingly quiet; but it was never muddy or stagnant. At other times it flowed gently, with slight ripple and scarcely audible murmur. Its general flow, however, was strong, steady and musical. But there were times, when, breaking away from all restraints of timidity, and overflowing all the barriers and boundaries of logical and rhetorical caution, amid dashing spray and tempestuous roar, it rushed with impetuous impulse adown the rocky rapids of impassioned feeling; bearing irresistibly on its loving torrent, whither it would, the thoughts and hearts of his captive auditors.

Such a ministry is not yet ended. In its blessed results it will never end. His voice, even now, is floating down to us on the evening zephyrs. I seem to hear its utterances:—"The salutation of me, Lucius, with mine own voice. Be perfect; be of good comfort; be of one mind; live in peace, and the God of love and peace shall be with you. All that are with me salute you. Greet them that love us in the faith. The grace of our Lord Jesus Christ be with you all. Amen."

Lucius C. Matlack was a patriot. Not such a patriot as mistakes love of party for love of country. Not such a patriot as follows the leadership of politicians or statesmen for the loaves and fishes they throw to the hungry, scrambling crowd. But such a patriot—such a lover of his country and of humanity as was willing to have no leader but Christ, and to lead no one but himself—to stand alone, if need be, so he maintained his honest, conscientious convictions.

As a young minister he stood knocking for admission at the door of the chosen conference of his chosen church. The alternative was presented: "Refrain from the public expression of your sentiments as to slavery, or step down." He stepped—up! Soon thereafter, he was stripped of ministerial authority, and remanded to the ranks of private church membership. He sought and found a sphere of unfettered utterance in the ministry of a sister Church. But there came a day when the Philadelphia Conference discovered its mistake, and made the *amende honorable* by adopting a resolution, reversing its former action; and, throwing wide its doors, it welcomed to membership the nationally recognized philanthropist, patriot, hero and Christian apostle.

Nor was Dr. Matlack such a patriot as contented himself with paying his stipend to support the government. But when the existence of that government and his country was threatened, he rushed to the front, and put his prayers and his manly, loving heart between it and the bullets of the foe. And, when the struggle was over, and safety and peace assured, his brotherly hand was ready to extend help to our impoverished and suffering brothers and their loved ones in the South; and he would as readily have fought for them, had they been unrighteously oppressed, as he had entered the lists against them when he esteemed them in the wrong.

The struggle over and the question of our civil conflict settled, Dr. Matlack resumed his place in the work of the Church; and no one would have ever known, from his voluntary showing, that he had filled any such prominent place in that great and portentous drama.

In presenting, at his funeral obsequies, the resolutions passed by the Delaware Conference, then in session, in reference to his decease; Rev. Wesley J. Parker, looking down from the platform, upon the casket containing his form, modestly and beautifully said: "Farewell, my friend! Farewell, friend of my race! Farewell, friend of the oppressed of all races! I will meet you in the resurrection morning!"

For reasons that may be gathered from what I have said, I nominated Dr. Matlack as a suitable appointee for the important Church at Cambridge, at the last conference. For similar reasons, Bishop Simpson confirmed that nomination. Whatever doubts any, at that time, may have entertained as to the wisdom of the appointment, were speedily dissipated as he became known to these dear brethren; and, to-day, I speak to a Church in which all are bereft—all are mourners. With tearful eyes, bowed heads and throbbing, aching hearts, you are all sighing, in one tremulous whisper, "The Lord gave" us this holy man of God. And doubtless, my brethren, despite the darkness of his mysterious dealings, you will be enabled to add—"And the Lord hath taken away; blessed be the name of the Lord!"

But why should God have taken away the precious gift so soon? In answer, I can only bid you hearken to His voice, who speaks to us from the night of his own sorrow: "What thou knowest not now, thou shalt know hereafter."

But Lucius Matlack is not dead. Only his body died. It sleepeth. "*He yet speaketh.*" The sound-waves set in motion by his faithful words are still quivering along through the corridors of your being. They are echoed from these temple walls. They are murmuring in your dwellings. They mingle with the tramp of the multitudes along your streets. They are heard, soft as falling snow-flakes, in the chambers where the sick are pining and the watchers wait. They still seek to soothe the remorse and agony that wails in yonder felon's dungeon.* They are heard and appreciated in our sister churches. And when and where shall be the limit of their Christly utterance? The worker has finished his task, and laid him down to rest, but his work goes on. As in the case of Samson, Heaven grant that the slain of Israel's enemies by his death may be more than by his life.

Allow me to refer to a few sentences in a letter written me by Dr. Matlack, about one month after our parting at conference. "We have been so busy in house-fixing,

---

* Dr. Matlack was on his return from a visit to a convict, under sentence of death, when he was stricken with the apoplectic stroke, that, a few hours thereafter, terminated his life and his Christly work.

garden-making, tree-planting, and getting acquainted in the homes of more than seventy families, that friendly letters have been postponed." Then, after speaking most tenderly of my recent bereavement in the death of a dear boy, he says: "I shall be glad to have an occasional letter, and to send one, which shall be a brotherly expression of our old time formula respecting the duty of preachers to God, to themselves and one another. A few more years, and our work is ended. I would live with the end distinctly in view. That is to live in the present tense, rather than in the future tense; walking closely with God, and having the work greatly at heart." Then follows an account of his prayer-meeting talks and services since conference, concluding as follows: "I enjoy my work. The people are kind and appreciative. To you I owe thanks for your commendations of me to these brethren."

To this, in due season, I replied, enclosing an invitation to the Woodlawn Camp-meeting. In response I received a postal card, written three days before he ascended, on which was traced: "Your letter received and welcomed; to be answered hereafter." The answer never came; but, oh! were there postal communications betwixt this and the country where he is gone, what a glowing letter I should some day receive, descriptive of his new appointment; of his mansion; of the trees and flowers planted by the Forerunner, growing luxuriantly and bending under their burden of blossom and fruit; of the new acquaintances made and the great meetings and conferences attended! Well; bye-and-bye we will sit down under the trees by the river side, and he will give me verbally the promised answer.

He continues: "Invitation to Woodlawn accepted. Expect to be there at the beginning, and to stay through to the end with *my crowd!*" The last two words emphasized and with the exclamation mark. Woodlawn is within sight of where his dust reposes. May not his expectation be realized? May not his glorified spirit be among the ministering hosts, assured by God's promise, to the heirs of salvation? "Expect to be there * * with *my crowd!*" To our dear brother the precious wife and darling boy constituted a crowd. They were enough to satisfy his home and his heart. The light of their smiles filled his horizon, and made all the earth-side of his life luminous with holy joy. Wait, Lucius; the little crowd is coming to you!

Well; we shall not see his manly form, or hear his well-remembered voice at Woodlawn. He is camped—

"On the other side of Jordan,
In the sweet fields of Eden,
Where the tree of life is blooming."

He is "there to stay through to the end!" He is there with *his crowd!* See! The fields of glory are covered with them! "They have white robes, and palms in their hands." They are "ten thousand times ten thousand, and thousands of thousands!" Hear their victorious shout! Listen to their glad song, as the very foundations of glory tremble with the melodious anthem—"Unto him who hath loved us, and washed us from our sins in his own blood, and hath made us kings and priests unto God and his Father, unto him be glory forever and ever." Amen!

Warrior, farewell! Thy earthly strife is ended;
  With thee, we say "God's holy will be done:"
From earth released, by angel hosts attended,
  Thy triumph and thy glory is begun.

Though fierce the charge the stealthy foe thrust on thee;
  And dark the night, and wild the howling storm;
Thou wert "not surprised;" Christ's armor was upon thee,
  And thou a victor, crowned on Sabbath morn.

On Sabbath morn, thy week of life and labor
  Dawned to its endless Sabbath in the skies;
The battle fought, sheathed is thy shining sabre,
  And glory-visions meet thy wand'ring eyes.

Lovely on earth:—though great yet meek and lowly—
  Thou'rt nobler, lovelier still where thou art gone;
Unstained in life, thy home is with the holy,
  Where sin nor sorrow's blight shall ever come.

Sleep, sweetly sleep! On Hopewell's couch reclining,
  Thy precious dust is guarded from on high:
Shout, victor, shout! Thy armor all resigning,
  And wait our welcome coming bye and bye.

THE END.

www.ingramcontent.com/pod-product-compliance
Lightning Source LLC
Chambersburg PA
CBHW050836230426
43667CB00012B/2021